SPORT COMPACT
NITROUS
INJECTION

JOE PETTITT

P9-CEU-912

Edited By:
Steve Hendrickson

Production By:
Rachelle Raphael

ISBN 1-884089-74-7

Order No. SA73

Printed in the United States of America

CarTech®, Inc.,
39966 Grand Avenue
North Branch, MN 55056
Telephone (651) 277-1200 • (800) 551-4754 • Fax: (651) 277-1203
www.cartechbooks.com

OVERSEAS DISTRIBUTION BY:

Brooklands Books Ltd.
P.O. BOX 146, Cobham, Surrey, KT11 1LG, England
Telephone 01932 865051 • Fax 01932 868803
www.brooklands-books.com

Brooklands Books Ltd.
1/81 Darley Street, P.O. Box 199, Mona Vale, NSW 2103, Australia
Telephone 2 9997 8428 • Fax 2 9997 5799

Front and Back Cover Photos: The PacMotorSports.com stroked B16A engine features a custom crankshaft with 89-mm stroke, and a custom rod to produce 1.61 rod ratio. You can choose between 10.5:1 or 9.0:1 compression ratios. The engine also includes O-ringed Darton cylinder sleeves with integrated block guard in either 81-mm or 84-mm bores. Because of the extreme stroke, the oil system had to be modified using a new oil high efficiency oil pump. The B16A head has massaged chambers, Manley valves and Crower cams and valve train.

Title Page Photo: When it comes to spooling up a turbo, nitrous is one of the most effective tuning tools available. That's why several performance manufacturers have entered the nitrous market with new system designs and product. This is definitely good for the enthusiasts. The competition on the race track brings more powerful, more reliable, safer and easier to install systems to the market.

TABLE OF CONTENTS

PREFACE

ACKNOWLEDGMENTS

Writing a book is a huge undertaking. One that challenges the endurance, memory, and patience of not only the author, but of family, of editors, and of colleagues as well. It takes late nights at the keyboard; follow-up calls to re-ask questions to make sure what is reported is correct; hours spent in the garage and various shops and race tracks to capture images of the technique and action of this fast-paced segment of automotive enthusiasts. And most difficult of all, there's the mind-numbing but critical task of keeping track of the facts, figures, formulas and photographs so they may be presented in an intelligible, logical way that teaches, informs, and sometimes entertains the reader.

To those who helped me in this endeavor, thank you. Of particular importance is the crew at NOS. Much of what I learned came from this company's long experience with nitrous oxide. Also the guys at Venom provided invaluable insight and great racing action which enhanced the look and technical content of this book. I also appreciate the effort of the folks at Nitrous Express and Nitrous Works in answering my questions and furnishing imagery. And I can't neglect the ZEX man, Matt Patrick. His insight and experience with his turbo and nitrous were enlightening and much of what we discussed is found in this book. Thanks also to the editor of this book, Steve Hendrickson, for his perseverance in searching out mistakes and rough transitions, and for his suggestions of story elements and angles. His input and effort, along with that of the entire CarTech production staff, have made this book much, much better than I could have created alone.

I wish to especially thank my wife, Patricia, who was so completely understanding and accepting of the odd schedule I assumed during this project, that she was willing to sleep in the glare of a computer monitor and rustle of a keyboard without complaint.

ABOUT THE AUTHOR

Joe Pettitt is a veteran automotive photojournalist. He's written hundreds of articles for the automotive perform-

ance media including *Hot Rod Magazine*, Hot Rod.Com, *Sport Compact Car*, *Drag Racer* magazine, *Car Craft*, *Circle Track* magazine, and *Motor Trend*. He also wrote for Autotronics magazine where he indulged his passion for great cars and great music. His automotive related adventures include piloting IROC cars around the famous ovals of Daytona and Talladega, and strapping into the world's fastest open road race record holder as a journalist/passenger. This mind-warping experience offered 27 minutes of sheer terror at up to 220 miles per hour while making the 90-mile Silver State Challenge run from Ely, Nevada to Lund, Nevada with an average speed of over 194 mph.

Pettitt has modified and tuned numerous sports cars, hot rods and street machines, installing sound systems in all of them. His favorite was a '59 XK 150 Jag. He says he didn't have the most expensive gear in that car, but installed it right and it made wonderful music as it moved swiftly through the turns and twist of the canyons of Southern California. Every time you build a car, says Pettitt, you learn something new. You learn how to do it a little smarter and a little easier; and you learn how to find the right people to answer your questions. Finding good information about building a car or super tuning your engine isn't easy; but once you have it, it makes your high performance projects run much smoother.

Joe Pettitt currently lives in southern California with wife Patricia, and two daughters, Vanessa and Jordan.

In terms of ease of installation and power output, nitrous oxide is the most efficient power adder on the market. Firms such as Nitrous Oxide Systems have been instrumental in developing and marketing well engineered nitrous systems. Over the years, firms involved in developing nitrous oxide as a predictable power adder have provided performance enthusiasts with tuning information as well as recommendations on the proper techniques in applying this technology. This book is an attempt to bring the collective experience of racers using nitrous into one volume.

Nitrous oxide's efficiency as a power adder comes from the fact that, unlike belt-driven superchargers or exhaust-driven turbos, the engine doesn't have to do any work to supply the additional oxygen. The energy expended to compress nitrous oxide into a liquid state isn't performed by the engine, so nitrous has an edge. Just add fuel and nitrous together in the proper amounts and you can create impressive power levels with very little engineering effort.

WHAT IS NITROUS OXIDE ?

Nitrous oxide has a reputation for either being too easy to make horsepower, and therefore less sophisticated, or for being too unpredictable and therefore too easy to destroy your engine. Depending on whom you may have talked to or what you may have read in all of your exposure to nitrous oxide, your personal opinion about nitrous could be shaped by either of these two concepts.

Some people, at the first sign of problems, will instantly blame the nitrous system for everything. On the other hand, there are those who are willing to spend a little extra time and effort to learn how nitrous works. Then they can make an educated choice when the time comes to buy the correct type of system for their application, or to track down a problem they may have with their current system.

Once you know how nitrous works, then you can begin to play with the concept of tuning. That's how you get to go faster and quicker. It doesn't matter if you're using nitrous, turbos, superchargers, or all-motor. The only way to find power, and control it to minimize the risk to your engine and yourself, is to learn how to tune.

If you're still reading, you're probably a tuner. That's good because, if you're interested in tuning a nitrous oxide system, you're reading the right book. This isn't a recipe book; we don't give you canned nitrous jet sizes and engine combinations. If we did, they would most likely be obsolete before the ink dried. What we have included are the theory and physics that explain how you make power with nitrous by tuning it to your combination and the circumstances in which you're tuning. Into the mix we throw some practical experience of real racers with real cars.

WHAT IS NITROUS OXIDE?

Nitrous oxide is a colorless, odorless gas, composed of two nitrogen atoms stuck to one oxygen atom. The scientific abbreviation for nitrogen is N, and O for oxygen. The correct abbreviation for one nitrous oxide molecule is N_2O. This is where the familiar phrase "N-2-O" comes from when people talk about nitrous oxide. A number of different molecules composed of nitrogen and oxygen are all grouped under the name "oxides of nitrogen." One of these combinations may be familiar to you, as it's one of the compounds monitored by the EPA (Environmental Protection Agency) as a major component of air pollution and is commonly referred to as NOx, which is a different combination

of nitrogen and oxygen, this one being poisonous to anything that depends on breathing air.

Nitrous oxide, however, is not poisonous and is not harmful to the atmosphere or the ozone layer like some refrigerants, such as R-12 and R-22. The method recommended by the CGA (Compressed Gas Association) for disposing of nitrous oxide is to simply vent it slowly to atmosphere in an open area with no one close enough to be able to breathe it in any significant concentrations. OSHA (Occupational Safety and Health Administration) lists nitrous oxide as a simple asphyxiant. This means you can't breathe it in moderate to high concentrations without the risk of being suffocated. Just like CO_2, nitrous oxide does not support life because it displaces the oxygen that you should be breathing. There is oxygen in nitrous oxide, but it's

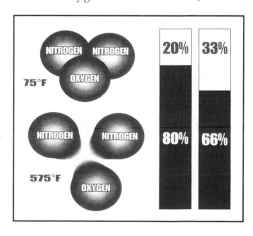

Regular air contains approximately 20 percent oxygen (O_2) by volume. Nitrous oxide contains approximately 33 percent oxygen by volume, so nitrous is comparatively oxygen rich. It provides your engine with additional oxygen in a relatively safe chemical form, with two nitrogen atoms bonded to one oxygen atom. (In this state it will not react with fuel.) The compression of your engine raises the temperature of the fuel/air mix. Above approximately 575 degrees F., the N20's molecular bond is broken, freeing the oxygen atoms, which are now free to react with fuel.

Here's an example of an extremely popular class, Pro 4. Notice the Lexan windows, extensive structural tubing in the car, and the big intercooler. These cars compete in one of the quicker classes with turbo and nitrous combos.

stuck to the nitrogen and your lungs don't have the ability to take it apart.

Performance enthusiasts use a commercial grade of nitrous oxide in their engines. The only type of nitrous oxide that you are likely to find is a commercial grade marketed and sold under the trademarked name, Nytrous+, by the Puritan-Bennett Corporation. This particular brand of nitrous oxide contains 99.9 percent nitrous oxide and 0.01 percent sulfur dioxide. Sulfur dioxide is added as an odorizing agent and as an irritant to discourage substance abuse. Sulfur dioxide is highly irritating to the eyes, throat, and respiratory tract, but has no effect on your engine and no detrimental effect on performance. Use only this type of Nitrous when getting your nitrous tank refilled.

Nitrous oxide is stored by pumping it into a pressure vessel. The legal specifications for a nitrous oxide tank are the same as that used for carbon dioxide gas. It must have a certified working limit of 1800 pounds of pressure per square inch. The tanks must have a certification date stamped into the tank near the outlet and must be current within 5 years. Your dealer will not refill your nitrous tank if it is out of date. If this happens you will need to pay a small fee for recertification. Depending on the resources of your dealer, recertification can be done at the dealer's location with the proper equipment, or the tank may have to be sent out.

Nitrous oxide, like many other substances, is stored in its tank in a liquid form. This is only possible if the nitrous is stored at a high enough pressure to liquefy it. At room temperature and normal atmospheric pressure (14.7 psi @ sea level) nitrous oxide exists in a gaseous form. There are two ways to get nitrous oxide into a liquid state. You can cool it down until it liquifies, or compress it until it liquifies. In order to cool it down enough, you would have to lower the temperature of the nitrous to minus 127 degrees Fahrenheit. That would be very difficult to do and not very practical for the automotive world. The other choice is to compress it. If the nitrous oxide were at a temperature of 70 degrees F, then you would have to compress it to 760 psi to change it to a liquid state. As the temperature of the nitrous oxide increases, the pressure required to keep it in a liquid state goes up. At 80 degrees F it takes 865 psi to keep it in a liquid state. This is far easier to accomplish than the cooling method.

Pressure tanks are commonly available for this type of pressure, and this is how the automotive industry has handled this problem from the very first use of nitrous oxide in the mid 1960s. The main advantage of storing nitrous oxide under pressure in a liquid state is that it occupies much less space. In addition, no pump is needed for pressurized

Before Chris Rado campaigned his Toyota Celica, he piloted the world's fastest drag racing unibody Acura and competed in IDRC Outlaw class and NIRA Pro FWD class. This brute puts nearly 800 horsepower of turbocharged, nitrous enhanced power to the wheels to put the quarter mile behind it in 8 seconds.

A hard charge off the line for a Pro 4 car. The nitrous gets the car moving and spools up the turbo to make 9-second quarter-mile blasts. Some racers like to use "back up" nitrous stages, even with turbos. If the turbo and the initial shot of nitrous isn't enough, they'll activate a second and sometimes a third stage to add to the power of the turbo.

nitrous oxide, as the pressure supplies all the force necessary to make the nitrous oxide flow.

Valves operated by electric solenoids start and stop the flow of nitrous and the additional fuel. A solenoid opens a passage by creating a strong magnetic field that moves a small plunger away from a hole and allows the nitrous or fuel to flow. When the electrical current is shut off, the plunger closes, sealing the hole to stop the flow.

In a modern nitrous system there are several ways to control the opening and closing of the solenoids. In the first years of automotive uses of nitrous oxide, the solenoids were controlled with a simple momentary push-button that you would operate manually whenever you wanted the system to come on. Today, there are components available that will do this for you at a predetermined RPM point or time. There are even systems that will start the operation of the nitrous system at a low power level and smoothly reach full power according to the time you preset it for. This works best with high-power systems that would otherwise have traction problems when the vehicle is just beginning to move.

All nitrous systems should only be activated at wide-open throttle. You normally control the engine's power by throttling it. This means that you are controlling how much air and fuel enters the engine by varying the position of the accelerator pedal. As you drive the vehicle, you open the throttle more and more until you reach the necessary power level. If you get to the point of maximum throttle opening and that isn't enough, then you activate the nitrous system. Since there is a limited amount of nitrous in the nitrous tank, you would just be wasting it if you used it at part throttle.

Once the system is on and flowing, the nitrous oxide and additional fuel are introduced into the intake system of the engine and carried to the individual cylinders along with the normal air/fuel mixture. The ratio and quantity of nitrous and additional fuel is regulated by jets within the nitrous and fuel plumbing circuits. The jets allow an exact amount of nitrous and fuel flow at specific pressures. Typically the nitrous jetting is based on 850-psi bottle pressure and the fuel jetting is based on 5 psi at the jet. Calibration changes for various power levels are implemented by the use of removable jets of various sizes.

There are many different ways to get the nitrous and additional fuel into the engine. Systems range from a simple spacer-type plate installed between the carburetor base and the intake manifold, to individual mixer-type nozzles

The high tech attitude that rules most of the sport compact drag racing associations, allows an exciting mix of Nitrous, turbos, and exotic fuel blends. This makes Sport Compact drag racing one of the most interesting and fun forms of motor sport today. Nitrous helps spool up the big turbos needed for top end power and can partially compensate for packaging compromises such as the 90-degree bend at the turbo outlet.

installed into each intake runner passage. The individual pod nozzle arrangement allows for tuning any one cylinder differently than the others. This can be a very valuable tuning tool for serious racing setups.

Nitrous oxide itself does not make any power. In fact, engines in general don't make power. All of the power comes from the fuel that you put in the fuel tank. An engine can only release the potential energy contained in the fuel.

Lisa Kubo is one of the more competitive racers in NIRA's Power 4-Cylinder class. Here she's on the return lane, responding to fan's cheers after a nine-second blast. The wheelie bars on front drive cars inhibit weight transfer off the front wheels to provide more grip off the starting line for quicker e.t.'s.

The import drag racing scene features an exciting mix of rear-drive, all-wheel drive, and front-drive vehicles with various engine configurations, ranging all the way to turbocharged, alcohol fueled, nitrous-enhanced rotary rockets, such as Flaco Racing's Pro car, seen here on its way to a mid-8-second e.t.

Nitrous at Work
K&N and Turbonetics Ford Focus Wagons

Ford's Focus is getting a lot of grassroots and factory support these days. The body shape's very attractive and aerodynamically advantageous. Plus the Ford Zetec engine responds well to performance mods. For serious performance, though you'll have to replace the composite intake manifold. It tends to break if the engine backfires, which most engines tend to do when they bounce on the rev limiter.

This flamed Focus is a street piece, tuned and styled to give sport compact performance enthusiasts ideas about how the shape responds aesthetically. Ken Dutweiller, far left, is working with Ford engineers to explore the performance limits of the Zetec engine and develop performance strategies and tactics for building performance levels of the engine. This effort of course includes nitrous.

The K&N, Turbonetics, Edelbrock Performer RPM nitrous system enhanced Turbocharged Focus wagon blends old school drag racing technique with new gen's penchant for high-specific output engines. The rear drive machine sports big's 'n' littles rear to front in traditional style and with the help of the modified north-south engine configuration and lots of turbo with a quick shot of nitrous, it should easily pound the quarter-mile into submission in eight seconds and change.

With the exception of the safety gear and the Precision Performance Products shifter, it looks pretty darn close to stock ... inside.

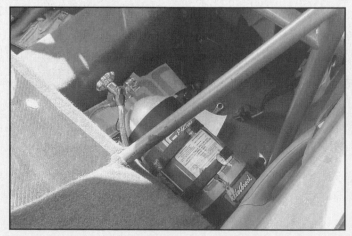

A small bottle of nitrous, the right jetting and bottle temps ... shake the ground with a few pounds of turbo boost, and the lights go by in nine seconds or less.

The engine provides the proper environment to convert the potential energy of the fuel into motion. If there is very little potential energy in the fuel, there will be very little power available.

Nitrous oxide supplies additional oxygen to the engine, which allows the engine to burn the fuel at a faster rate. This additional oxygen also allows more fuel to be burned in the same time period than the engine would without the additional oxygen that comes from the nitrous oxide. As we just stated, the power is released from the fuel, not the nitrous oxide. The nitrous oxide provides you with a tool to control how much and how quickly the fuel is burned. When fuel burns it expands. This expansion creates the pressure that pushes the piston down. The greater the force of the expansion, the greater is the available power placed on the top of the piston —to a point. This brings us to the last portion of your introduction to nitrous oxide, the limitations of the engine itself.

The issue of nitrous breaking engines isn't about nitrous as much as it is about making tuning mistakes and mistuned combinations. Anything can be broken with enough force. Since most adjustable nitrous systems can be calibrated for some very high potential power levels, the user must be acutely aware of the

Nitrous is one of the most versatile power adders on the market. It's easy to install and can be configured to fit just about any vehicle and performance level. The BMW 12 cylinder in the 850 requires two separate nitrous systems because it uses two separate fuel systems. A challenge for the installer, but very fast once installed. Would you expect the suit driving this BMW850 to have the squeeze on tap? Take a look at the purge valve in action.

point at which the engine's components are going to fail. It can be very much like an addiction. Once you are used to a certain power level, you begin to want more. If you ignore the maximum capabilities of the engine, then you have only yourself to blame if it breaks. The nitrous system did what it was supposed to do: release more power. If that power level exceeds the strength of the engine's components, damage will occur.

This, probably more than any other reason, is where nitrous gets a reputation for tearing up engines. Over estimating the power level the engine can adequate-

ly and reliably handle is what breaks engines, not nitrous oxide. The nitrous companies are responsible for delivering to you the amount of additional power you request. The container you provide to capture and transform this power is your responsibility, so it makes good sense to learn as much as you can about using and tuning nitrous as a power enhancer as well as your particular engine and its realistic limitations. Only then can you make an intelligent choice about which type of nitrous system best serves your purpose. We hope this book will help you do just that.

The wide open power-adder rules for most sport compact drag racing classes have provided exciting racing and technically advanced cars. The racers are always figuring out ways to use turbos and nitrous to go quicker and faster. Two of the fastest tube frame front drive cars are Stephan Papadakis' Honda and Shaun Carlson's Ford Focus. These cars run in a class that allows nitrous.

Lisa Kubo, the only woman in the sport compact drag racing scene to run consistent 9-second e.t.'s, shows off her driving talents as she leaps off the line, all cameras on her car as her competition experiences technical difficulties.

Quick Start Reference Guide
The Most Important Points to Remember

- **Work Safely**: Always wear eye protection and gloves when working with lines or hoses that contain pressurized nitrous oxide or fuel. Never transport nitrous cylinders loose in a trunk or the back of a pick-up truck and especially NOT within a vehicle's interior whether the cylinder is full OR empty. Always disconnect the GROUND side of the battery when working on any electrical components.

- **Be Realistic About the Amount of Additional Power Your Engine Can Reliably Handle**: If you're in doubt, it's always better to guess less than more. The various nitrous companies can lend some very valuable information concerning particular engine and component strength and durability. They don't want you to reach the point of damage any more than you do.

- **Consistency is Everything**: Fluctuating fuel pressure, different nitrous cylinder temperatures, worn or sticky mechanical advance mechanisms, intermittent wiring problems, etc., can all lead to erratic system performance and possibly engine damage.

- **Nitrous Oxide Won't Fix Problems You Already Have**: Before you install your nitrous system, be sure your engine is in good mechanical condition. Ignition problems and carburetor calibration problems become bigger problems when combined with nitrous oxide.

- **Install as Many Safety Devices as You Can**: Power relays, oil pressure safety switches, wide-open-throttle switches, rpm activated switches, and low fuel pressure safety switches are just a few examples of things you can install to ensure that your system can only be activated when the engine is running and is at wide-open-throttle.

- **Never Defeat the Operation of the Safety Relief Disc in the Nitrous Cylinder's Valve Stem**: It's required by law and is there for your safety. Don't be stupid.

- **Never Drill, Machine, Weld, Deform, Scratch, Drop, or Modify a Nitrous Oxide Tank in ANY Way Whatsoever!** Although some people have polished their tanks to a chrome-like appearance, even this is not recommended because it removes a non-uniform layer of the tank's material that may or may not affect its integrity. Certainly, never attempt to subject a nitrous tank to any type of plating process because this often affects the strength of the tank's material.

- **Never Overfill Nitrous Cylinders**: That tiny little bit extra will put you and others at great risk for injury. More often than not, when the cylinder warms up, the pressure goes above the limit of the safety relief disc and you lose all the nitrous you just paid for. If you are a retail dealer and you overfill a cylinder beyond its rated capacity in weight, whether intentional or not, you could be held liable for the consequences of any damages or injury. If your customer specifically requests an overfill, don't do it.

- **All the Power Comes From the Fuel, Not the Nitrous**: Nitrous oxide is simply a tool that allows you to adjust how much and how quickly the engine burns the fuel. If the fuel isn't there, the power won't be either.

- **Avoid Detonation at All Times**: Nitrous enhanced detonation is much more damaging than detonation that occurs when naturally-aspirated due to the increased amount of fuel available for releasing energy and the fact that more oxygen is present.

- **When You Check the Spark Plugs, Check EVERY Plug**: Don't just "spot check" the easiest plug you can get to. Due to the wide possibility of air/fuel mixture variations, you need to check every single plug for signs of detonation or other problems.

- **Always Start With the Recommended Calibration That Came With Your System**: If your system is an adjustable type, begin with the lowest supplied level of calibration. The 'calibration' is the combination of nitrous and fuel jets that determine how much nitrous and fuel will flow when the system is activated.

- **At the First Sign of Detonation, Backfire, or Misfire, ALWAYS REDUCE THE NITROUS JET FIRST!** Don't think that you'll "cool things down" by adding more fuel. Since nitrous oxide is an oxidizer, the safest approach is to reduce the nitrous first, identity the problem, and go from there.

- **Check the Fuel and Nitrous Filter Screens on a Regular Basis**: This rates right up there with the most common problems that can lead you in circles for days. It doesn't take much to alter the calibration. Even a small scrap of pipe sealing tape can cause big problems.

- **If, When Your System is Activated, Something Doesn't Feel or Sound Right, BACK OFF**: If you hear any detonation or feel anything unusual, get off the throttle. It's a lot easier to check everything over than it is to just try to drive through it and break a lot of expensive parts.

PUSHING THE LIMITS

HOW MUCH POWER CAN YOUR ENGINE TAKE?

How much power? That question is usually the first asked when considering the purchase of a nitrous oxide injection system. The short answer is, "How much power can your engine take?" A more complete answer will require a modest investment of your time and attention.

We mentioned this briefly in the introduction but it bears repeating and expanding here. Over-estimating the power level that the engine can adequately and reliably handle as well as mistuning the system is what breaks engines, not nitrous oxide. This is what gives nitrous systems a reputation for destroying engines. The firms providing nitrous systems deliver to you the amount of additional power you request. The strength of the container you provide to capture and transform this power is your responsibility.

There are limits to the power that your engine can produce without being harmed. Defining those limits is the goal for this chapter.

It's vital to appreciate that these limits fall within a range. There are too many variables interacting, each with its own range of uncertainty, to state unequivocally the precise limit where an engine will fail, with or without the use of nitrous oxide.

TWO LIMITS: FUEL AND MECHANICAL

The power level you can expect from a nitrous system is limited by two things: The mechanical/physical strength of the materials from which your engine is made, and the power producing potential of the engine and its components. The material limitations have to do with containing the forces produced by introducing nitrous oxide and additional fuel into the combustion chamber. The power-producing component combination has to do with the airflow potential of your engine. Intake manifold, head, cam, and exhaust flow potential limit power output, though not usually with the catastrophic results associated with material failures.

As we shall explain in more detail later in the book, horsepower is a rate of work that is directly related to the rate of air an engine is capable of flowing. The connection of this flow rate and nitrous oxide is this: how much power a nitrous system will produce is directly related to the power potential, i.e. air flow potential of the engine. In other words, nitrous systems work best when they enhance your engine's power combination. If you have a high-flowing intake, cam, head, and exhaust components, your engine will produce high levels of horsepower. Adding a properly tuned nitrous system will make even more power.

While it is true that most failures result from trying to get more power from an engine than its materials can physically contain, many failures occur from trying to use the nitrous system to overcome the air flow potential of the engine. This is really a tuning issue because the cause behind the failure can almost always be traced to creating the conditions that result in detonation. When fuel detonates instead of burning in a controlled manner, it no longer produces power at the wheels. It simply destroys pistons, rods, and bearings, and ultimately your engine. Detonation, its causes, and how to avoid it are discussed in great detail in subsequent chapters.

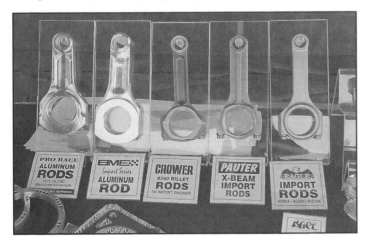

Cast connecting rods tend to break under the high compressive loads generated with large doses of nitrous oxide. For most applications factory forged connecting rods are acceptable. For very high output applications, a steel billet or aluminum rod is suggested.

With the theoretical reasoning out of the way, here are some practical methods and observations that will help you make the most efficient and safest use of your nitrous system.

DRY SYSTEM POWER LIMITS

A dry manifold system delivers a specific amount of nitrous by virtue of its jetting and bottle pressure. That amount of nitrous needs to be mixed with an additional amount of fuel in order to maintain the appropriate oxygen-to-fuel ratios.

In a dry manifold system, the fuel injectors deliver the enrichment fuel. Instead of having a second fuel supply calibrated by pressure and jetting, the fuel injectors deliver more fuel by increasing their fuel pressure. The formula for this is given in the engine management chapter. But we'll repeat it here:

$$F_2 = \sqrt{P_2/P_1} * F_1$$

Where:

F2 = New Fuel Flow Rate
F1 = Original Fuel Flow Rate
P2 = New Fuel Pressure
P1 = Original Fuel Pressure

Since the power comes from the fuel, the limit in this case is going to be the stock fuel system. To find the approximate power limit of the stock system, we can work from the rated power output of the engine and make a few assumptions about the fuel injectors. (For a greater discussion of this, refer to the *High Performance Honda Builder's Handbook*. In that book is a section on fuel injection where Russ Collins tells you about most stock fuel injectors and their pressure limits and behaviors above 80-85% duty cycles.)

The assumptions we'll use, in addition to a Brake Specific Fuel Consumption (BSFC) of .5, is that the max duty cycle of the stock injector is 80% @ 7000 rpm; max fuel pressure is 55 psi, with a limit of a 30% increase over stock fuel pressure.

Using a 1996 Acura Integra 1.8 liter RS as an example, we first note the

power rating of the engine. It is rated at 142 horsepower at 6300 rpm. That means the engine makes approximately 35.5 horsepower per cylinder.

The formula for finding the power potential of an injector is:

$$HORSEPOWER = \frac{Flow\ rate \times \%\ duty\ cycle}{BSFC}$$

For our example then:

$$35.5 = \frac{Flow\ rate \times .8}{.5}$$

Which changes form when we solve for flow rate:

$$Flow\ Rate = \frac{35.5 \times .5}{.8}$$

Which is solved as:

$$Flow\ Rate = 22.19\ lbs./hr.\ of\ fuel$$
at max horsepower

This figure (22.19 lbs/hr.) is the rate of flow for each injector at the maxi-

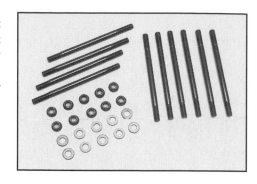

Tru-Torque Head Studs from AEM are made to handle the extreme cylinder pressures encountered during high rpm performance driving. These fasteners are made from 8740 chrome-moly steel to withstand the massive pressures of racing. (AEM)

mum rated power of the engine. It is not the advertised flow rating of the injector. The advertised flow rating is based on fuel flow through a locked open (100% duty cycle) injector at a specified fuel pressure. Ours is a working flow rate from which you can estimate the rated flow of the injector by adding 20%. In this case, to find our estimated injector

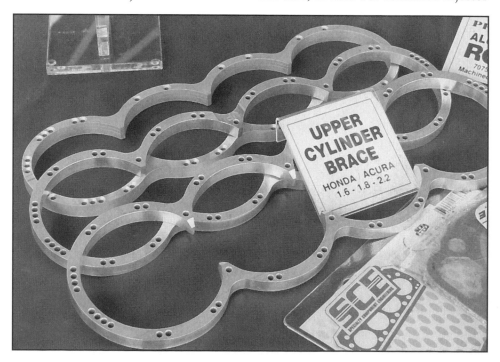

Floating style cylinders need to be stabilized when running heavy doses of nitrous and/or boost. These stabilizer plates work great, or you can fill the block old school style. In addition, four-bolt main cap blocks reduce the tendency for the main caps to "walk" under high output loading. Cylinder head studs decrease the chance of cylinder heads lifting or moving relative to the cylinder block deck surface.

flow rate we add 20% to 22.19 lbs./hr., for a flow rate of 26.6 lbs./hr.

Now that we know the naturally aspirated fuel flow rate, we can find the power limits of the stock fuel system with the required increase in fuel line pressure with a nitrous system.

Using the formula above to determine the potential fuel flow from the stock system and therefore the additional power it will support, we find:

P1 = 55 psi (assumed)
P2 = 71.5 psi (30% increase)
F1 = 22.19 lbs./hr.
F2 = 25.30 lbs./hr.

So you can raise the fuel pressure to 71.5 psi and deliver 25.3 lbs./hr. of fuel with a reasonable expectation of reliability from the fuel injectors.

The 25.3 lbs./hr. figures out to:

$$(25.3*.8)/.5 = 40.5 \text{ horsepower}$$

Remember, that number is per cylinder. So with nitrous oxide, our 4-cylinder, 1.8 liter engine with the stock fuel system has a potential of 162 horsepower or just over a 14% increase in total power. Per cylinder, we're up from 35.5 horsepower to 40.48 horsepower.

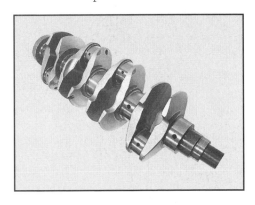

Stock cast crankshafts may break. For most applications a factory forging is acceptable, but aftermarket units are recommended for very high-output applications. Crower offers a billet stroker crank or reworked factory crank for Honda B16 blocks. Custom billet crankshafts are available for any make (Nissan, Toyota, Mitsubishi, Porsche, etc.), however lead times are 2-3 months for delivery. (Crower)

Cast pistons are prone to failure at the elevated temperatures and pressures a nitrous-enhanced engine generates. Fortunately Race Engineering and other manufacturers are supplying quality forged pistons for just about any engine combo. If you don't see it on the shelf, ask, and they'll make it for you. Just be prepared to pay for it.

This is the limit if you want to maintain any assurance of reliability from the injectors. If you want to take a chance and step up the fuel pressure by 50%, 75%, or 100%, you're asking for an injector failure which could lean one or more cylinders and force detonation. We don't recommend it, but we'll run the numbers at 50% fuel pressure increase to see if it's worth the risk.

P1 = 55 psi
P2 = 82.5 psi (55 x 1.5= 82.5)
F1 = 22.19 lbs./hr.
F2 = 27.18 lbs./hr.

With a 50-percent increase in fuel pressure across the stock injectors, horsepower increases to 43.48/cylinder or 174 hp total for all four. This represents a net gain per cylinder of 3 horsepower per cylinder. In terms of percentage increase over stock, tuning in a 50-percent increase in fuel pressure gives you a 22.5% increase in power.

We don't suggest adding any further power than this, and only add what we've suggested if you understand that you are operating beyond what is considered stable and reliable injector oper-ation and are increasing the risk of damaging your engine.

Stock ignition systems are prone to producing misfires at high-rpm, when subjected to high cylinder pressures. A quality aftermarket racing ignition is suggested. The Accel 300+ ignition system was designed to be the most compact, lightest, most powerful and most reliable ignition system available. It's fully epoxy encapsulated for water and vibration resistance in extremely demanding environments. The unit also features a low operating current draw, and an integral rev limiter, which can easily be changed with a rotary dial. (Accel)

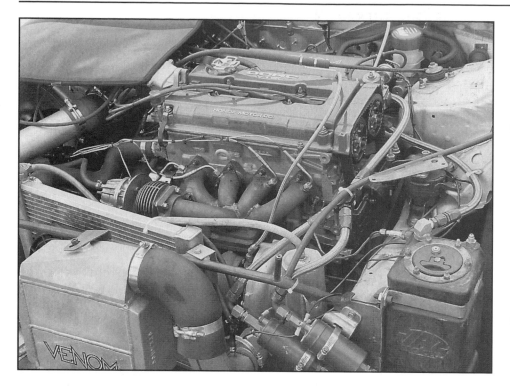

This Turbocharged GS-R engine is part of Venom's R&D efforts behind the company's nitrous system product line. Venom, along with NOS, NX, and Edelbrock, provide performance enthusiasts with reliable, tunable hardware and electronic controllers to realize nitrous' enormous power potential.

You can also use these formulas to guide your fuel injector size choice and the fuel pressure you need to run in order to meet your nitrous enhanced perform-ance goals. Just plug in the numbers and do math before you try to go fast.

If you increase the flow capacity of the fuel system, you can increase the power of most stock combinations to the level supported by the additional fuel. This assumes that the additional capacity is managed effectively and efficiently. Additional injectors and controllers are available on the after market.

Mechanically, most stock combinations will support a 40 to 50% increase in power output. If you intend to increase engine output by more than 40%-50%, the following engine modifications are suggested:

- **Rotary Engine Apex Seals.** In rotary engines, standard apex seals tend to be brittle and can break under high combustion pressures. High-perform-ance iron (not carbon) apex seals will provide superior durability.
- **Forged Pistons.** Cast pistons are very prone to failure at elevated cylinder temperatures and pressures.
- **Connecting Rods.** Cast connecting rods tend to break under the high compressive loads generated with large doses of nitrous oxide. For most applications, factory-forged connect-ing rods are acceptable. For very high output applications, use steel billet or aluminum rods.
- **Cylinder Block.** Floating-style cylin-ders need to be stabilized when run-ning heavy doses of nitrous and/or boost. Adding a deck plate works great, or you can fill the block old-school style. Four-bolt main cap blocks reduce the tendency for the main caps to "walk" under high out-put loading. Cylinder head studs decrease the chance of cylinder heads lifting or moving relative to the cylin-der block deck surface.
- **Crankshaft.** Stock cast crankshafts may break. For most applications a factory forging is acceptable. Aftermarket cranks are recommended for very high output applications.
- **High-Output Ignition System.** Stock ignition systems are prone to produc-ing misfires at high RPM, when sub-jected to high cylinder pressures. A quality aftermarket racing ignition is suggested.

Much of the allure of the Honda/Acura engines comes from the robust, reliable design. Lots of webbing strengthens the aluminum alloy block, which allows it to contain more force. The floating siamese cylinder bank is a concern for serious all-out racing engines, but upper cylinder bracing and filling the block are time-proven tactics to stabilize this area.

The crankshaft on this modified B-18 engine features five main bearings for plenty of support; the stock rods and pistons have been replaced with Carrillo rods and Ross forged pistons. The assembly has been balanced and is good to contain at least 500 horsepow-er, assuming it is properly tuned and not experiencing detonation.

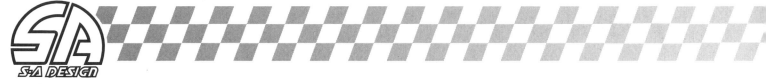

NITROUS SYSTEMS FOR EVERY NEED

Nitrous systems come in several configurations that support any performance need, from mild street system to monster multi-stage 1500 hp racing systems. For our purposes we'll divide the categories into street/strip, supercharging and turbo charging applications, and race-only competition systems. Within these categories, two methods are used to deliver the nitrous and fuel mix to the engine: a plate system and mixing nozzles. Using variations of these two delivery systems allows a nitrous tuner to generate incredible power for professional racing competitions or mild to wild street/strip systems for the performance enthusiast.

A BASIC NITROUS SYSTEM

A nitrous oxide system begins with the bottle of nitrous. The most common bottle is an aluminum tank containing 10 pounds of nitrous oxide. A bottle's weight is how you determine how much nitrous it contains. The bottle will have a label on it that tells you the weight of the bottle when empty and when full. The bottle has a safety pressure-relief disc mounted in the valve. This disc is required by law to relieve the pressure in the bottle if it gets too high. At room temperature the pressure of a typical nitrous bottle is about 850 psi. The safety disc will rupture at somewhere around 1200 psi. Each bottle also carries a certification date stamped into it. When you get your bottle refilled, the refill vendor cannot legally refill your bottle if it's out of date. An out-of-date bottle has to pass a pressure test and get recertified before being refilled.

Inside each bottle is a tube that is attached to the bottle valve and extends to the bottom of the inside of the bottle. More nitrous can be transferred in liquid form than in gaseous form. This fact permits small hoses and lines to carry the nitrous toward the engine. The tube

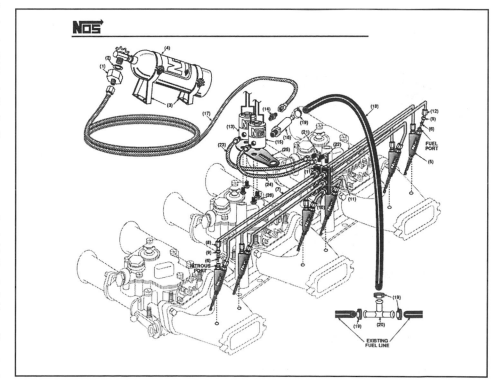

Here is the basic layout of the nitrous side of a nitrous system. The bottle contains the pressurized nitrous. A high-pressure hose delivers it to the injection nozzle(s). Delivery is controlled by electrical solenoids and flow rates are controlled by jets. (NOS)

inside the bottle is called a siphon tube. It sucks up liquid nitrous until there is very little left. Each manufacturer supplies instructions for mounting the bottle. The instructions show how to properly position the siphon tube so the liquid nitrous flows during acceleration.

The bottle is usually mounted in the trunk for convenience — and also because it doesn't fit well anywhere else. A high-pressure hose gets the nitrous from the bottle to the rest of the system under the hood. This is a special hose that has a Teflon inner liner and a braided-steel outer covering. The ends are power-crimped. Don't replace this hose with a standard neoprene-rubber-lined braided-steel hose, especially one that has screw-together-type ends. These types of hoses cannot take the high pressures of a nitrous system, and they will become very brittle at the extremely low temperatures of nitrous.

The solenoids are the next step. There is one solenoid for nitrous and one for fuel in a typical system. Systems designed for factory fuel-injected cars often don't use a fuel solenoid. These

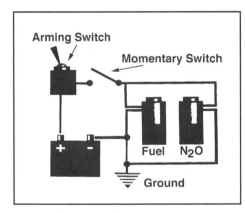

The most basic, bare-bones nitrous systems have only two switches between the battery and the solenoids. The "arming switch," makes 12 volts from the battery available to the second switch. The second switch is a momentary, spring-loaded switch that is manually operated. With the arming switch "on" and the momentary switch depressed, or squeezed (hence the slang terminology "on the squeeze"), the solenoids open and the system is activated. This style of actuation circuitry was the first used to control nitrous systems. (NOS)

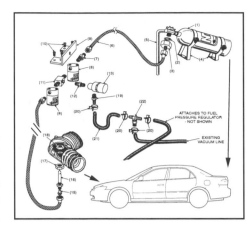

Since dry manifold systems use the fuel injectors to deliver the enrichment fuel, some means must be devised to adjust the fuel pressure to force the injectors to deliver the proper amount of additional fuel. This is accomplished by a feedback circuit, which uses the nitrous system's pressure to provide a signal to a pressure-sensitive adjustable fuel pressure regulator. (NOS)

systems are known as dry manifold systems. They supply the additional fuel during nitrous-assisted operation by raising the fuel pressure to the fuel injectors. The solenoids are the valves that control the on/off operation of the system. These electromechanical valves use 12 volts to create a strong magnetic field, which in turn pulls open a small plunger. The solenoids are designed so that the supply pressure assists in keeping the valve closed. The arrangement works similar to a ball covering the drain in a bathtub. As the water gets deeper the pressure on the ball increases, thereby increasing the sealing action. In a solenoid, the magnetism created by the wire windings of the coil must be strong enough to pull open the plunger. A solenoid is simply an electrically operated valve.

The most basic, bare-bones nitrous systems have only two switches between the battery and the solenoids (see Basic Wiring diagram). The "arming switch" makes 12 volts from the battery available to the second switch. The second switch is a momentary, spring-loaded switch that is manually operated by hand. With the arming switch "on" and the momentary switch depressed, or

squeezed (hence the slang terminology "on the squeeze"), the solenoids open and the system is activated. This style of actuation circuitry was the first used to control nitrous systems.

From the solenoids, the nitrous and the fuel — which are still completely separated from each other — travel to the small jets that control how much nitrous oxide and fuel are delivered to the engine. These jets are typically small brass inserts that can be easily changed for tuning purposes. After passing through the jets, the nitrous and the fuel enter the engine.

There are various schemes for introducing these substances to the engine. The most common method for carbureted applications involves a thin plate, which is plumbed to deliver both nitrous and fuel. Another method of getting nitrous and fuel into the engine involves a mixer nozzle that combines the nitrous and the fuel as they are injected into the engine. It can be used as a single nozzle for the entire engine or as individual nozzles per cylinder. The individual nozzles allow you to tune each cylinder differently if necessary.

In a wet manifold system, one circuit delivers nitrous; the other delivers fuel. Solenoids control the flow, on or off. It's easy to build a two stage or

Several types of pressure sensitive fuel pressure regulators are available with a variety of pressure rise curves to accommodate your engine's fuel needs. Though this is more important and sensitive with turbos and superchargers, it is still vital to get the correct pressure rise at the injector as required by the nitrous jetting and bottle pressure in order to generate the proper mixture ratio.

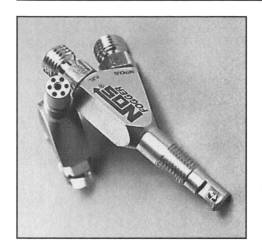

NOS offers these annular discharge nozzles. They produce a specific plume shape that can improve performance depending on the flow behavior of your combination. (NOS)

three stage system. Add another layer of nitrous and fuel delivery circuits and you've got a two-stage system. Actually, by adding the second set of nitrous and fuel circuits, you've got a three-stage system.

Here's how it works: activate the first system; when the second stage activates, usually the first switches off. To activate the third stage, both circuits flow nitrous and fuel. Designing the electrical circuits to control each circuit can add a certain level of complexity, but not so complex that it's beyond the average enthusiast's abilities.

For every type of nitrous system, it is extremely important that the fuel supply from the fuel side of the system is reliable and stable. The calibration accuracy of any nitrous system depends on the ability of the fuel side to deliver a consistent flow of fuel at a consistent pressure. Most carbureted systems tap the fuel line into the carburetor to supply fuel to the fuel solenoid. This method is adequate up to a certain power level. At higher power levels a separate fuel pump, usually electric, supplies an adequate amount of fuel. A fuel-pressure regulator, which keeps the fuel pressure at a constant level, may be required to maintain the calibration accuracy. A majority of the problems encountered with nitrous systems can be traced to an inconsistent fuel supply.

TYPES OF NITROUS SYSTEMS

Today, the most common system for sport compact applications is a dry manifold system. It is called a dry manifold system because there isn't any fuel present in the intake manifold. Such systems use a spray nozzle to deliver nitrous oxide (but no fuel) to the intake. The additional fuel is supplied by increasing fuel pressure when the nitrous system is activated. A dry manifold system is safer than a wet manifold system because nitrous by itself is not explosive. It's when you mix nitrous with fuel in the manifold that you get spectacular manifold and hood removals.

The next most common delivery method is a plate. This method involves a thin plate, which mounts downstream of a carburetor or at some point in the intake of a fuel-injected engine. These plates have two thin brass tubes paired together, one over the other. The upper tube usually delivers the nitrous and the lower tube usually delivers the fuel. This is the most common arrangement and uses the high velocity of the nitrous as it comes out of the upper tube to atomize the fuel.

Systems that use individual mixer nozzles, such as NOS's Direct Port systems, as well as others, are third most common and are usually found in very high-horsepower racing systems. This type of nozzle combines the nitrous and the fuel as they are injected into the engine. These systems use individual nozzles for each cylinder, allowing you to tune each cylinder differently if necessary. These systems are found on both carbureted and fuel-injected engines.

Nitrous systems designed for use with turbochargers have become very popular because they provide the low-end power traditionally missing from small-displacement, high-output turbocharged engines. The best systems have devices, RPM switches, boost-level switches, etc. that automatically stop the system when the turbochargers have "spun up" to carry the air flow and power demand of the engine.

Nitrous can also be used with superchargers. Typically, nitrous application on supercharged engines is to provide an intercooler effect. However, enrichment fuel has to be added to control combustion and avoid detonation. In addition, the fuel octane and energy content must be selected carefully.

The least common delivery method is found in hybrid racing systems, which use a plate and individual mixing nozzle schemes. Such systems are usually staged, i.e., the plate system is active off the start, then it is switched off and the second stage, usually the mixer nozzle system, is activated. Serious nitrous racers can also activate both first and second stages creating a third stage. Staged nitrous systems evolved from the fixed flow characteristics of nitrous systems. Because each stage delivers a fixed rate of fuel and nitrous, the engine demands more flow as it revs higher. The second and third stages are calibrated and tuned to be switched on as engine demand increases.

SYSTEM BUYERS GUIDE

The aftermarket industry makes it extremely easy and reasonably safe to use nitrous oxide to enhance your engine performance. While not an exhaustive list of manufactures that supply nitrous kits and components, the following will provide a good over view

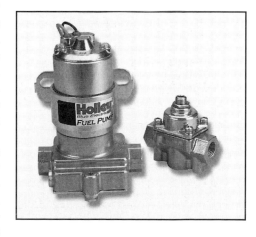

The Holley "Blue" electric fuel pump is a low-pressure unit perfect for an NOS wet system. The unit has a new lower housing casting for enhanced fuel flow. It's rated at 110 GPH in free flow and 70 GPH at 9 psi. It's not compatible with alcohol fuels and is not designed to supply high-pressure fuel-injection systems. (Holley)

NOS has developed safe and reliable dry manifold nitrous kits to fit most popular sport compact cars with EFI. These kits are easy to install and make very impressive power gains without impacting drivability. (NOS)

of the types of systems and kits available on the market. In addition, we'll explore some of the more important accessories and components.

NOS Factory Fuel-Injected Engine Kits

Nitrous Oxide Systems Inc. (NOS) kit number 5120 is intended for use on 2.8 – 3.4L multi-port injected engines that are equipped with return-style fuel systems. Kit number 5122 is intended for use on late model passenger car engines displacing 1.3 – 2.3L. Kit number 5123 is designed for use on late model passenger car engines displacing 2.4 – 3.0L. Kit number 5124 is intended for use on late model passenger car engines displacing 3.1 - 4.0L.

Kit numbers 5122, 5123, and 5124 all flow fuel through an engine's stock fuel injectors. Necessary fuel flow is accomplished by increasing the fuel pressure and fuel flow rate. Stock fuel injection systems typically operate at 38 - 45 psi. Kit numbers 5122, 5123, and 5124 increase fuel pressure to 60 - 70 psi. Always use high-pressure fuel hose when replacing or repairing fuel lines.

Horsepower and torque increases due to these kits will vary with engine displacement and modifications. Approximate power increase estimates can be made based upon the mass flow of nitrous oxide into the engine. The following table is provided to allow you to

estimate the power increase you can expect for your application. NOS strongly suggests an upper limit of about 40% to 50% increase in power output from your stock engine. Exceeding this can result in premature engine failure. Drivability, fuel economy, and exhaust emission should not be affected under normal (part-throttle) vehicle operation.

System Requirements: When used according to instructions, these kits will work with stock internal engine components. For vehicles with manual transmissions and those that will be exposed to severe operating conditions, such as drag strip use, the standard clutch should be replaced with a high-performance unit to ensure proper performance and drive line longevity. For vehicles with automatic transmissions that will be exposed to severe operating conditions, such as drag strip use, the automatic transmission should be serviced by a reputable high-performance transmission shop.

NOS Kits for Honda VTEC Engines NOS's VTEC system features the company's highly effective Big Shot injector plate, which attaches to the OEM Honda plenum. The Big Shot benefits from a unique "fogging" plate design that vastly improves nitrous flow, fuel atomization, and mixture distribution. How much of a difference can nitrous make? Kurt Gordon's street-driven Honda Civic runs

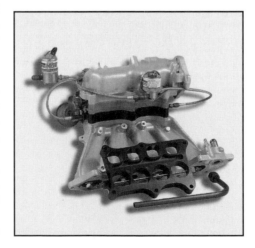

The NOS Prelude kit #02045 (A,B) fits 1997-1999 Honda Prelude with 2.2 VTEC engines. The plate system is specifically designed to fit the dual path manifold of the Prelude's VTEC engine. (NOS)

NOS offers a killer system for competition-spec import 4-cylinder and rotary engines. The adjustable, state of the art Pro Race Fogger system provides from 80 to 225 additional horsepower on properly built race engines. The Pro Race Fogger features the industry's best flowing valves, stainless hard lines, and the Pro Race bottom discharge solenoid. (NOS)

11.55 at 122 mph in the quarter mile, thanks to an NOS #2040 nitrous system.

NOS's new VTEC kit includes a 10-pound nitrous bottle, the Big Shot injector plate, fuel and nitrous solenoids, high-quality fittings and braided stainless lines, wiring, jets to adjust the amount of nitrous flowing through the system, hardware. In other words, everything needed for a professional-quality installation is included in this kit.

Part #	Description
02040 (A,B)	.1997-1999 Acura Integra GSR (1.8 VTEC)
02045 (A,B)	.1997-1999 Honda Prelude (2.2 VTEC)

Power levels for the NOS Sportsman Fogger systems are adjustable by changing fuel and nitrous jets on each Fogger2 Nozzle. The latest in high-tech solenoid technology allows for an extreme degree of reliability with adjustability ranging from a 30 to a 50% HP gain. All Sportsman Fogger Systems include a 10-lb. capacity nitrous bottle, nitrous and fuel solenoids, Fogger2 nozzles (including the tap for plumbing Fogger2 nozzles, #15990), filters, fittings, tubing, distribution blocks, jets, switches, aircraft quality steel braided hose, and all other necessary hardware for a complete installation (requires removal of intake manifold for plumbing).

Horsepower increases from these kits will vary with engine displacement and configuration. However, approximate power increases can be estimated based upon the mass flow of nitrous oxide into the engine.

Part #	Description
05030	4 cyl., (in-line) carbureted applications
05030-FI	4 cyl., (in-line) fuel-injected applications
05040	6 cyl., (in-line) carbureted applications
05080	VW/Porsche, 4 cyl., air-cooled, carbureted applications
05082	VW Competition Fogger, air-cooled, carbureted applications
05085	6 cyl., Porsche carb
05086	Mazda rotary, carbureted

Opposed 4/6 Cylinder Sportsman Fogger

NOS Kits 5080 and 5082 are designed for opposed 4-cylinder engines. Kit 5085 is designed for opposed 6-cylinder engines.

Nitrous Express

Dry manifold kits are available from Nitrous Express for the following:

Part #	Description
20413	Acura
20413	Acura EFI (50-75 hp)
20814	BMW 4- & 6-cylinder EFI, all models (50-75 hp)
20815	BMW 8-cylinder EFI, all models (50-75-100-150 hp)
20816	BMW 12-cylinder EFI, all models (50-75-100-150 hp)
20817	BMW M3 2.3L (35-50-75 hp)
20313	Dodge Neon, all
20414	Honda
20414	Honda EFI, all (50-75 hp)
20816	Infinity EFI, all models (50-75-100 hp)
20913	Lexus V-8 EFI (50-75-100-150 hp)
20914	Lexus EFI, all models (50-75 hp)
20416	Mazda Miata, all

Part #	Description
20416	Mazda Miata, all models (50-75 hp)
20415	Mazda RX
20415	Mazda RX EFI, all (50-75 hp)
20714	Mitsubishi Eclipse (50-75 hp)
20716	Mitsubishi Eclipse EFI, turbo (35-50-75 hp)
20715	Mitsubishi 3000 GT, all models including VR4 (50-75 hp)
20614	Nissan EFI (50-75 hp)
20615	Nissan (all EFI ZX & SX series, except turbo) (50-75 hp)
20616	Nissan 300ZX twin turbo (35-50-75 hp)
20010	Porsche EFI, all models, non-turbo (50-75 hp)
20011	Porsche EFI, all models, turbo (50-75 hp)
20514	Toyota (all) including turbo
20417	Toyota MR2, all models (50-75 hp)
20514	Toyota EFI, all models including turbo (50-75 hp)
20917	VW EFI Corrado/Golf/Jetta, all models (50-75 hp)
20918	VW Beetle, water-cooled
20915	All Other EFI Sport Compact Cars
15499	Pro Wiring Kit (Includes all hardware to wire and 2 solenoid system)
UP215	Upsize (from 10-lb. to 15-lb. bottle)
00011	Bottle Downsize (from 15-lb. to 10-lb. bottle)
00010	10-lb. Bottle Discount (for use with preexisting bottle)
00015	15-lb. Bottle Discount (for use with preexisting bottle)

System Contents

- 10-lb. bottle with Pure-Flo valve
- Lifetime guaranteed large solenoids
- Hinged steel bottle brackets
- 14-foot stainless steel braided supply line
- Heavy-duty 40-amp anti-flyback relay
- All necessary hardware

Jim Wolf Technology (JWT)

JWT's Nitrous Oxide system eliminates the need for add-on fuel injectors or

The Zex Nitrous Oxide Kit is so simple to install, your mom could do it. When armed, the Zex Nitrous Kit kicks in electronically off the throttle position sensor and tells the fuel pressure regulator how much extra fuel to deliver. Results are the most constant nitrous-to-fuel ratio of any kit available. So while the other guy is trying to find the Nitrous switch, you have already won! The Zex Nitrous Oxide Kit is the ultimate in plug & play performance.

spray nozzles, since additional fuel is added through the existing injectors, as intended by the engine designer. A custom program module is installed inside the ECU that switches between two engine control programs. Program #1 is a normal performance program, used for maximum power when nitrous oxide is not used. Program #2 is activated only when the nitrous arming switch is on, and the throttle has been fully depressed.

On turbo cars, this system is designed as a supplemental system to fill in the low-end power missing from high-output turbocharged cars. The system automatically shuts itself off when the turbochargers have sufficiently spun up to carry the power demand.

The JWT Nitrous kit as installed in a 300ZX twin turbo uses one jet for each intake track for optimum distribution. While costing more, only pro-grade nitrous solenoids are used for maximum reliability.

JWT has integrated, computer controlled, Nitrous Oxide applications for the Infiniti G20, Infiniti Q45, Sentra, Sentra SE-R, 200SX SE-R, NX2000, 240SX, Maxima, Pathfinder, and Nissan trucks.

Nitrous at Work
Chris Rado's Acura: Fastest Unibody on the Planet

Christian Rado's awesome unibody Acura churns out well over 800 horsepower from its diminutive 1.8 liters of displacement. The Rob Smith-built engine is a marvelous blend of high-tech and traditional hot rod techniques. Chris chose to use alcohol as a fuel because it generates more horsepower than gasoline, it has a higher resistance to detonation, and alcohol motors run cooler. These characteristics are all suited to the use of high boost levels and nitrous injection. Rado uses the nitrous both to spool up the turbo and as a full-on max-effort "back up." When faced with a tough competitor, he'll hit a second stage of nitrous to increase the power output of the engine to the redline.

Here's an in-depth look at the Christian Rado nitrous-assisted combination that makes his car the quickest unibody on the planet.

Chris Rado's Acura ran in the low-9s at near 160 mph. The turbo/nitrous alcohol-fueled machine puts well over 800 ponies to the ground to pull 9-second e.t.s

Alcohol has about half the energy density per volume, so you have to run twice the amount compared to gasoline. The large single fuel delivery line splits at the Y-block that also contains the fuel pressure gauge. Then each line runs to an injector rail. Two rails support two sets of injectors. To supply over 800 horsepower and allow the car to idle requires two sets of injectors.

This detail shot of the intake shows the fuel rails and the fabricated intake plenum. Plenum size is a critical dimension that has a major impact on power output as does intake runner dimension.

An efficient exhaust system leading to the turbo helps make this motor very powerful. Horsepower is a rate of work and air flow so anything that makes the engine more flow-efficient helps it make power.

Rado's crew is an important part of the formula for this "World's Fastest Unibody Front-Drive Drag Racer," but nitrous is the key to the car's incredible performance. A quick shot of nitrous spools up the turbo to make the power. In addition, an override switch lets Rado keep the nitrous pumping to provide additional oxygen and intercooling. When tuned properly, the result is one very fast Acura.

Under the hood of Rado's super-fast Unibody Acura. Every effort is made to get as much weight forward so that the tires provide more grip on launch. The air-to-water intercooler reservoir and the radiator are positioned in front of the front axle.

THE FUEL SYSTEM

To reinforce the importance of this concept, we'll say it one more time: Fuel is the source of engine power. This chapter addresses how much fuel your engine will demand at various power levels; as well as how to design a fuel system to reliably and consistently supply the fuel. We discuss carbureted applications in this section because they are an inexpensive alternative to aftermarket engine management systems, and when tuned properly, they make horsepower reliably and efficiently.

The air-to-fuel ratio (a/f ratio) that is accepted as safe and will produce the most acceleration from a naturally aspirated, gasoline-fueled, four-stroke engine is 12.8:1. At this air/fuel ratio, if your component combination is good and the engine tuned properly, you will get a brake specific fuel consumption (BSFC) of approximately .5 lb./horsepower/hour. Advanced engine tuners can run an a/f ratio of 13:1 and .45 BSFC to get the most steady state power from an engine. Keep in mind you're getting closer to the lean side of the fuel curve, and if you're not completely dialed in you can get into detonation. By the way, these ratios are for full-throttle, high-load situations. When you're cruising under low-load conditions, you can run right at 14.7:1 (the theoretical ratio that allows complete reaction of fuel and available oxygen) or lower, depending on the engine load.

When you add nitrous to the mix, you need to add fuel because of the high oxygen content of nitrous and the super-cooled state in which it arrives at the combustion chamber. The fuel flow-to-horsepower chart shows the relationship between fuel flow and horsepower requirements for a particular power level at a BSFC of .50.

Fuel Consumption and Horsepower @ BSFC = 0.50					
Horsepower	Gas lbs./hr	Gas Gals./hr	Gas Gals./min.	Mins. to flow 1-gal	Secs. to flow 1-gal
500	250	37.93	0.63	1.58	94.90
480	240	36.41	0.60	1.64	98.85
460	230	34.90	0.58	1.71	103.15
440	220	33.38	0.55	1.79	107.84
420	210	31.86	0.53	1.88	112.97
400	200	30.34	0.50	1.97	118.62
380	190	28.83	0.48	2.08	124.86
360	180	27.31	0.45	2.19	131.80
340	170	25.79	0.42	2.32	139.55
320	160	24.27	0.40	2.47	148.28
300	150	22.76	0.37	2.63	158.16
280	140	21.24	0.35	2.82	169.46
260	130	19.726	0.32	3.04	182.49
240	120	18.20	0.30	3.29	197.70
220	110	16.69	0.27	3.59	215.67
200	100	15.17	0.25	3.95	237.24
180	90	13.657	0.22	4.39	263.60
160	80	12.13	0.20	4.94	296.55
140	70	10.62	0.17	5.64	338.91
120	60	9.10	0.15	6.59	395.40
100	50	7.58	0.12	7.90	474.48

An engine's power output comes from the fuel. It takes a certain amount of fuel to make a certain amount of power. This chart details the accepted average brake specific fuel consumption of a properly tuned gasoline fueled engine. Use the chart as a guide to aid in nitrous-to-fuel jetting at different power levels and to design your fuel system's flow capacity.

Most experienced nitrous tuners recommend starting with a 5:1 nitrous-to-fuel ratio. This is on the rich side, but it has a very low probability of detonation and yet makes good power. From this ratio a racer should tune toward a 6:1 nitrous-to-fuel ratio. At these levels of nitrous consumption, Harold Bettes of Super Flow Corp., suggested I include a chart displaying the flow rates at .7 BSFC, a rate he says is a good rule of thumb value for the total fuel flow demands placed on the fuel system of a gasoline-fueled engine using nitrous. (These charts are included in the engine tuning reference chapter.) If you use methanol you'll need about double the flow capacity because of methanol's low energy density compared to gasoline.

The reason you need to build a fuel system with more capacity than you need is because maintenance of adequate fuel pressure and delivery is an absolute must to ensure proper performance and engine life. Most carburetors are designed to operate at 5-10 psi. When designing your fuel system, plan on your pumps and lines flowing at least 0.1 gallon of gasoline per hour per horsepower at 5 psi. For example, an engine that makes 350 hp when the nitrous system is activated will require a fuel pump that flows at least 35 gallons per hour at 5 psi. Fuel pumps tend to be rated at free flowing conditions; at 5-psi fuel pressure, their flow rates may be greatly reduced. Stock fuel injection systems typically operate at 35-40 psi and most nitrous kits for fuel-injected engines increase fuel pressure to 80 psi. Remember to always use quality high-pressure fuel hose when installing such kits.

DESIGNING A FUEL SYSTEM

Two types of fuel pumps are produced for gasoline engines: low pressure (4 - 10 psi) and high pressure (30 - 90 psi). Low-pressure pumps are intended for carbureted engines. You can also use them for wet nitrous systems. Common examples are the 110 and 140 gallon per hour (gph) units marketed by a number of manufacturers. These pumps are rated under free flow exit conditions (no outlet restriction). When the outlet of the pump is restricted (real world conditions) the flow capacity is usually significantly less than the rated performance. Low-pressure pumps are the most economical to produce. In most carbureted applications a low-pressure pump will provide adequate performance and enjoy a cost advantage. Flow capabilities of high-pressure pumps are specified at typical real world pressure levels. This results in pumps performing much closer to the manufacturer's claim than most low-pressure units.

High-pressure pumps will work well in carbureted applications when matched with the correct bypassing fuel pressure regulator. Never attempt to use a high-pressure pump with a dead-heading fuel pressure regulator. (Note: For more information on regulators see "Choosing the Correct Fuel Pressure Regulator.") High-pressure pumps are constructed with closer tolerances and more costly production techniques. High-pressure pumps will tolerate more severe operating conditions and last longer than low-pressure units.

Choosing a Fuel Pump

When purchasing a fuel pump there are two factors to consider: performance and cost. By correctly matching a fuel pump to your requirements, you can fill your needs without spending money needlessly. Using the tips below you should be able to choose the correct pump for your vehicle.

1. Determine the horsepower the pump will have to support (be realistic — no inflated values).
2. Estimate the number of gallons of fuel per hour required to support that horsepower figure. Note: these figures are for gasoline, for alcohol double them. For four-cycle engines: multiply horsepower by 0.08 to 0.095. For two-cycle engines: multiply horsepower by 0.095 to 0.11. The result is the number of gallons of fuel per hour (gph) required.
3. Determine the fuel pressure at which the pump will operate. For carbureted engines this should be 6 to 10 psi. For fuel-injected applications you will have to determine the required pressure.
4. Examine the flow-versus-pressure curve for the pump you are considering. Your flow requirements should be on or below the pump's plotted performance. Note: In some instances it is impractical to use a single fuel pump. It is possible to run two pumps in parallel, resulting in an approximate doubling of flow rate if done correctly. In high-pressure applications two pumps may be run in a series. This occurs when trying to increase the fuel flow rate in a late-model fuel-injected vehicle. The resulting flow of this arrangement is not equal to the sum of the flow rates of the two pumps (it will be less).

Now let's look at the proper way to check fuel flow. All reputable pump manufacturers rate their fuel pumps at gallons per hour at a specific pressure. First, estimate the horsepower of the engine you are trying to feed. Divide the estimated horsepower by 2 to get a fuel flow rate required to support that maximum horsepower at a BSFC of .50. Once you have your theoretical fuel requirement in lb./hr. convert it to gallons per hour by dividing pounds of fuel by 6.2-6.8 lb./gal., depending on the density of the fuel. Now take this number (let's use 100 gal./hr.) and divide it by 60 to get the required flow in 1 minute. (Which would work out to be 1.66 gal./min.). If we take the reciprocal of this (1 divided by 1.66) we would get the fraction of a minute required to flow 1 gallon. This would be .6 minutes or 36 seconds.

Now let's get practical. Plumb a pressure gauge into a fuel line just before the carburetor or injectors followed by a small petcock or needle valve. Once you have safely attached the fuel line to a sealed vented measuring container of at least two gallons, turn on the pump and adjust the petcock valve until the pressure reads whatever pressure the pump is rated at. At this point, stop the pump, drain the container, and then get ready to measure the time required to fill one gallon in the container with flow at rated pressure! This method will ensure accu-

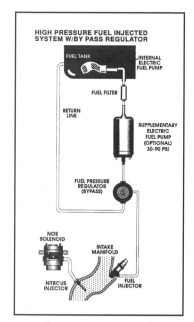

HIGH PRESSURE FUEL INJECTED SYSTEM W/BY PASS REGULATOR

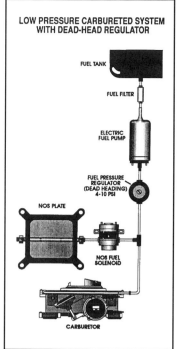

LOW PRESSURE CARBURETED SYSTEM WITH DEAD-HEAD REGULATOR

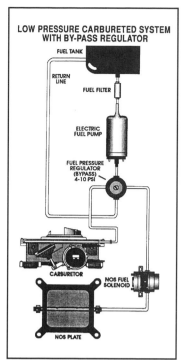

LOW PRESSURE CARBURETED SYSTEM WITH BY-PASS REGULATOR

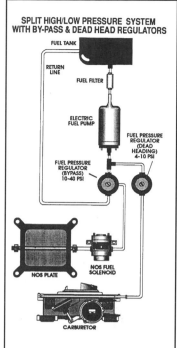

SPLIT HIGH/LOW PRESSURE SYSTEM WITH BY-PASS & DEAD HEAD REGULATORS

This high-pressure bypass fuel circuit provides steady fuel pressure to the injector. Adjustable bypass fuel pressure regulators receive a vacuum signal from the intake to raise pressure at the injector in order to deliver more fuel enabling more nitrous to be used to create a more powerful dry manifold system. (NOS)

A low-pressure system with a dead-headed fuel pressure regulator is the least stable fuel system for nitrous. While it'll work okay at low power levels, you don't want to use such a system when you're pushing the limits. (NOS)

A low-pressure bypass fuel system is a good system for low to moderate street systems on carbureted vehicles. You can still get variations in fuel delivery during launch, but at these power levels you should be safe. (NOS)

For all out racing apps with carburetion, this split high/low pressure system is ideal. You'll get rock steady fuel delivery on the fuel side of the nitrous system and very steady delivery on the carburetor side as well. (NOS)

rate results and cut through all the claims and counter claims.

TIP: If using an electric pump, make sure that you monitor voltage to the pump and make sure that the hot wire feeding the pump and ground wire will carry the amperage necessary to achieve full rated flow. Once you qualify your entire fuel delivery system using this method you will be amazed at how many "gremlins" disappear. – *From "Uncommon Sense in Engine Development," presented at the Super Flow Advanced Engine Technology Conference.*

Next, perform the same flow check of the enrichment fuel circuit of your nitrous system. That's the only way to be sure you're getting the fuel you think you are when you change fuel jets or pressure at the regulator.

A convenient way to accomplish this is to use a scale to measure the change in weight of the fuel and nitrous containers over the time of your test.

The procedure is rather simple in concept and can be performed with the full nitrous system as installed in your car. You just have to arrange to have enough length of nitrous line and an extension of fuel intake line to reach a remote fuel container sitting on a scale. If you can't do this with the fuel system you can capture and measure the fuel escaping at the nozzles in measured containers.

Choosing a Pressure Regulator

Two types of fuel pressure regulators are available: Dead-heading and bypassing. When working with a low-pressure pump, either type of pressure regulator can be used successfully. When using a high-pressure pump you must use a bypassing regulator. Using a dead-heading regulator with a high-pressure pump will result in premature pump failure and/or ruptured fuel lines. Regardless of which type of regulator

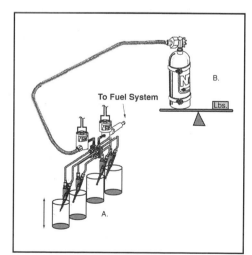

The only way to verify the actual mass fuel flow through the nitrous system is to measure it. One way to do this is to put the nozzles in a jig, place them in measured containers, and activate the system for a specific time. This is especially important on multi port designs as it confirms fuel flow to each cylinder.

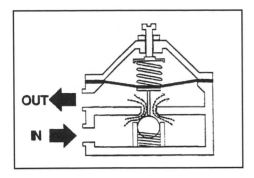

A dead-head fuel pressure regulator pulses the fuel flow. This isn't a problem when feeding a carburetor because of the fuel reserve in the fuel bowl. When regulating fuel to the fuel side of a nitrous system this pulsing causes fluctuations in the nitrous-to-fuel ratio. (NOS)

you choose, it is important that the regulator be matched to the flow capabilities of your fuel pump. Listed below are the characteristics of the two types of regulators available.

Dead-Heading: A dead-heading regulator works by regulating fuel pressure in the line down to a set value using a diaphragm/spring arrangement. Only fuel that passes through the regulator goes into the engine. If fuel requirement goes to zero, such as when the engine stops, fuel flow through the regulator ceases. If the fuel pump remains on, the fuel pressure in the line upstream of the regulator will climb to the value at which the pump stalls. Dead-heading regulators are relatively inexpensive, yet provide acceptable performance in most carbureted applications.

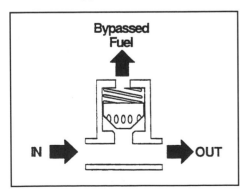

Bypass fuel pressure regulators provides stable fuel pressure. This is the preferred regulator to feed the fuel side of your nitrous system. (NOS)

Bypassing: A bypassing regulator controls fuel pressure by returning excess fuel to the fuel tank or the fuel line upstream of the fuel pump. This offers several advantages over the dead-heading regulator. Stress on the fuel pump is reduced by lowering the fuel pressure at which the pump operates. (The fuel pump will not see pressures above that of the regulator setting.) Fuel pressure is also more constant with a bypassing regulator (dead-heading regulators allow fuel pressure to pulse). When using nitrous oxide injection it is desirable to eliminate fuel pressure pulsing, or the nitrous/fuel ratio will fluctuate.

HIGH-PRESSURE RETURN-STYLE FUEL SYSTEMS

The fuel circuits of most nitrous oxide injection systems are usually configured to operate with 4 to 10 psi fuel pressure. They are set up to operate at

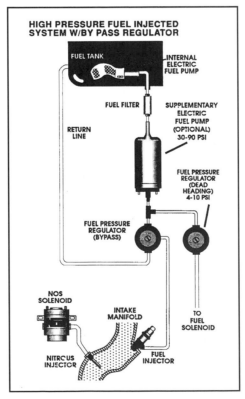

For a combination dry/wet nitrous system this fuel pressure regulator scheme works well. The dead-head regulator feeding the nitrous fuel side only sees on or off, so fluctuations shouldn't be an issue. (NOS)

these levels to be compatible with typical carbureted fuel systems. In most low-to-moderate output applications, this works fine.

In high-output and competition environments there are performance and tuning advantages from using elevated fuel pressure for these systems. Here's how it works. The fuel enrichment side of a nitrous kit is a fixed orifice/constant flow device. When the system is activated, the fuel solenoid opens fully and variations in fuel flow will only result from changes in fuel pressure.

The relationship between fuel pressure and fuel flow follows a fundamental law of fluid mechanics, i.e. flow is proportional to the square root of fuel pressure. In practical terms this means that at fuel pressure levels used with carburetors, small changes in fuel pressure produce significant changes in fuel flow rate. At fuel pressure levels used with fuel injection, the same size pressure fluctuations produce much smaller changes in flow rate. Examples one and two provide a comparison of the effects of typical fuel pressure fluctuations.

Example One

Fuel Pressure = 5 psi
Fuel Pressure Fluctuation = ±1 psi
This can produce flow deviations of:
1. Sq. rt. of 4/5 = .89, or 89 percent of baseline
2. Sq. rt. of 5/6 = 1.09, or 109 percent of baseline.

This means just a ±1 psi fluctuation in fuel pressure can change fuel flow up to 20 percent.

Example Two

Fuel Pressure = 30 psi.
Fuel Pressure Fluctuation = ±1 psi
This can produce flow changes of:
1. The square root of 4/5 = .983 or 98.3 percent of baseline
2. The square root of 5/6 = 101.6 or 101.6 percent of baseline

So, a change in fuel pressure of +/- 1 psi only changes actual fuel flow about 3.5 percent with the higher pressure.

It's obvious that higher fuel pressures reduce the potential variation in fuel flow rate to the nitrous system, keeping the nitrous/fuel ratio much more constant. Thus, lost horsepower due to overly rich conditions is minimized and engine damage from excessively lean mixtures is prevented. This lets you make much finer adjustments to nitrous/fuel ratio so you can walk right to the edge and not fall off.

UNDERSTANDING FUEL DELIVERY

Building and tuning a performance sport compact is a process that involves chasing down and correcting weak links in the performance chain. On the mechanical side, a car is a collection of systems that work together to produce power and motion. If any of these systems fail to deliver a required function, the performance of the whole machine suffers.

As displacement, RPM, nitrous flow increase, so does the engine's need for fuel. If the fuel system on your car fails to deliver an adequate fuel supply to the carburetor or fuel injection, then the air-to-fuel and nitrous-to-fuel ratios

This all new NOS high-pressure, high-volume electric fuel pump (Part # 15763) was specially designed to provide the ultimate in critical fuel delivery for nitrous-system applications. With dyno tested flow rates of 46 gph @ 40 psi, this NOS fuel pump can be used as a booster pump or stand-alone pump for EFI applications and, when coupled with a quality bypass regulator, the pump may be used with carbureted applications up to 550+ horsepower! Comes complete with anodized mounting bracket, isolating sock, and all necessary fittings for easy installation. (NOS)

will be affected, usually toward the lean side. However, it is possible to have too much pressure leading to an over-rich condition. Lean air/fuel ratios tend to cause cylinder temperatures to rise and can, in extreme conditions, lead to detonation and destroy your engine. A rich condition lowers cylinder temperatures and reduces power output.

Though a faulty fuel delivery system is not the only cause for lean or rich air/fuel ratios, it is a primary system that must function properly. If the fuel system doesn't deliver enough fuel to your carburetor and nitrous system, then no amount of tuning will achieve optimum engine performance.

There are three basic fuel delivery concepts to consider. One is the rated volume of the pump, the second is the inside diameter of the fuel line, and third is the fuel pressure, which is measured in pounds per square inch. Pressure and volume are related in that a higher pressure, for a given diameter of fuel line, will yield more volume, at least up to a point. Obviously a larger diameter line will have a higher-volume capacity.

Delivering an adequate fuel supply requires that the system overcome the force of gravity (since the carburetor is usually located higher than the fuel tank), the acceleration of the car, and the friction within the fuel line. As a general rule, a fuel line with a horizontal length of 13 feet between the tank and carburetor will lose 4 psi per G of acceleration. Losing pressure means you are also losing volume, and that means you might be losing performance.

The solution to this performance problem is to design a system that has an adequate reserve of pressure to overcome the effects of gravity and acceleration, and to install a fuel line that is of adequate diameter and is as free of needless bends as possible. Bends in the fuel lines and connections cause turbulence and friction, which reduce flow.

The trend in fuel system design has been toward high-pressure systems to overcome the obstacles stated above. In drag racing, Warren Johnson is credited with starting this move in the early '80s. His crew designed a high-torque fuel pump which revolutionized the way rac-

Holley in-line fuel pumps are designed to work in-line, not in the tank. Installation is quick and easy and these are available in several capacities to provide fuel at most levels. (Holley)

ers thought about fuel systems. Since then, using a high-torque, high-pressure, high-flow pump has been refined with the concept of using return lines, which offer advantages in fuel pressure stability, cooling, and bleeding off air in the fuel.

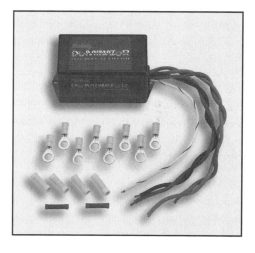

The Holley Pulse-Modulated Fuel Pump Controller provides efficient power management for high amperage-draw racing fuel pumps. Reducing electrical drain by the fuel pump allows the use of a smaller, lighter battery. This is a must for drag racers with high-energy electronic ignition systems that run without a charging system. The unit is driver activated and reduces electric flow current to the pump to prevent engine floods while at idle or part throttle. This unit provides reliability and longevity to any race pump by allowing the pump to operate at less than 100% when not racing. This pump is not for use with EFI systems. (Holley)

Holley's External EFI fuel pumps are engineered to provide the tremendous fuel volumes and pressures required by race motors. They are compatible with gasoline and methanol, accept 12v and 14v input, are rated for continuous duty, and accept -AN fittings. These pumps are available in free flow ratings of 600, 900, and, 1,200 lbs./hr. (Holley)

The old way — using a big Holley pump and regulators near the carbs — was very hard on the fuel pump's electric motor. With this kind of system you have a long column of fuel that constantly stops and starts as the regulator opened and closed to maintain its pressure setting. At the same time, the fuel pump's motor, being part of a hydraulic system,

This Holley EFI in-tank high-performance replacement pump #12-906 is rated at 255 liters per hour. These units provide more flow and use existing factory hangers and hardware. Holley has a version designed to support turbocharged/supercharged engines with a flow rating of 255 liters per hour. (Holley)

would stop and start with the fuel. Stopping an electric pump motor is very hard on the unit. Depending on where in its cycle it stopped it could create a closed circuit and burn out, which was a big problem with these early systems. By using a return line, the pump is allowed to stay in constant motion, thus delivering consistent pressure in the fuel line.

TIPS FOR TWEAKING AND TUNING YOUR FUEL SYSTEM

If you want a state of the art fuel system for a carbureted car, the following ideas will help you. Most, but not all, of the concepts apply to fuel-injected cars, which is why these tips are in this book. Of course, you'll still have to do the testing and tuning at the race track.

1. Delivering a consistent supply of fuel begins with choosing a proper fuel tank. Choose a tank with baffles to keep the fuel from sloshing away from the outlet during acceleration. It should also have fuel outlet bungs that are positioned at the rear of the tank, so that acceleration forces fuel into the fuel line before the pump.

2. Electric fuel pumps do not pull fuel well, they're better at pushing it. So the less restriction you have before the pump, the more efficient and stable your fuel supply will be. Low-pressure, high-volume systems are more sensitive to restrictions than high-pressure, low-volume systems. Since the system is gravity fed at this end by accelerating off the line, restrictions here can really impede the flow of fuel.

3. You can reduce the turbulence in the fuel line exiting the fuel tank by massaging the insides of the fitting to improve flow. It's similar to porting the heads. Drill out the I.D. of the fitting, then hand blend the angles of the male and female fittings. You have to be careful not to enlarge the I.D. too much or you'll compromise the integrity of the seal. This process is helpful if you have a fuel delivery problem.
   The inner diameter of the fuel line should be as big as the inner diameter of the fuel pump fittings. If two lines need to be split or joined in a "Y" or

"T" arrangement, the cross sectional area of the two lines should be equivalent to the cross sectional area of the single line. Lines should be kept as short and free of tight bends as practical.

4. Filter debris from the fuel before the pump so it can't cause a restriction or hurt the pump. It's best to position the fuel filter to make it easy to inspect and clean. Use a filter with lots of capacity reserve so it doesn't restrict fuel flow.

5. Pro's use high-torque fuel pumps to generate reliable high pressure. A weak pump motor tends to stop at lower pressures, and when it does, it will draw more current from the battery and wear out quickly. Pump pressures are related to the amount of voltage available. If you need more pressure, run a 16-volt battery, but remember that a 16-volt battery is heavy. Another tactic is to use a lighter 12-volt battery with a 10-gauge wire from the kill switch directly to the pump to deliver the maximum voltage offered by the battery. Stock fuel pump wiring can restrict voltage and reduce fuel pressure and flow.

   In addition, products such as the B&M Power Plus Voltage Control Unit provide 18 volts for fuel pumps. It handles 15 amps continuous, 20 amps peak. The Power Plus is for any vehicle with electronic fuel injection. Designed and engineered for ultra-high performance racing applications, this unit provides up to 50% more energy for electric fuel pumps. The Power Plus' internal voltage regulator keeps a constant 18-volt output and will provide full output even when input voltage drops below 12 volts! It is fully epoxy encapsulated to survive the toughest racing environments, and the anodized-aluminum case requires only a 3" x 5" space to mount. It's ideal for drag racing with the alternator belt removed, as it maintains voltage and therefore fuel pump performance.

6. You need a second pressure regulator to reduce pressure to the carburetors. Too much pressure to the carburetor and it will blow past the needle valve and raise the level in the fuel bowl, causing a rich fuel mixture. Run a

return line off the regulator block to a T-fitting just before the fuel pump. The amount of fuel returned is controlled by a jet; this further bleeds off air and also cools the fuel, as the fuel line is very close to the engine at this point.

7. Pro racers use a plug in the regulator block to install a fuel pressure gauge, allowing them to check fuel pressure between rounds. Use a second plug to check the low pressure side (near carbs if you have them). We know one very successful bracket racer who likes to run pressure to the carb at approximately 9.5 psi —as high as he can without fuel pressure blowing off the needle valves and upsetting fuel bowl levels. This racer has found that fuel pressure only varies by .2-.3-psi when he runs it this high. He used to run 8 - 8.5 psi and pressure would drop about 1 psi when the car left, then slowly recover. He's not sure if dropping a pound hurts that much, but eliminating a variable can't hurt when tuning the car for track conditions.

8. If you can't science out a starting line bog, try this. Run -10 fuel lines to the carbs. Most racers use -8, but we've heard reports that after installing a high-pressure fuel system a -10 line seemed to help. Basically, you get a reserve in the lines to feed the carbs during the initial launch G-shock. You need this reserve, because when the G-shock adds to the psi in the lines, the regulator, which is set at 9 psi, will shut fuel flow off, and momentarily starve the carb. The preceding scenario assumes the lines are laid so the force of the launch pushes the fuel in the lines toward the carb and regulator. You can also drill out the opening in the carb by .050 inch and blend the angles. Don't use a larger diameter bit because you won't get a secure seal.

FUEL INJECTOR TUNING FACTORS

The point of building a reliable, consistent fuel system is to allow you to mix fuel with air and nitrous to make

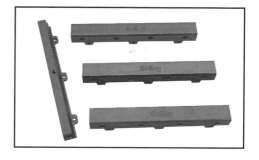

Holley CNC-machined fuel rails have the capacity to deliver high fuel flows to feed your hungry nitrous-enhanced engine. They have a 9/16-inch inner bore allowing up to 1100 hp flow rate using gasoline. (Holley)

power. To do that safely and efficiently you have to know how much fuel and oxygen you're delivering into the combustion chamber. Here we talk about some of the components and concepts of fuel injection. A more in-depth explanation can be found in the *Honda Builder's Handbook, Volumes 1 & 2*. Read what Russ Collins has to say about fuel injec-

Flow Rates, Power Potential, and Idle Requirements of Representative Lucas Fuel Injectors

@psi/bar	lbs/hr	lb/min	lb/millisec	lb/sec	max power	CFM air @ 90% duty w/bfsc 0.5 per injector	min CFM air req'd for horsepower per injector	min lb/sec air req'd for idle a/f 12.25:1
43.50/3.0	52.07	0.87	0.00001446	0.01446389	93.73	149.96	2.43	0.177
43.50/3.0	42.29	0.70	0.00001175	0.01174722	76.12	121.80	1.97	0.144
43.50/3.0	37.27	0.62	0.00001035	0.01035278	67.09	107.34	1.74	0.127
39.15/2.7	35.81	0.60	0.00000995	0.00994722	64.46	103.13	1.67	0.122
43.50/3.0	26.43	0.44	0.00000734	0.00734167	47.57	76.12	1.23	0.090
50.75/3.5	21.41	0.36	0.00000595	0.00594722	38.54	61.66	1.00	0.073
43.50/3.0	21.28	0.35	0.00000591	0.00591111	38.30	61.29	0.99	0.072
43.50/3.0	19.82	0.33	0.00000551	0.00550556	35.68	57.08	0.92	0.067

	Grams per min.	mg per pulse			@ 80% duty	
	394	11.80			83.31	133.30
	320	9.96			67.66	108.26
	282	8.42			59.63	95.40
	271	8.13			57.30	91.67
	200	6.10			42.29	67.66
	162	5.28			34.26	54.81
	161	4.50			34.05	54.48
	150	3.28			31.71	50.74

Injector Time Schedule:
Batch-Fire – Once per Rev

RPM	Millisecs per Rev	90% Duty	Time Closed (millisecs)	80% Duty	Time closed (millisecs)	Revs per Second
11,000	5.45	4.91	0.55	4.36	1.09	183.33
10,000	6.00	5.40	0.60	4.80	1.20	166.67
9,000	6.67	6.00	0.67	5.33	1.33	150.00
8,000	7.50	6.75	0.75	6.00	1.50	133.33
7,000	8.57	7.71	0.86	6.86	1.71	116.67
6,000	10.00	9.00	1.00	8.00	2.00	100.00
5,000	12.00	10.80	1.20	9.60	2.40	83.33
4,000	15.00	13.50	1.50	12.00	3.00	66.67
3,000	20.00	18.00	2.00	16.00	4.00	50.00
2,000	30.00	27.00	3.00	24.00	6.00	33.33
1,000	60.00	54.00	6.00	48.00	12.00	16.67
500	120.00	108.00	12.00	96.00	24.00	8.33

Injector Time Schedule:
Sequential – Once per Intake Valve Opening

RPM	Millisecs per Intake Opening	90% Duty	Time Closed (millisecs)	80% Duty	Time Closed (millisecs)	Revs per Second
11,000	10.91	9.82	1.09	8.73	2.18	183.33
10,000	12.00	10.80	1.20	9.60	2.40	166.67
9,000	13.33	12.00	1.33	10.67	2.67	150.00
8,000	15.00	13.50	1.50	12.00	3.00	133.33
7,000	17.14	15.43	1.71	13.71	3.43	116.67
6,000	20.00	18.00	2.00	16.00	4.00	100.00
5,000	24.00	21.60	2.40	19.20	4.80	83.33
4,000	30.00	27.00	8.40	13.71	16.29	66.67
3,000	40.00	36.00	4.00	32.00	8.00	50.00
2,000	60.00	54.00	6.00	48.00	12.00	33.33
1,000	120.00	108.00	12.00	96.00	24.00	16.67
500	240.00	216.00	24.00	192.00	48.00	8.33

tor behavior at duty cycles over 85 percent in the *Honda Builder's Handbook Vol. 1*. In the same book, take a look at the series of charts given in the chapter on fuel — especially if you're running nitrous, a turbo, a supercharger, or some combination of those.

By now you should know that though power comes from the fuel, it has to be mixed with appropriate amounts of oxygen to make good power. To use a dry manifold nitrous system, turbo, or supercharger successfully you have to tune the ratio of nitrous to fuel. The only way to do that with a fuel-injected engine is to know how much fuel your injectors are able to deliver, in addition

to knowing how much additional oxygen the nitrous system, turbo, or supercharger is delivering.

The Flow Rates, Power Potential and Idle Requirements chart show a breakdown of the stats on several Lucas injectors with typical flow rates. We give the maximum horsepower ratings for each injector, the amount of air flow each will support, as well as the minimum air flow required to keep an air/fuel ratio that will keep an engine idling. That should give you a feel of how the injector's fuel flow rating influences air/fuel ratios at maximum power and idle RPM.

There are also two charts that dis-

play the time schedules of batch-fire and sequential injectors. The batch-fire schedule presents the time relationship between engine speed and injector firing frequency for a batch-fire injection system. Batch-fire systems fire the injectors every revolution so the time between injector pulses is much shorter than sequential systems, which fire only on the intake cycle.

We've also crunched the numbers to generate a volumetric efficiency table for each of the popular four-cylinder engine sizes. Charts detailing the 1.6 liter engine, 1.7 liter engine, 1.8 liter engine, and 2.2 liter engine, show the air flow at a couple of percentages of volumetric efficiency so you can see how they'll influence injector sizing. For turbo applications, you can estimate the flow rate by multiplying the 100% rates by whatever percent of boost psi over the standard atmospheric pressure. For example, if you're running 7 psi boost, multiply the 100% VE rate by 1.5 (50%).

Because dry manifold nitrous systems, turbos, and superchargers pump up the fuel pressure to the injector to increase fuel delivery, we've included the correct formula to predict the flow rate change.

Due to space limitations, we can't include the tuning information for all the Sport Compact marquees on the market. Just focus on the concepts presented. These apply to other engine makes as long as they are four-stroke engines using gasoline. Remember the goal is to maintain the proper air-to-fuel ratio, even when "air" is nitrous. It's the oxygen content that counts. See the nitrous tuning reference section for more info.

Fuel Injection Pressure
Change Equation
Duty Cycle

$$F_2 = \sqrt{P_2/P_1} * F_1$$

Where:

F2 = New Fuel Flow Rate
F1 = Original Fuel Flow Rate
P2 = New Fuel Pressure
P1 = Original Fuel Pressure

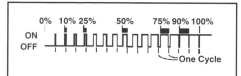

Duty cycle is how fuel injectors control fuel delivery. A 0% duty cycle is completely off; a 100% duty cycle is locked open. Duty cycle is a constantly changing amount of time controlled by the RPM of the engine. The injector has only so much time before the intake valve opens again. The limits to the injector control how quickly it can close and open. The time unit is usually milliseconds. The Injector Time Schedule charts display the time cycles for RPM and duty cycle.

Flow Ratings of
RC Engineering Injectors
Low Resistance — 2.5 / 3 Ohms
(measured at 43 P.S.I.G.)

155 cc / min.
185 cc / min.
195 cc / min.
210 cc / min.
220 cc / min.
250 cc / min.
270 cc / min.
320 cc / min.
370 cc / min.
400 cc / min.
450 cc / min.
500 cc / min.
550 cc / min.
650–800 cc / min.
800–1200 cc / min.
1400–1600 cc / min.

Saturated Injectors
High Resistance approx. 12 - 16 Ohms
(measured at 43 P.S.I.G.)

160 cc / min.
185 cc / min.
200 cc / min.
210 cc / min.
225 cc / min.
240 cc / min.
270 cc / min.
310 cc / min.
370 cc / min.
440 cc / min.
500 cc / min.
600–800 cc + / min.

Computer Interface Tuning Aids

If you step up to larger injectors, you're going to need to tune your combination. Computer interfaces are one way to achieve optimum tuning. Two examples of this are the Venom 400™ and the Hypertech Shogun. The Venom unit would be a great addition to a moderate street dry-manifold nitrous system, while the Hypertech unit offers a wider range of tuning for heavier doses of laughing gas. Keep in mind there are several other computer interfaces on the market, so do your shopping wisely.

VENOM 400 PERFORMANCE CONTROL MODULE

The Venom 400 Performance Control Module is an add-on control unit that features its own micro-controller. This module is connected to the vehicle's sensors and increases engine performance by monitoring the sensors' output characteristics and modifying the input to the vehicle's computer. The Venom 400 improves horsepower by as much as 25% through the range of approximately 1,000 to 5,000 rpm. The Venom 400 is OBD II compatible. Besides a substantial increase of torque, the Venom 400 reduces flat spots or delay time during sudden acceleration. The Venom 400 incorporates an 8-bit micro-controller that is capable of monitoring the various sensor inputs and modifying their output at more than 40 times per second.

If you have already installed a performance PROM, the Venom 400 will enhance the vehicle's performance beyond the parameters set by the performance PROM.

The Venom 400 is only active when peak performance is required. During normal driving, the unit remains passive until the microcomputer determines that engine airflow and throttle position warrants increased performance. Normal fuel economy prevails while under normal load.

The Venom 400 has an off switch so smog certification is achieved when not racing, and the unit will not trigger the emission safeguards of today's vehicles.

HYPERTECH SHOGUN POWER TUNER

Hypertech's Shogun Power Tuner™ allows the operator to optimize the ignition timing and air/fuel ratio, over the entire RPM range, for stock or modified Japanese imports, at the touch of a button. It allows maximum power tuning for any combination of modifications, and readjustment of the factory rev-limiter.

The unit's controller allows you to adjust timing in 1-degree increments. Air/fuel ratio is adjustable as a percentage (+/-%) of baseline settings, and the factory rev limiter is adjustable in 500 rpm increments.

The Shogun installs by simply plugging its adapter between the stock computer and the stock wiring harness, snap the cable into the controller, and you are ready to tune. When you're done tuning, the Shogun controller displays real-time RPM, ignition timing, and fuel settings. The controller can be permanently mounted, or removed and stored after tuning is complete.

This universal by-pass type fuel pressure regulator from Holley is designed for use on fuel-injected and turbocharged engines. It features a pressure sensor to raise fuel pressure to accommodate the fuel demands of turbocharged engines as boost increases. (Holley)

Volumetric Efficiency of
Popular Engine Displacements

RPM	Air Flow at 100% Vol. Eff. CFM	lb./min.	Air Flow at 85% Vol. Eff. CFM	lb./min
1.6 Liter Engine (total)				
11,000	311.92	22.77	265.13	19.35
10,000	283.56	20.70	241.03	17.60
9,000	255.21	18.63	216.93	15.84
8,000	226.85	16.56	192.82	14.08
7,000	198.50	14.49	168.72	12.32
6,000	170.14	12.42	144.62	10.56
5,000	141.78	10.35	120.52	8.80
4,000	113.43	8.28	96.41	7.04
3,000	85.07	6.21	72.31	5.28
2,000	56.71	4.14	48.21	3.52
1,000	28.36	2.07	24.10	1.76
500	14.18	1.04	12.05	0.88
1.7 Liter Engine (total)				
11,000	331.02	24.16	281.37	20.54
10,000	300.93	21.97	255.79	18.67
9,000	270.83	19.77	230.21	16.81
8,000	240.74	17.57	204.63	14.94
7,000	210.65	15.38	179.05	13.07
6,000	180.56	13.18	153.47	11.2
5,000	150.46	10.98	127.89	9.34
4,000	120.37	8.79	102.31	7.47
3,000	90.28	6.59	76.74	5.60
2,000	60.19	4.39	51.16	3.73
1,000	30.09	2.20	25.58	1.87
500	15.05	1.10	12.79	0.93
1.8 Liter Engine (total)				
11,000	350.12	25.56	297.60	21.72
10,000	318.29	23.23	270.54	19.75
9,000	286.46	20.91	243.49	17.77
8,000	254.63	18.59	216.44	15.80
7,000	222.80	16.26	189.38	13.82
6,000	190.97	13.94	162.33	11.85
5,000	159.14	11.62	135.27	9.87
4,000	127.31	9.29	108.22	7.90
3,000	95.49	6.97	81.16	5.92
2,000	63.66	4.65	54.11	3.95
1,000	31.83	2.32	27.05	1.97
500	15.91	1.16	13.53	0.99
2.2 Liter Engine (total)				
11,000	426.5	31.13	362.53	26.46
10,000	387.73	28.30	329.57	24.06
9,000	348.96	25.47	296.61	21.65
8,000	310.19	22.64	263.66	19.25
7,000	271.41	19.81	230.70	16.84
6,000	232.64	16.98	197.74	14.44
5,000	193.87	14.15	164.79	12.03
4,000	155.09	11.32	131.83	9.62
3,000	116.32	8.49	98.87	7.22
2,000	77.55	5.66	65.91	4.81
1,000	38.77	2.83	32.96	2.41
500	19.39	1.42	16.48	1.20

RPM	Air Flow at 100% Vol. Eff. CFM	lb./min.	Air Flow at 85% Vol. Eff. CFM	lb./min
1.6 Liter Engine (per cylinder)				
11,000	77.98	5.69	66.28	4.84
10,000	70.89	5.18	60.26	4.40
9,000	63.80	4.66	54.23	3.96
8,000	56.71	4.14	48.21	3.52
7,000	49.62	3.62	42.18	3.08
6,000	42.53	3.11	36.15	2.64
5,000	35.45	2.59	30.13	2.20
4,000	28.36	2.07	24.10	1.76
3,000	21.27	1.55	18.08	1.32
2,000	14.18	1.04	12.05	0.88
1,000	7.09	0.52	6.03	0.44
500	3.54	0.26	3.01	0.22
1.7 Liter Engine (per cylinder)				
11,000	82.75	6.04	70.34	5.13
10,000	75.23	5.49	63.95	4.67
9,000	67.71	4.94	57.55	4.20
8,000	60.19	4.39	51.16	3.73
7,000	52.66	3.84	44.76	3.27
6,000	45.14	3.30	38.37	2.80
5,000	37.62	2.75	31.97	2.33
4,000	30.09	2.20	25.58	1.87
3,000	22.57	1.65	19.18	1.40
2,000	15.05	1.10	12.79	0.93
1,000	7.52	0.55	6.39	0.47
500	3.76	0.27	3.20	0.23
1.8 Liter Engine (per cylinder)				
11,000	87.53	6.39	74.40	5.43
10,000	79.57	5.81	67.64	4.94
9,000	71.61	5.23	60.87	4.44
8,000	63.66	4.65	54.11	3.95
7,000	55.70	4.07	47.35	3.46
6,000	47.74	3.49	40.58	2.96
5,000	39.79	2.90	33.82	2.47
4,000	31.83	2.32	27.05	1.97
3,000	23.87	1.74	20.29	1.48
2,000	15.91	1.16	13.53	0.99
1,000	7.96	0.58	6.76	0.49
500	3.98	0.29	3.38	0.25
2.2 Liter Engine (per cylinder)				
11,000	106.63	7.78	90.63	6.62
10,000	96.93	7.08	82.39	6.01
9,000	87.24	6.37	74.15	5.41
8,000	77.55	5.66	65.91	4.81
7,000	67.85	4.95	57.68	4.21
6,000	58.16	4.25	49.44	3.61
5,000	48.47	3.54	41.20	3.01
4,000	38.77	2.83	32.96	2.41
3,000	29.08	2.12	24.72	1.80
2,000	19.39	1.42	16.48	1.20
1,000	9.69	0.71	8.24	0.60
500	4.85	0.35	4.12	0.30

Sport Compact Nitrous Injection

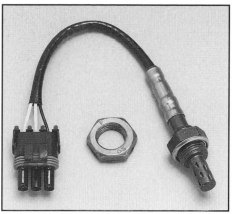

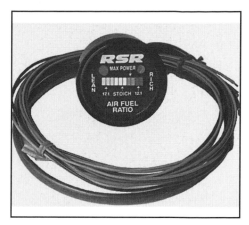

Wet systems make the most power with turbos. Greddy makes it a little easier to build a powerful turbo/nitrous system with its injector holders. Following is a list of applications for Greddy injector holders. (Greddy)

Air/Fuel Ratio Meters are an excellent tuning aid for immediate response to air/fuel mixture changes. Several units are on the market, including models that use wide-band sensor technology. Wide-band units are expensive, but they tend to be more accurate. Units such as this one from RSR, while using OE replacement style sensors such as the Holley shown unit, still provide excellent tuning information. (Holley/RSR)

Greddy Injectors/ Injector Holders

Part #	Description
13500036	360 cc Injector
13500055	550 cc Injector
13500072	720 cc Injector
13900001	Dummy Injector
13540001	Mazda RX-7 Turbo '87-92 1 (one) Injector Holder
13540002	Mazda RX-7 T/T '93-97 1 (one) Injector Holder
13530001	Mitsubishi Galant VR-4 1 (one) Injector Holder
13551011	Nissan 300 ZX T/T '90-96 2 (Two) Injector Holders
13510006	Toyota MR-2 Turbo '90-96 2 (Two) Injector Holders
13510021	Toyota Supra Turbo '87-92 2 (Two) Injector Holders
360558	Toyota Supra T/T '92-97 2 (Two) Injector Holders
13900451	Steel Injector Boss
13900452	Aluminum Injector Holder

Holley also offers Bosch-style injectors in a variety of sizes to fit a wide range of applications. (Holley)

TMW Induction Injector Selector

S·A DESIGN

Fuel Pressure psi (= lbs/hr)				Driver Type	Resistance in Ohms	Manufacturer's Part Number
43.5	60	65	73.5			
19	22	23	25	Sat	16	Rochester 2900-2016
19	22	23	25	Sat		Bosch 2900-3302
20	23	24	25	Sat	16	Lucas 2500-1014
20	23	24	25	P & H	2.2	Lucas 2500-1028
20	23	24	26	P & H	2.2	Lucas 2500-1033
20	24	25	26	Sat	16	Lucas 2500-1012
21	24	25	27	Sat	16	Lucas 2500-1004
21	25	26	27	P & H	2.4	Lucas 2500-1001
21	25	26	27	Sat	12	Rochester 2900-2010
21	25	26	28	Sat	16	Lucas 2500-1000
21	25	26	28	P & H	2.4	Lucas 2500-1013
22	26	27	29	Sat	16	Rochester 2900-2017
24	28	29	31	Sat	16	Lucas 2500-1022
25	29	30	32	Sat		Bosch 2900 1302
25	29	30	32	P & H	2.2	Lucas 2500-1025
26	31	32	34	P & H	2.0	Rochester 2900-2011
26	31	32	34	Sat	16	Lucas 2500-1008
31	36	38	40	Sat		Bosch 2900-2302
31	37	38	40	Sat	16	Lucas 2500-1021
32	38	40	42	P & H	2.2	Lucas 2500-1016
34	40	42	44	P & H	2.0	Rochester 2900-2012
36	38	44	47	P & H		Bosch 2900-0803
37	43	45	47	Sat		Bosch 2900-4302
37	43	45	48	P & H	2.2	Lucas 2500-1018
37	44	46	49	Sat	16	Lucas 2500-1031
38	45	46	49	Sat	12	Rochester 2900-2018
41	48	50	53	Sat	16	Lucas 2500-1009
42	49	51	54	Sat	16	Lucas 2500-1030
50	59	61	65	Sat	12	Rochester 2900-2013
51	60	63	67	P & H	2.2	Lucas 2500-1032
72	85	88	94	P & H	2	Rochester 2900-2014
96	113	117	125	P & H	2	Rochester 2900-2015

The NOS Glycerin-Filled Fuel Pressure Gauge (Part # 15905) dampens vibration and allows a more accurate and uniform reading. Although performing the same function as a standard gauge, this gauge measures fuel pressure from 0-15 psi and can withstand far greater abuse from vibration. NOS also offers regular (Part #15906) and glycerin-filled (Part #15907) fuel gauges specifically for EFI nitrous systems where much higher fuel pressures are used. These gauges are accurate from 0 to 120 psi. (NOS)

These are Accel's highest-flowing, high-impedance injectors, but they're still compatible with the OE computer injector drivers. They also provide a full 30 degrees of cone spray angle, which results in excellent fuel atomization, improved fuel economy and throttle response. The Performance Injectors are also the new anti-plugging type, which eliminate problems associated with carbon build up. They're available in flow rates of 22, 30, and 36 lb/hr. Low-impedance models are available with flow rates of 55 and 83 lb/hr, but should only be used with the SEFI system. (Accel)

Nitrous Tip
A quick Way to Estimate HP

Injector size (lbs/hr) x 2 x number of cylinders = Horsepower

The tech tip above is a good way to quickly estimate the horsepower a set of injectors can provide. But remember, horsepower comes from fuel flow and fuel flow is a product of the pressure at the injector and its duty cycle. Regulating the pressure to the injectors is critical for optimum performance on or off the bottle. Manufacturers such as Holley provide fuel-injection regulators that have an adjustment range up to 65 psi and provide all the fuel pressure a high-performance, fuel-injected vehicle requires. Holley offers two universal regulators: Part # 512-504 is for fuel-injected, non-turbocharged vehicles. It is machined from billet aluminum and is adjustable from 15-65 psi. It comes equipped with two -8AN inlet fittings and one -6 AN outlet fitting, and it can be used on any import or domestic fuel-injected vehicle. The other universal regulator is part # 512-505, designed for fuel-injected, nitrous enhanced and turbocharged engines. Because of its boost compensating design, it can provide more fuel under turbocharger boost and or nitrous enhanced conditions. Its range of adjustability is from 20-65 psi.

Six regulators for dedicated applications round out Holley's current product line. They each feature a range of adjustability from 35-65 psi and can accommodate engine modifications from the mild to the wild side. They're made to bolt in the stock regulator's location so installation problems are greatly simplified. These Holley-designed regulators use a special wave spring to maintain constant fuel pressure to enhance the performance of other horsepower-creating components on your vehicle.

RC Engineering can provide fuel injectors in any format, any type of mounting or fuel rail configuration. These include hose end, large O-ring American / European fuel rail, small O-ring Japanese fuel rail, and custom additional controller units. A partial listing of available injector sizes is on page 31. All flow numbers are taken at static settings. Most Gally or Side feed injectors can be modified up to rates of 100%.

The Venom Stage I Injector is an off-the-shelf, high-performance, exact-fit injector with an OEM design. Flow rate is increased up to 10% in order to maximize horsepower increase, while minimizing against too rich fuel mixture. Idle is maintained, while increasing overall performance throughout the RPM range. The Venom Stage II Injector is an OEM-style exact fit injector with matched specific flow rates balanced to required horsepower gains. Venom Injectors are standard 8-9% upgrades above stock flow and also are offered in the flow rates ranging from 32 to 120 lb/hr. (Venom)

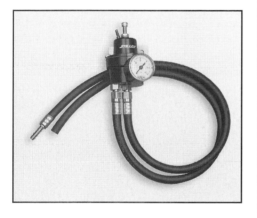

Stillen's R&D department has been analyzing ways to enrich the fuel mixture for a power gain on vehicles equipped with intake, headers, and exhaust. Such equipment leans out a motor and the typical cure is to update the fuel delivery schedule hidden within the engine's computer. The Fuel Pressure Riser (FPR) offered by the company has proven to be the answer. Tested and tuned on a Honda Civic equipped with intake, headers, and exhaust, Stillen's FPR showed a maximum gain of 6 horsepower on the company's DynoJet. The billet aluminum component is shipped with gauge, clamps, hoses, fittings, and instructions. The FPR installs in 30 minutes. (Stillen)

NOS Fuel Injector Kits

These injector kits will enable you to upgrade your engine's fuel delivery system. This is a definite necessity when you begin modifying a stock engine with such items as a performance fuel pump and camshaft, or modifying the stock cylinder heads or upgrading to new performance cylinder heads, adding headers, high-flow throttle bodies, etc. The fuel injectors here are all top-fed, Bosch-style with various flow ratings as shown below. The chart also equates the injector fuel flow potential to an engine horsepower rating. All NOS injectors are engraved with the PPH rating for easier identification. Example: H - 24 = 24 pph, H - 36 = 36 pph, etc.

NOTE: To convert pounds per hour fuel flow to cc per minute, multiply the pounds per hour by 10.5092. For example, 42 lb./hr. is equal to 441.3 cc/min. fuel flow.

Part #	Horsepower Rec. Max	Qty	Injector Flow (lbs./hr)	Impedance
922-1404	up to 125	4	14	High
922-1406	up to 185	6	14	High
922-1408	up to 250	8	14	High
922-1904	125 – 175	4	19	High
922-1906	185 – 260	6	19	High
922-1908	250 – 350	8	19	High
922-2404	175 – 225	4	24	High
922-2406	260 – 335	6	24	High
922-2408	350 – 450	8	24	High
922-3004	225 – 275	4	30	High
922-3006	335 – 415	6	30	High
922-3008	450 – 550	8	30	High
922-3604	275 – 325	4	36	High
922-3606	415 – 490	6	36	High
922-3608	550 – 650	8	36	High
922-4204	325 – 375	4	42	High
922-4206	490 – 565	6	42	High
922-4208	650 – 750	8	42	High
922-5004	375 – 425	4	50	High
922-5006	565 – 640	6	50	High
922-5008	750 – 850	8	50	High
922-5504	425 – 475	4	55	Low
922-5506	640 – 715	6	55	Low
922-5508	850 – 950	8	55	Low
922-6504	475 – 550	4	65	Low
922-6506	715 – 825	6	65	Low
922-6508	950 – 1100	8	65	Low
922-7504	550 – 600	4	75	Low
922-7506	825 – 900	6	75	Low
922-7508	1100 – 1200	8	75	Low
922-8504	600 – 700	4	85	Low
922-8506	900 – 1050	6	85	Low
922-8508	1200 – 1400	8	85	Low
922-9504	700 – 800	4	95	Low
922-9506	1050 – 1200	6	95	Low
922-9508	1400 – 1600	8	95	Low

* Horsepower figures are calculated at 80% duty cycle and 100% duty cycle (static) at 43 psi based on BSFC of 0.44.

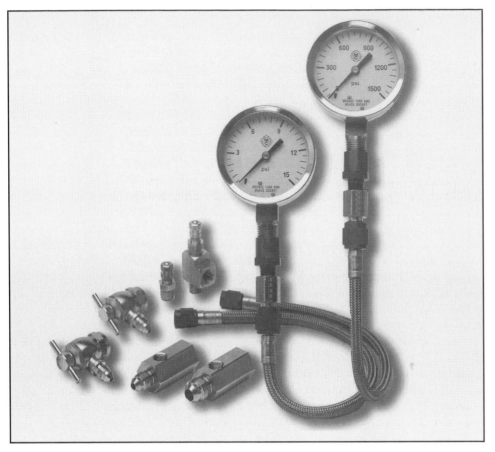

The NOS Fuel Pressure Gauge (Part #15900) can be an important component for maximizing and tuning your nitrous system. This gauge measures fuel pressure from 0-15 psi and is designed primarily for use with a carburetor plate and direct port nitrous systems. In most cases it is advisable to run between 5-8 psi of fuel pressure for best results. Comes with adapter fittings.(NOS)

The NOS Pinch Valve electronically controls fuel system richness/leanness with a switch or push button. It enables the use of exotic racing fuels such as alcohol or nitro. Each kit includes battery pack (single action only), dual-action switch or single-action push button, solenoid, wiring, and instructions. (NOS)

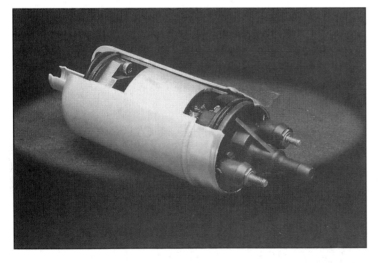

The electronic fuel pump is central to the fuel management system. It must deliver precisely pressurized fuel in exacting quantities at each and every level of performance. Venom has applications for the following vehicles: Acura, Audi, BMW, Chevrolet, Honda, Mazda, Mitsubishi, Nissan, Saturn, Subaru, Toyota, and Volkswagen. (Venom)

Holley offers this billet adjustable pressure regulator for fuel-injected non-turbocharged engines. It comes with –8 AN inlet/outlets and provides pressure adjustment from 15 to 65 psi. (Holley)

THE NITROUS CIRCUIT

We discussed the basics of nitrous oxide in the Introduction and in chapter two. In this chapter, we'll focus on the nitrous circuit— from bottle to nozzle. After reading this chapter you should be very familiar with the various components that are combined to make a safe, reliable nitrous system that will flow the amount of nitrous your system requires.

The function of the nitrous circuit is, obviously enough, to deliver nitrous from the bottle to the nozzle in the intake of your engine. Simple and straightforward. It must also be reasonably robust, physically and mechanically to endure the severe temperature changes and ultra high pressures that come with liquid nitrous oxide. Of course the better know manufacturers have plenty of experience designing system components that are compatible with the temperatures and pressures of nitrous. You just have to make sure your using the right component in the proper manner, and you're pretty much assured your system will perform properly.

If you're making very large horsepower increases using nitrous, you want to pay attention to the flow capacity of the nitrous circuit. The only restriction you want in the system is the jets with which you control the flow rate for tuning. If the bottle valve does not flow as much as you are demanding, or the orientation of the pick-up tube is misaligned, then you can get very different flow rates than you planned. This is not good and can potentially cause engine damage.

Fortunately there are a lot of goodies and extra add-ons for nitrous systems these days, including high-flow capacity valves and solenoids. Of all the products available, there is one item that can be worth its weight in gold if you live where it gets cold during the winter — which means everywhere except Hawaii. It's a bottle heater. NOS sells a fully automatic, thermostatically-controlled, strap-type heater that maintains the bottle temperature at a toasty 75 degrees, even if the temperature outside is below zero.

Before getting into details of the nitrous circuit, we'll start with a description of the circuit and its components.

The nitrous circuit begins with the nitrous bottle (1). A Teflon bottle nut washer (2) provides a high pressure seal between the bottle nut(3) and the bottle valve. The bottle is secured the vehicle by mounting brackets(4). The blow down (5) tube is a safety device that vents nitrous from the vehicle's interior if the bottle pressure exceeds that of the pressure disc.

The purge valve line splices off the nitrous feed line just before the nitrous solenoid. Nitrous racers use a purge valve to clear the feed line of boiled or gaseous nitrous. By doing so they get super-cooled liquid nitrous oxide to the solenoid valve, thus delivering the most nitrous in the least amount of time.

Once the valve is opened, pressurized nitrous flows up the siphon tube through the valve and into a length of nitrous supply hose(6) through a nitrous filter(7) to a nitrous solenoid(8). The designers at NOS prefer to use two nitrous solenoids on dry systems. The second solenoid is a backup to prevent nitrous from being introduced into the engine should a single solenoid fail.

The T-block (11) provides a port for the nitrous pressure regulator (13). This unit reduces line pressure to a level that is usable by an adjustable fuel pressure regulator/pressure riser. We covered this circuit in chapter three.

After the nitrous solenoids, another length of nitrous delivery hose connects the nitrous path to the jet(15) and spray nozzle (16). The nitrous flow rate is determined by the diameter of the jet selected and the bottle/line pressure of the nitrous circuit. The nozzle/jet assembly is mounted to the intake by means of a nut (17) and collar (18) fastener.

NITROUS BOTTLES

As we discussed in the introduction, the bottle's temperature is important. We'll talk more about the temperature/pressure relationship of compressed nitrous, positioning the bottle for a correct install, and several other intricacies in other sections of the book. There are a few things you should know

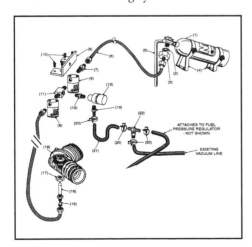

The nitrous circuit comprises a pressurized bottle of nitrous, lengths of delivery hose, control solenoids, metering jet, and spray nozzle.

about nitrous bottles though. So before we go on, here a few tips on how to treat your nitrous bottle.

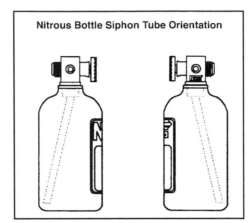

How you position the bottle in your vehicle is key to proper performance of the nitrous system. Most nitrous system makers have an offset siphon tube as illustrated on this drawing of an NOS arrangement. On NOS bottles the tip of the internal siphon tube is always on the same side as the valve opening. (NOS)

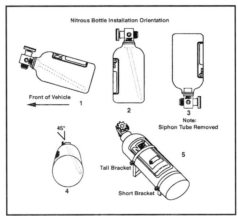

The offset siphon tube allows proper installation and orientation for almost any packaging challenge. You can even mount the bottle upside down by removing the internal siphon tube. (NOS)

Never drill, machine, weld, deform, scratch, drop, or modify a nitrous oxide tank or the valve in ANY way! Although some people have polished their tanks to a chrome-like appearance, even this is not recommended because it removes a non-uniform layer of the tank's material that may or may not affect its integrity. Certainly, never attempt to subject a

nitrous tank to any type of plating process because this often affects the strength of the tank's material.

Never overfill nitrous cylinders. That tiny little bit extra will put you and others at great risk for injury. More often than not, when the cylinder warms up, the pressure goes above the limit of the safety relief disc and you lose all the nitrous you just paid for. If you are a retail dealer and you overfill a cylinder beyond its rated capacity in weight, whether intentional or not, you could be held liable for the consequences of any damages or injury. Don't do it.

NOS offers D.O.T. approved aluminum nitrous bottles in a variety of sizes to suit your needs. There's no mistaking an NOS system with the famous blue bottle, the CGA approved Hi-Flo Valve and built-in siphon tube on all bottles except the 10 oz. units. For extra safety, NOS has designed an exclusive blow-off venting system if your bottle is overfilled or if pressure increases beyond the maximum safety level. All bottles are shipped full and ready to use.

When you are handling nitrous be sure to remember that the liquid contents will cause severe burns (frostbite) upon contact with skin. Use caution

NOS Bottle Specifications

Part #	Capacity	Length	Diameter
14700	10 oz.	14 1/4"	2"
14705	1 lb.	9"	3 1/8"
14710	2 lb.	10 1/4"	4 3/8"
14720	2 1/2 lb.	11 1/2"	4 3/8"
14730	5 lb.	16 1/2"	5 1/4"
14745	10 lb.(std)	19"	7"
14750	15 lb.	25 1/2"	7"
14760	20 lb.	25 3/4"	8"
14770	35 lb.	40 1/8"	8"
14780	50 lb.	48 5/8"	8 5/8"

NOTE: All bottle measurements include the bottle valve. Bottles must be shipped empty for air freight. For Super Hi-Flo valve on 5 lb. and larger bottles, add "SHF" to the bottle part number.

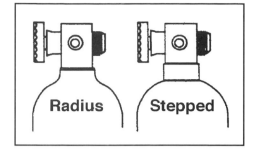

Radius   **Stepped**

NOS has produced 10 lb. bottles in three different weights. The reduced neck bottle (6.2 inches in diameter) weighs 23.6 pounds full. The stepped neck bottle (6.2 inches in diameter) weighs 25.0 pounds full. The short, fat bottle (6.9 inches in diameter) weighs 24.7 pounds full. (NOS)

The Nitrous Express Next Generation is guaranteed not to affect horsepower output or cause surging. This powerful servo motor unit is furnished with all installation hardware and weather-pack wiring kit. (Nitrous Express)

Bottle jackets, like this one from NX Next Generation, keep the bottle pressure stabilized by preserving the heat in winter; in the summer they insulate to keep the sun and excessive ambient temperatures out. NX jackets are available for both 10- and 15-lb. bottles. (Nitrous Express)

Nitrous Bottle Empty and Filled Weights

The following is a list of the weights of NOS nitrous oxide cylinders.

Bottle Size	Weight Empty (Pounds)	Weight Full (Pounds)
10 oz.	2.0	2.6
2 lb.	4.3 or 3.7	6.3 or 5.7
5 lb.*	8.3 or 9.7	6.3 or 5.7
10 lb.**	15.0, 14.7, or 13.6	25.0, 24.7, or 23.6
15 lb.	23.9	38.9
20 lb.	27.0	47.0

There is a "Tare Weight" (marked TW) on the cylinders. This is the weight of the bottle when empty. The label also has this info. Remember, the bottle has weight, which is why we included the "empty weight" in the chart above. For example a 10-lb. bottle of nitrous weights 15 lbs. empty and 25 lbs. filled.

* NOS has produced two different weight 5 lb. bottles. Visually they appear the same. Regardless of what the bottle label says, always weigh the bottle completely empty to determine which unit you have before filling.

** NOS has produced three different weight 10 lb. bottles. The reduced neck bottle (6.2 inches in diameter) weighs 23.6 pounds full. The stepped neck bottle (6.2 inches in diameter) weighs 25.0 pounds full. The short, fat bottle (6.9 inches in diameter) weighs 24.7 pounds full.

when handling bottle in the valve area. Safety disc on valve may relieve contents at any time. Do not ever overfill bottle, do not puncture, incinerate, use near heat, or store above 120° F (49° C). For racing use only, do not breathe as nitrous may cause damage to your respiratory tract. Refill only with Nytrous+ (a brand name for nitrous oxide with 100 ppm sulfur oxide added).

BOTTLE VALVES

The bottle valve is typically a standard industrial unit. Its job is to provide a means to contain the pressure within the vessel until you've got the nitrous line connected to the solenoids and finally to the injecting device. The also house the safety disc that allows an over heated, or over filled bottle to vent pressure non-explosively. These units work quite well for low to moderate power increases.

But when you need enough nitrous flow to support serious horsepower, you need to think about stepping up to a high flow valve. These valves are essentially the

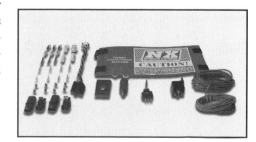

Nitrous Express produces this "fully automatic bottle heater." This huge (5.25 by 12.75 inch) heater is pressure-transducer controlled (not thermostatically) and keeps the bottle pressure between 1,020 psi and 1,050 psi at all times. Its 240-watt, 400-degree temperature is a key to consistent performance out of your nitrous system. (Nitrous Express)

cannot take the high pressures of nitrous, and they will become very brittle at the extremely low temperatures of liquid nitrous.

In addition to surviving the low temps and high pressures of nitrous, the delivery hose has to be laced through the chassis and engine bay to reach the engine intake. This means it'll have to perform some bends, rest on sharp metal edges, and resist vibration caused sawing effects on those sharp metal edges. Fortunately the aftermarket has you covered with quality hose ends and bends, bulk head adaptors and all sorts of hardware to make your nitrous delivery hose safe and reliable.

FILTERS

Among the most important components of a nitrous system are the nitrous (and fuel) filters. Because of the pressures involved, the diameter of the jet orifice is very small. It doesn't take much debris to clog the jet. If the nitrous

In racing, every bit of weight counts, so Nitrous Express produces these lightweight nitrous bottles with the added benefit of extra nitrous volume. (Nitrous Express)

same as the generic industrial units except the diameter of the passage through the valve is markedly greater.

HOSES

Because of the high pressures and severely low temperatures that the pressurized liquid nitrous places on the delivery hoses, you have to use only manufacturer recommended or approved hose. Generally this means a hose with a Teflon inner liner and hose ends that are power-crimped. Don't replace this hose with a standard neoprene-rubber-lined braided-steel hose, especially one that has screw-together-type ends. These types of hoses

Super HiFlo Valve features an orifice that flows 249% more than the standard industrial valve. This allows the new Super HiFlo valve to provide better flow for more consistency and power in today's monster engines. The Super HiFlo valve features specially designed passages to maximize flow rate and velocity, twin-gauge ports for the attachment of a nitrous pressure gauge or other performance accessories, the exclusive NOS safety venting system with -8AN fitting for professional in-car blowdown tube, and a standard 660 automotive connection. A must for the serious professional. Valves may be custom ordered to fit any bottle 5 pounds or larger. (NOS)

When you step up and start flowing high-horsepower doses of nitrous, you will need a valve that can keep up. The DF5 features a .5-inch orifice good to flow 2,000 HP worth of nitrous. It comes with a .625-inch stainless siphon tube that connects to the straight-through design of the valve. (Nitrous Express)

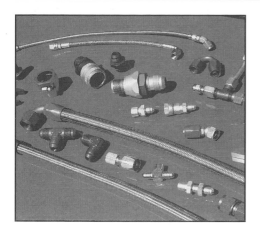

A high-pressure hose gets the nitrous from the bottle to the rest of the system under the hood. This is a special hose that has a Teflon inner liner and a braided-steel outer covering.

When you have to make sharp bends, or pass through a firewall or around other vehicle component/obstacles, Aeroquip and other manufacturers have elbows and hard line connections to do the job right. (Aeroquip)

side gets clogged, typically, it's not catastrophic though you'll lose power dramatically. If the fuel side becomes clogged it can hurt your engine.

SOLENOIDS

The solenoids are the next component in the nitrous flow path. There is one for nitrous and one for fuel in a typical wet system. The solenoids are the valves that control the on/off operation

of the system. These electromechanical valves use 12 volts to create a strong magnetic field, which in turn pulls open a small plunger. The solenoids are designed so that the supply pressure assists in keeping the valve closed. The arrangement works similar to a ball covering the drain in a bathtub. As the water gets deeper the pressure on the ball increases, thereby increasing the sealing action. In a solenoid, the magnetism created by the wire windings of the coil must be strong enough to pull open the plunger.

INJECTING NITROUS

There are three basic styles of nitrous injection devices. The first systems used a plate system with a tube with small holes that broadcast the nitrous into the engine intake air flow. Then came individual nozzles that combined fuel and nitrous directing the mixture into an individual cylinder intake runner. The most popular style of injection nozzle is the dry manifold nozzle. This nozzle directs nitrous only into the intake passage of the engine. It's most popular because until recently it was the easiest approach to injecting nitrous on a fuel injected street car.

The new NOSzle system from NOS may change that. The NOSzle Direct Port EFI systems allow precise fuel/nitrous distribution without the chance of fuel puddling, and huge horsepower gains with no intake manifold modifications or hard line routing

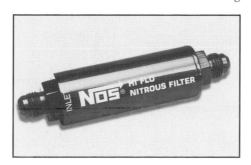

NOS offers their Hi Flo nitrous filter to compliment the NOS Hi Flo nitrous bottle valve. The durable canister holds the filter element securely and withstands the high pressures of the nitrous. It also features AN style inlet and outlet.

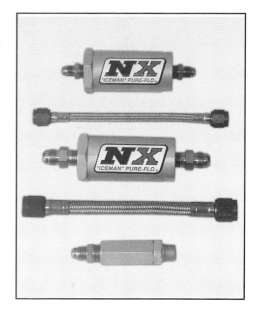

Nitrous Express offers nitrous filters designed to keep debris from clogging your jets. Installing a nitrous filter between the bottle and any metering devices just makes sense and will keep your machine running strong. (Nitrous Express)

required. Instead of the hard line, the new NOS system employs high-pressure rated poly tubing.

Systems designed for factory fuel-injected cars, as depicted here, don't use a fuel solenoid. These systems are known as dry manifold systems; they supply the additional fuel during nitrous-assisted operation by raising the fuel pressure to the fuel injectors. One solenoid supplies the nitrous to the engine, a second solenoid diverts pressure to the adjustable fuel pressure regulator.

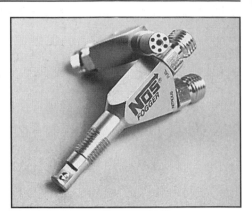

The NOSzle is a 3-piece billet aluminum unit that channels additional fuel and nitrous while housing your existing fuel injector. This method of distributing fuel and nitrous takes the danger out of single-nozzle fogger systems and the hassle out of traditional direct port fogger kits.

There are various schemes for introducing these substances to the engine. One of the most powerful methods involves a plate mounted below the carburetor with thin brass tubes that are paired together. One tube is positioned over the other. The upper tube is usually nitrous and the lower tube is usually fuel. The high velocity of the nitrous as it comes out of the upper tube helps to atomize the fuel. Wet systems, such as this VTEC, offer an uncomplicated means to inject enough nitrous and fuel to support additional horsepower. (Stock motors should be restricted to a 75 horsepower increase.) (NOS)

Another method of getting nitrous and fuel into the engine involves a mixer nozzle. This type of nozzle combines the nitrous and the fuel as they are injected into the engine. It can be used as a single nozzle for the entire engine or as individual nozzles per cylinder. The individual nozzles allow you to tune each cylinder differently if necessary. Shown are the annular discharge nozzle and the soft plume nozzle available on the NOS Pro Race Fogger Import system. (NOS)

From this view of the new NOSzle, you can see the mixing holes. The unit looks to be very efficient and dyno tests seem to confirm the reported horsepower increases with the system.

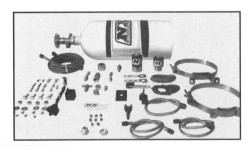

For the Honda / Acura crowd Nitrous Express offers the Stage One EFI. This system is designed to work with your vehicle's stock components. The kit is adjustable from 35-50-75 HP and is guaranteed to make within 2% of the advertised HP at the wheels. System includes 10-lb. bottle, fuel and nitrous solenoid, bottle brackets, 16 ft. of line, filter, patented Shark nozzle, all electrical, WOT switch, and instructions. (Nitrous Express)

The Shark SX2 (US Patent 5699776) is the world's first, and only dual-stage single nozzle. With only one nozzle in the intake-port, turbulence of the natural airflow is greatly reduced. No more drilling two sets of holes, hoping your nozzles will clear when installed. The SX2 is the most advanced nozzle on the market. (Nitrous Express)

The Carbon Fiber NOS bottle is DOT approved and weighs about half as much as a standard bottle. Its high-tech cosmetic appeal complements race-inspired interiors. (NOS)

Maintaining Nitrous Systems

CLEANING THE NITROUS SOLENOID FILTER

When nitrous bottles are refilled they can become contaminated with debris. If the retailer does not have an adequate filter in his transfer pump mechanism, contaminants in the bottle will eventually become lodged in the nitrous solenoid filter fitting. Periodically, after every 20 to 30 pounds of nitrous usage, examine the mesh in the nitrous filter for debris. Clean the filter using the following procedure.

1. Close valve on nitrous bottle.
2. Empty main nitrous feed line.
3. Disconnect main nitrous feed line from nitrous solenoid.
4. Remove nitrous filter fitting from nitrous solenoids.
5. Remove all Teflon paste debris from solenoids inlet port threads and from nitrous solenoid filter pipe threads.
6. Examine the mesh in the nitrous filter fitting for contaminants. Blow out debris with compressed air, if necessary.
7. Apply fresh Teflon paste to nitrous filter pipe threads. Reinstall filter in nitrous solenoid.
8. Reconnect main nitrous supply line to nitrous solenoid.

NITROUS SOLENOID PLUNGER MAINTENANCE

The seals used in Nitrous Oxide Systems solenoid plungers are constructed from materials designed for use with nitrous oxide. When kept free from fuel contaminants or from being over-pressurized, they should provide trouble-free performance. However, you should examine the seal in the nitrous solenoid plunger periodically; after using about 20 to 30 pounds of nitrous.

The seals are designed to work at pressures of up to 1100 psi. Exposing the plunger to excessive pressure (whether the vehicle is sitting or in use) can result in the seal in the plunger swelling, or in extreme cases disintegrating. The seals have a fail-safe feature. If they fail they will not leak, nor will they flow nitrous. If the nitrous solenoid plunger seals swell, that will reduce nitrous flow and cause the nitrous / fuel ratio to become overly rich and reduce engine power.

If an NOS solenoid fails to operate correctly, the problem usually stems from chemical incompatibility, contamination from debris, or coil failure due to overheating. Chemical or debris contamination can result in flow reduction or flow stoppage. Coil failure will cause flow stoppage. Occasionally plunger seals chip or crack from contamination, resulting in solenoid leakage.

An engine which suddenly is running lean may indicate a problem in the NOS fuel solenoid. Suddenly running rich is characteristic of trouble in the NOS nitrous solenoid.

Disassembly and inspection of NOS solenoids is easy.

1. Close valve on nitrous bottle.
2. Empty main nitrous supply line.
3. Remove retaining nut from nitrous solenoid.
4. Remove coil and housing from nitrous solenoid base.
5. Unscrew stem from nitrous solenoid base. Do this by double nutting the stem, or by using a solenoid stem removal tool. Do not use pliers on the solenoid stem or you will damage it.
6. Remove stem, spring, and plunger from the solenoid base.
7. Examine the plunger seal for swelling. The seal service should be flat, except for a small circular indentation in the center of the seal. A chemically-contaminated seal will protrude from the plunger and be dome shaped.

A chemically-contaminated seal will return to its original shape if left out in fresh air for several days. It may then be returned to service. Seals which are damaged should be replaced.

A persistent seal swelling problem will require corrective action. Some fuel additives are not compatible with NOS gasoline solenoids. Changing brands of fuel may cure this condition. NOS nitrous plunger seals will swell when exposed to fuel. A swollen nitrous seal is indicative of fuel collecting in the NOS nitrous solenoid. This problem can be cured by moving the NOS nitrous solenoid higher and/or further from the injection orifice.

Solenoid Basic Tech

SOLENOID CHARACTERISTICS

NOS offers ten unique solenoids. Each is designed for a specific set of operating conditions, liquid medium (i.e., nitrous, gasoline, alcohol, nitromethane, etc.), flow rate, and operating pressure. When installed with the correct components and used as intended, they are effective and reliable. If used incorrectly or in the wrong application, the solenoid may fail to work, or have a drastically reduced life expectancy. To correctly select a solenoid for an application, keep the following parameters in mind:

SEAL COMPOSITION

The seals in NOS solenoids are made of materials compatible with their intended operating environments. Flowing fluids other than those for which a solenoid was designed may result in seal failure. So don't try to run methanol through a gasoline solenoid.

When a solenoid is cycled, a large amount of force can be placed on the solenoid seal. The durometer or "toughness" of the seal is varied depending upon the pressure at which the solenoid is intended to operate. Use of a soft seal in a high-pressure application will result in the seal being cut. If a hard seal is used in a low-temperature environment (such as with nitrous oxide), the seal may chip or shatter. Use of an excessively hard seal in a low-pressure environment may result in solenoid leakage.

MAXIMUM OPENING PRESSURE

NOS solenoids use electronic coils for opening and closing the solenoid orifices. The strength of the coil is determined by the size of the solenoid orifice and the pressure at which it will operate. When selecting a solenoid, the maximum pressure capability of the unit should exceed the operating pressure it will experience by 20 percent.

MAXIMUM OPERATING TIME

NOS solenoids are intended for momentary usage. High-pressure solenoids should not be held open for more than 60 seconds, and if used in a "flutter" system, not more than a 33-percent duty cycle. Low-pressure solenoids should not be operated for more than five minutes continuously, with a 50-percent duty cycle.

AMPERAGE DRAW

The current draw required by an NOS solenoid is determined by the strength of the opening and closing coil. All wiring switches and relays must be rated for the amperage draw of the solenoids they are to operate. Note: If solenoids are left on for extended periods, the coil will heat up. As a coil gets hot, the amperage required to operate it increases dramatically.

ORIFICE SIZE

Orifice size dictates solenoid flow capability. The solenoid orifice should always be bigger than the combined area of all downstream metering jets. Solenoid efficiency is significantly degraded if this condition is violated.

NOS solenoid orifices should never be enlarged. Increasing the solenoid orifice will result in premature failure of the solenoid coil and plunger seal.

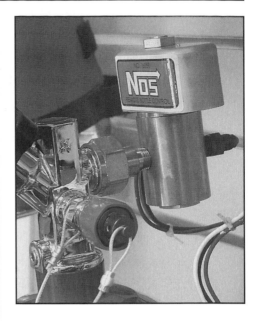

The NOS remote bottle valve opener opens your nitrous bottle valve at the flick of a switch, eliminating the need to get out, open the trunk, and open the valve. When the system's not in use, the bottle valve is closed for safety. When you need it, just activate and you're ready to rock. Also great as a safety shut-off valve, it operates on 12 volts DC and fits in line with 5 lb. or larger nitrous bottles.

The NOS Bottle Blanket helps stabilize nitrous bottle temperatures by keeping heat in and cold out. It is also an excellent companion to the NOS bottle heater and a great cosmetic item to dress up your bottle and hide all those scrapes and scratches. Features include Velcro fasteners, attractive heavy-duty blue nylon material with lining for insulation, and NOS Logo patch. Blankets are available to fit most NOS bottles.

ACTIVATING AND CONTROLLING NITROUS

The first nitrous system activation schemes involved two switches between the battery and the solenoids. The "arming switch," makes 12 volts from the battery available to the second switch. The second switch is a momentary, spring-loaded switch that is manually operated by hand. With the arming switch "on" and the momentary switch depressed, or squeezed (hence the slang term "on the squeeze"), the solenoids open and the system is activated.

Using nitrous is a little safer and more convenient when you add a switch mounted on the throttle linkage to sense wide-open throttle (WOT). This switch helps prevent the system from coming on at part throttle, but it is susceptible to activation without the engine running. A good way to avoid activating the system without the engine running is to wire the activation circuit through an oil-pressure switch. This setup assumes that if there is oil pressure, then the engine is running, and vice versa. Or, you can install a switch that senses fuel pressure.

All of this still leaves the ultimate timing of the system to the coordination of the driver, whose hand is holding the activation button and/or whose foot controls the throttle position. Accidental activation at too low an RPM or when the clutch is in can destroy your engine or some other component in the drive line.

One of the smoothest and most consistent means of activating any nitrous system is to use an electronic RPM-activated on/off switch. When used in conjunction with WOT switches, an RPM switch makes the easiest and safest way to wire up your nitrous. The system can only come on when it is running at WOT and somewhere between a

The NX Maximizer is a progressive nitrous controller that uses state-of-the-art circuitry to achieve a smooth application of nitrous power. With its single box, compact design, limitless adjustability, and rugged high-amp capacity, the Maximizer will handle all the solenoid amp load you can throw at it. The Maximizer allows your N$_2$O system to deliver full power on the 100% setting. (Nitrous Express)

low- and high-RPM point. You can select the RPM at which the system comes on as well as the RPM at which it turns off. This setup prevents backfires caused by activating the system at too low an RPM and over revving the engine while shifting gears. You just put your foot down and drive.

For turbo and supercharged motors, NOS, Nitrous Express, and others offer several adjustable pressure switches to disengage the nitrous system at a particular manifold pressures. If you're running nitrous on a turbo motor, these switches are a must. In addition, both NOS and Nitrous Express offer "incrementally" adjustable systems, i.e., they come in gradually, for an extra fine measure of launch tuning.

In addition there are systems on the market such as the Zex and Venom systems that put microprocessor technology to work to make your nitrous experience more convenient, responsive, safe, and powerful.

NITROUS ACTIVATION COMPONENTS AND SYSTEMS

Basically all a nitrous system does is deliver a constant amount of fuel and nitrous. This property is the primary reason for activating nitrous systems within a specific RPM band and the use of multi-stage systems. It is also the rea-

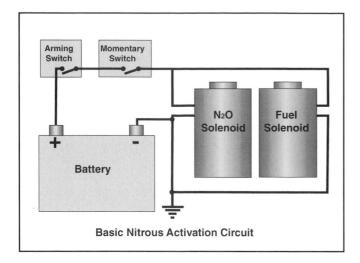

Basic Nitrous Activation Circuit

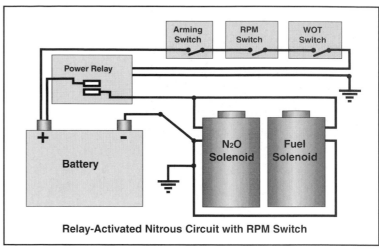

Relay-Activated Nitrous Circuit with RPM Switch

The most basic nitrous activation scheme is illustrated above. You have two switches, one to arm the system, and one to activate it. The activation switch is a momentary device meaning that when your release pressure it breaks the circuit and deactivates the system.

Above is the most popular activation scheme for street nitrous systems. It uses an arming switch, an rpm sensitive switch and a switch that completes the circuit only when the throttle is wide open. When armed this system will activate when the throttle is wide open and when engine rpm is within a range set by the rpm switch.

son pulsing, or "flutter" systems were invented. Multi-stage systems add fuel and nitrous flow to keep up with the air flow rates as RPM increases. The manual switch in this diagram can be replaced with several other triggers, such as RPM, pressure, and timing switches.

This NOS micro switch allows for full-throttle activation of a nitrous system. It's excellent for use where a manual activation switch is inconvenient, or as a safety device to prevent the nitrous system from activating unless you are at full throttle. All NOS nitrous systems are designed for use under full-throttle conditions only.

Boats, personal water craft, and other nitrous applications require a waterproof switch for remote nitrous

activation. Features include heavy wall wire insulation, spring coiled cord, and hi-amp rating.

This super heavy-duty arming switch features a flip-up cover to help prevent accidental arming of your nitrous system. It's also built to take hard use in a racing environment. The lighted toggle switch is the standard arming switch in most NOS kits, and features a blue light when the nitrous system is armed.

The NOS key-operated nitrous arming switch is a great way to arm your nitrous system and replaces the standard toggle arming switch. Also a great fail-safe switch to prevent unauthorized use of your nitrous system.

The Fuel Pressure Safety Switch

prevents your nitrous system from engaging when the fuel pressure is below a safe level. The easy-to-install version for all carburetor and direct port nitrous systems (part #15750) is preset at 4 psi and is adjustable from 4 to 7 psi. For EFI applications NOS offers a safety switch (Part #15685) preset at 50 psi, which is adjustable from 30 to 70 psi.

Installing a fuel pressure safety switch is straightforward. Find a spot on the fuel line that's safe and out of the way with enough room to fit the switch and related plumbing. This underbody view of a BMW 850 shows the chosen

The NOS key-operated nitrous arming switch is a great way to arm your nitrous system and replaces the standard toggle arming switch. Also a great fail-safe switch to prevent unauthorized use of your nitrous system.

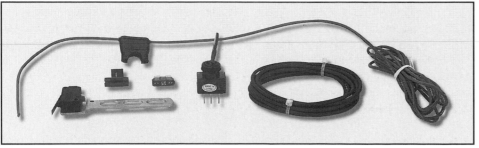

This NOS micro switch allows for full-throttle activation of a nitrous system. It's excellent for use where a manual activation switch is inconvenient, or as a safety device to prevent the nitrous system from activating unless you are at full throttle. All NOS nitrous systems are designed for use under full-throttle conditions only.

Boats, personal watercraft, and other nitrous applications require a water-proof switch for remote nitrous activation. Features include heavy wall wire insulation, spring coiled cord, and hi-amp rating.

This super heavy-duty arming switch (bottom right) features a flip-up cover to help prevent accidental arming of your nitrous system. It's also built to take hard use in a racing environment. The lighted toggle (middle) switch is the standard arming switch in most NOS kits, and features a blue light when the nitrous system is armed.

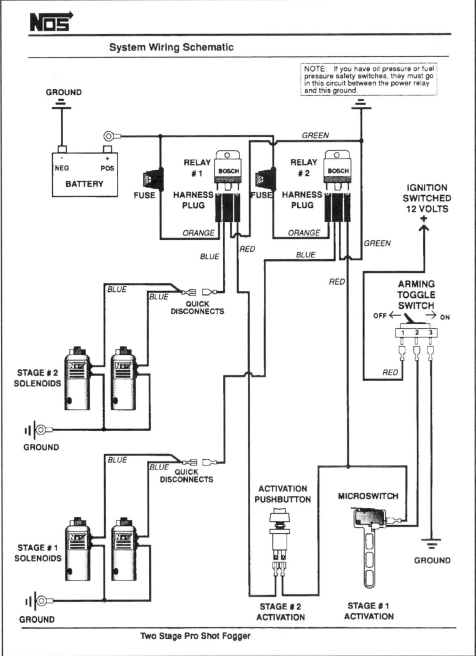

Basically all a nitrous system "stage" does is deliver a constant amount of fuel and nitrous while activated. This property is the primary reason for activating nitrous systems within a specific RPM band and the use of multi-stage systems. It is also the reason pulsing, or "flutter" systems were invented. Multi-stage systems add fuel and nitrous flow to keep up with the airflow rates as RPM increases. The manual switch in this diagram can be replaced with several other triggers, such as RPM, pressure, progressive controllers, and timing switches. (NOS)

mounting area. This car has a V-12 engine that uses two separate fuel systems fed by the two fuel lines in the center of the image.

After you run the wires to the switches from the nitrous controls, you have to cut out a length of fuel line to allow for fitting the switch hardware.

The NOS RPM-activated switch automatically turns your nitrous on and off under full throttle at predetermined RPM levels simply by plugging in inter-

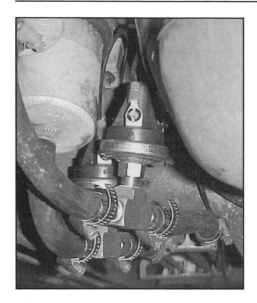

After you run the wires to the switches from the nitrous controls, you have to cut out a length of fuel line to allow for fitting the switch hardware.

The Fuel Pressure Safety Switch prevents your nitrous system from engaging when the fuel pressure is below a safe level. The easy-to-install version for all carburetor and direct port nitrous systems (part #15750) is preset at 4 psi and is adjustable from 4 to 7 psi. For EFI applications NOS offers a safety switch (Part #15685) preset at 50 psi, which is adjustable from 30 to 70 psi.

changeable RPM chips ranging from 3000 to 8000 rpm. Also excellent for use in conjunction with dual- or multi-stage nitrous systems for activating a second stage. The NOS RPM switch will only allow the nitrous system to operate at

Installing a fuel pressure safety switch is straightforward. Find a spot on the fuel line that's safe and out of the way with enough room to fit the switch and related plumbing. This underbody view of a BMW 850 shows the chosen mounting area. This car has a V-12 engine that uses two separate fuel systems fed by the two fuel lines in the center of the image.

wide-open throttle within its preselected RPM range. It also acts as a nitrous "rev limiter" in that it shuts off the flow of nitrous and fuel at the high limit point. Comes with 3000 & 6000 rpm chips.

VARIABLE DELIVERY CONTROL SCHEMES

The fixed flow rate of nitrous systems results in a tuning obstacle for extremely powerful combinations or those that are extremely traction limited. When the nitrous system is activated, it delivers a punch of torque. The system is instantly flowing all the fuel and oxygen it is jetted to deliver and this fact often leads to uncontrollable wheel spin off the line or mid-pass when the system is activated. To overcome this tuning and performance issue, several manufacturers have designed variable delivery control schemes.

NOS's Time Based Progressive Nitrous Control System starts nitrous flow at any level you set (from 0% to 100%) and then gradually brings in the full 100% flow of nitrous over a time period adjustable from 0 to 5 seconds. This allows you to start with a small shot of nitrous power (say 25 to 30%) to minimize wheel spin off the line; then smoothly transition to full nitrous power when the tires can hook up and handle it. The manufacturer claims ET improvements of up to 1/2 second and more can be achieved with the simple addition of an NOS Progressive Nitrous Control. It can be used with most single-stage nitrous systems.

Designed for the Pro racer, the NOS Time Based Progressive Control

comes in a black anodized, billet aluminum case. The control features adjustment knobs that lock into place, so the progressive settings can't be changed accidentally, and comes complete with all necessary hardware and instructions for easy installation.

In addition to the time based progressive controller, NOS offers two Progressive Nitrous Controls, which are activated by throttle position sensing. These kits offer an excellent method of bringing in nitrous gradually as the throttle is brought toward wide open.

The NOS RPM-activated switch automatically turns your nitrous on and off under full throttle at predetermined RPM levels simply by plugging in interchangeable RPM chips ranging from 3000 to 8000 rpm. Also excellent for use in conjunction with dual- or multi-stage nitrous systems for activating a second stage. The NOS RPM switch will only allow the nitrous system to operate at wide-open throttle within its preselected RPM range. It also acts as a nitrous "rev limiter" in that it shuts off the flow of nitrous and fuel at the high limit point. Comes with 3000 & 6000 rpm chips.

NOS's Time Based Progressive Nitrous Control System starts nitrous flow at any level you set (from 0% to 100%) and then gradually brings in the full 100% flow of nitrous over a time period adjustable from 0 to 5 seconds. This allows you to start with a small shot of nitrous power (say 25 to 30%) to minimize wheel spin off the line; then smoothly transition to full nitrous power when the tires can hook up and handle it.

Modifications may be required to mount the throttle position switch on your carburetor. The Progressive Control (Part#15835-C) may be used with virtually any nitrous systems using 2 solenoids and a TPS switch that produces a wide-open-throttle voltage between 4.7 and 5.0 volts. With the system armed,

The NX delay timer can be used to control a variety of devices. Its capabilities include delay at onset as well as its ability to turn off a device after a timed period. Its lowest setting is .10 seconds and it's adjustable in tenth of a second increments up to 9 minutes. (Nitrous Express)

nitrous oxide and supplemental fuel begins to flow when TPS voltage reaches about 2.5 volts.

Nitrous Express offers a product called Maximizer. The NX Maximizer is a progressive nitrous controller that uses state-of-the-art circuitry to achieve a smooth application of nitrous power to the ground. With its single box, compact design, limitless adjustability, and rugged high-amp capacity, the Maximizer will handle all the solenoid amp load you can throw at it. The Maximizer allows your N_2O system to deliver full power on the 100% setting.

Nitrous racers have also found it useful to use time delay boxes to activate systems. This is a different tuning approach and requires that the racer/tuner be very consistent and methodical in their approach to racing. Products such as the Nitrous Express delay timer are an excellent choice for this approach. The NX delay timer can be used to control a variety of devices. Its capabilities include delay at on-set as well as its ability to turn off a device after a timed period. With its lowest setting of .10 of a second and adjustability in .10s of a second up to 9 minutes, the NX delay timer could be the answer to your problems.

Some manufacturers have combined several tuning and activating tactics into a single product. For example Jacobs Electronics' Nitrous Mastermind and Venom's PC Nitrous System.

Jacobs Electronics' Nitrous Mastermind is a driver-adjustable nitrous injection system controller with a built-in rev limiter. The Nitrous Mastermind works by pulsing the nitrous solenoids at the onset of nitrous flow (which is adjustable) and gradually reducing the pulsing until the full flow setting is reached. Additionally, the Nitrous Mastermind monitors fuel pressure, engine RPM, and full-throttle conditions using a full-throttle switch. Should a drop in fuel pressure occur, the Nitrous Mastermind immediately reacts and shuts off the nitrous flow, thereby protecting the engine from damage. The rev-limiter also protects the engine by shutting down the nitrous before it cuts out the ignition. This prevents a buildup

NOS offers two Progressive Nitrous Controls that are activated by throttle position sensing. These kits offer an excellent method of bringing in nitrous gradually as the throttle is brought toward wide open.

of nitrous in the engine and exhaust that can cause damage when the ignition "cuts back in."

The Nitrous Mastermind must be used in conjunction with an aftermarket ignition system and is fully compatible with Jacobs Electronics "Ultra Teams" and secondary trigger applications (except EZ applications) by using a factory connection harness for the easiest integration/nitrous controller on the market.

The Venom™ PC Nitrous System has several key advantages. The system is completely programmable by the end user. The user simply plugs the Nitrous

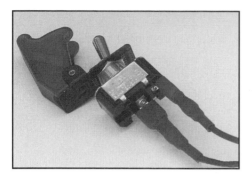

Designing a fail-safe control scheme doesn't have to involve an intricate mix of electronic devices. It can be simple. For example, a covered toggle switch will keep you from accidentally arming your nitrous system, or a keyed arming switch may be a better choice. (If others drive your car, you shouldn't have to think about a keyed arming switch, just buy it and install it.)

Controller into the serial port of a PC. Using Venom™ software, the user can configure the nitrous to operate in three various modes of operation.

Drag Mode. In this mode, the nitrous operates in the same mode as current nitrous systems operate. Full nitrous is delivered to the engine when the control mode has sensed wide-open throttle.

Linear Mode. In this mode, the user programs the throttle angle for the starting point to begin the introduction of nitrous. The control module then adds a proportionate amount of nitrous in relation to throttle angle. The higher the throttle angle, the greater the nitrous flow. This is expected to be the most popular mode of operation.

Timed Mode. In this mode, the user programs the throttle angle for when the nitrous should be introduced and how much nitrous should be added (in terms of %). The user also enters a time delay (pause after the throttle angle is reached) and an injection time (how long to inject the nitrous). This is ideal for turbocharged engines. The nitrous can be energized while the turbo reaches optimized boost levels and, after a certain amount of time, it is deactivated.

The Venom system has advanced features such as electronic low bottle detection. The control module monitors the vehicle's existing oxygen sensor to determine if proper nitrous was introduced. The module electronically detects when the bottle is low and automatically disables the system. A low bottle LED is illuminated on the control pad to inform the driver.

The Venom system also provides optimal air fuel ratio at any bottle pressure. When nitrous is introduced, additional fuel is required to ensure the proper air/fuel mixtures. Without this additional fuel, the mixture can become too lean, causing predetonation, which leads to severe engine damage. Venom's system uses the existing injectors to enrich the fuel mixture when nitrous is introduced. The system adds an injection pulse after the computer has finished its pulse. The pulse added is a product of how much nitrous is entering the engine. The user only needs to program the amount of nitrous, the control module will automatically calculate the additional amount of fuel required. The module ensures the proper air/fuel ratio by monitoring the vehicle's existing oxygen sensor. If bottle pressure becomes too low, the system is disabled and no additional fuel is needed.

With all these tuning aids on the market, there's just no excuse for not going fast. Whether or not you make to the winners circle is between you and the competition.

Nitrous Activation and Control for EFI

What makes the Zex dry-manifold nitrous system one of the smoothest, easiest-to-use systems on the market is how the firm designed the activation and enrichment fuel circuits. Most current nitrous systems use a throttle arm actuated micro-switch. That means you have to fabricate a mounting bracket for the switch and adjust the placement of the switch to make it work right. The Zex nitrous kit uses a wire that you simply clip on the

throttle position sensor (TPS) output voltage wire on your car's EFI system. The TPS voltage signal is sent to an electronic switch that engages and disengages the system at a predetermined voltage threshold. Above the threshold determined for wide-open throttle the system activates; below it, it remains dormant.

The Zex system automatically tunes the amount of enrichment fuel to the amount of nitrous the system is delivering. It does this with a feedback loop between the pressure of the nitrous circuit and the fuel pressure regulator. The nitrous oxide that is delivered to the engine's air inlet is conveyed via a delivery hose to an injection nozzle. The amount of nitrous oxide is adjustable by means of a metering jet installed in the injection nozzle itself. The nitrous oxide circuit communicates to the fuel control circuit through a small bleed orifice. This bleed orifice provides a reference source of bottle pressure and a controllable source of pressure to perform the needed function of fuel enrichment.

Fuel enrichment occurs by conveying this source of pressure through a delivery hose to a vacuum ported fuel pressure regulator. This source of pressure on the rubber diaphragm of the fuel pressure regulator causes an increase in inlet pressure. This increase in inlet pressure performs the function of adding fuel volume through the engine's own fuel injectors. The amount of additional fuel that is added can be changed by an adjustable metering jet in the fuel control circuit. This jet accomplishes the task by controlling the amount of pressure allowed to build in the delivery hose to the fuel pressure regulator. The jet bleeds off excess pressure in the fuel control circuit and vents it through a delivery tube, back to the intake manifold plenum.

BECOME AN EXPERT NITROUS TUNER

The goal in tuning a nitrous system is to control the burn rate of the fuel in order to avoid detonation and time peak cylinder pressure. There are four basic factors that influence that process: the compression ratio of the engine, the octane rating and chemistry of the fuel you choose, the amount and ratio of oxygen to fuel present in the combustion chamber, and ignition timing.

You can't really tune the compression ratio of the engine. Instead, it is a combination choice having more to do with the RPM range at which you want the engine to make power. An engine's compression influences tuning choices of ignition timing, cam specs, and fuel octane requirements. Fuel choice is another factor that influences the tune of your engine. You don't necessarily tune with fuel, but it does have a substantial impact on the tuning calibration of air, fuel, and nitrous ratios.

Therefore, your primary tuning channels are air/fuel/nitrous ratios and ignition timing. It is essential to learn how to properly use these channels. You always start with the calibration recommended by the manufacturer of your nitrous system. That means you'll have the recommended fuel and nitrous jet sizes installed. Make sure your bottle pressure is correct. Usually the recommended jet sizes will be conservative, i.e., they will provide a rich (more fuel)

nitrous-to-fuel ratio. Always adjust the power up as you tune by using small increases in the nitrous jet size. If you try dumping a ton of nitrous on your motor on the first shot, you'll be amazed at all the holes in your pistons.

Set your desired power level by providing the engine with the amount of fuel required for that much power. The power comes from the fuel, not the engine or the nitrous. If the fuel isn't there, the power won't be either. At the

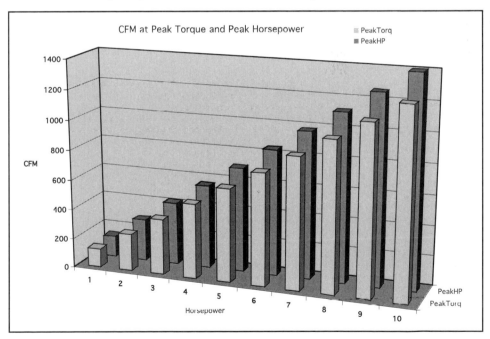

This chart is a graphic representation of the different flow rates required for peak torque and peak horsepower. It's another way to look at engine efficiency. An engine uses less air per peak ft.-lb. of torque compared to the rate required at peak horsepower. Torque is a measure of force and horsepower is measure of the rate of work. Peak horsepower usually occurs at a higher rpm and therefore at a point where some of the mass flow of air and fuel must be devoted to overcoming friction. Rate of mass flow is an important concept in tuning an engine.

first sign of detonation, backfire, or misfire, *always reduce the nitrous jet first!* Don't "cool things down" by adding more fuel. Since nitrous oxide is an oxidizer, the safest approach is to reduce the nitrous first, identity the problem, and go from there.

Very gradually adjust the nitrous, beginning with too little, until the fuel is burned at a normal rate. Read every spark plug just as you would without nitrous. Not enough nitrous results in a rich, sooty, black coloration of the plug. This coloration means the fuel is burning too slowly. Too much nitrous will exhibit high heat in the form of a bluish or rainbow-like coloring on the plug's metal surfaces. This means you're engine is about to begin, or is already, detonating. Detonation will destroy your engine. When you check the spark plugs, check EVERY plug. Don't just spot check the easiest plug you can get to. Due to the wide possibility of air/fuel mixture variations, you need to check every single plug for signs of detonation or other problems.

Nitrous oxide makes fuel burn more quickly. As you add nitrous, at some point you need to pull out ignition timing advance. The actual amount of ignition timing advance depends on your engine combination. Every engine is different and local conditions (i.e. temperature, humidity, altitude) will have an effect on a fine-tuned engine. If your combination isn't electronically controlled, adjust the timing down (less advance before TDC) until there is a noticeable loss of power, then go up 2 degrees. If you don't already have an electronic retard box, buy one and install it. Buy one that only comes on when the nitrous is on. Set it to retard the timing by the amount you just determined was correct. If you use one of these boxes, don't forget to set your timing to a normal, non-nitrous number so that it runs well without the nitrous system on.

Check and clean the fuel and nitrous filter screens on a regular basis. This is one of those common problems that can lead you in circles for days. It doesn't take much to alter the calibration. Even a small scrap of pipe-sealing tape can cause big problems.

When your system is activated, if something doesn't feel or sound right, back off. If you hear any detonation or feel anything unusual, get off the throttle. It's a lot easier to check everything over than it is to just try to drive through it and break a lot of expensive parts.

That's the basic procedure for tuning a nitrous system. The following information describes some of the finer points of tuning a nitrous system.

FLAT FLOW RATE OF NITROUS SYSTEMS VS. ENGINE AIR FLOW RATES

Nitrous systems, when properly calibrated and maintained, deliver a steady quantity of nitrous and fuel unrelated to engine speed. This concept and the fact that the power comes from the proper oxygen/fuel ratio are the fundamental tuning concepts of your nitrous system.

Optimum tuning is only achieved in a narrow RPM range because of the way your engine pumps air and the way a nitrous system delivers nitrous and fuel to your engine. Your engine flows progressively more air as engine speed increases whereas a nitrous system delivers a set flow virtually the instant it is activated.

The CFM/RPM/CID chart located in this chapter displays air flow compared to RPM and cubic inch displacement. The displacement sizes are large to give you a sense of what turbo/superchargers flow. At 14 psi boost (twice atmospheric pressure), your 2.5 liter engine is 5 liters, or 300 cid. You can see that at low RPM an engine pumps very little air; as engine speed increases so does air flow. This chart displays air flow in CFM per RPM at 100% volumetric efficiency (VE). Naturally-aspirated engines as a rule do not operate at 100% VE. A few combinations get close and some even surpass 100% VE within a very narrow RPM band. However, the average is closer to 80% VE for two-valved engines, and in the 90% to 95% for four-valved "active intake" systems. A good rule of thumb is that the VE curve of an engine closely follows the torque curve.

Horsepower is directly associated with air flow according to the techs at SuperFlow Corp., manufacturer of SuperFlow Dynos and flow benches. A naturally-aspirated engine will consume approximately 1.25 standard cubic feet

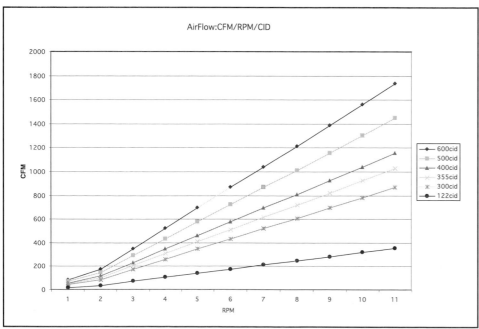

An engine is an air pump. The rate of flow it is capable of generating is determined by its cubic displacement and its speed in rpm. This chart shows the relationship of airflow in cfm relative to displacement and rpm.

per minute (SCFM) of air per horse-power at peak torque while using approximately 1.4 SCFM at peak power. SCFM is a measure of air flow with atmospheric conditions at a barometric pressure of 29.92 inches of mercury, 60 degrees F, and no water in the air (dry vapor pressure). This relationship is displayed in the CFM at Peak Torque and Peak Horsepower chart. In this instance we used SCFM as the unit of measure, however it is just as valid to use pounds per hour, or pounds per minute of air flow. The important idea though, is that power is directly proportional to mass flow through the engine, no matter what unit you use to measure. The mass flow is air (oxygen and other components) and fuel.

A nitrous system helps an engine leap to super power status in a single squeeze by injecting additional oxygen and fuel mass into the cylinders where it can react to make heat and power. Of course, a nitrous jet and a fuel jet are fixed orifices and as such they only flow a specific amount at a specific pressure. Which means when you activate the system, it's flowing, almost instantly, a specific rate of mass determined by the jets and pressure behind them. Putting it bluntly, most nitrous systems are plain flat-line systems. They are completely dumb to the increasing air/fuel demands of your engine as it spins faster.

If you compare the air flow curve with the flat line of a nitrous system in the N_2O Flow in Horsepower as CFM vs. RPM chart, you should be able to see the situation quite clearly. Basically all a nitrous system can do is deliver a constant amount of fuel and nitrous. This property is the primary reason for activating nitrous systems within a specific RPM band as well as giving rise to use of multi-stage systems. It is also the reason pulsing, or "flutter" systems were invented.

Activating the system at too low an RPM can create more cylinder pressure than the fuel can take, forcing it to detonate, because the piston isn't moving down the bore quick enough to relieve the pressure. If the fuel doesn't detonate, then the high pressure can cause other engine failures such as damaged rod

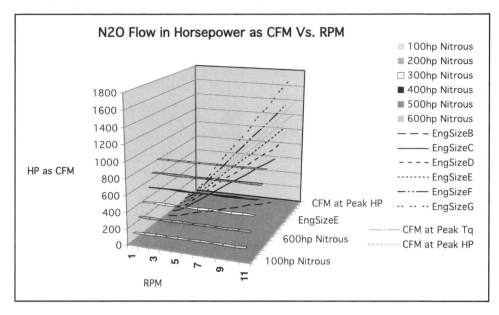

This chart compares the flat flow characteristics of a nitrous system to the rpm dependent flow characteristics of your piston engine. The faster your engine spins, (and this is true for turbos and superchargers as well) the more mass it is able to flow. A single stage of a nitrous system in contrast reaches its flow rates nearly instantly upon activation.

bearings, broken crankshafts, blown head gaskets, to mention a few. Additionally, since you're putting more nitrous and fuel into the manifold than the engine is consuming, you run the risk of igniting what amounts to a bomb in the intake, turning your trick manifold into shrapnel.

With multi-stage systems, you switch to the larger system to deliver more fuel and nitrous when your engine surpasses the flow capabilities of the system. Exactly when you make the shift depends on your combination and includes decisions on gearing and tire diameter, as well as the engine combination. In theory, it doesn't matter how many stages of nitrous you're using as long as you have them tuned to deliver the proper air-to-fuel ratios for the operating conditions. Just as when you're tuning the engine without nitrous, your goal is to achieve the same ratios of air and fuel, but you are putting a lot more mass through the engine. Pulse control of nitrous is an effort to tune how quickly the power comes on. By controlling the nitrous system in much the same way as a fuel-injection system, you can roll into the power and keep your tires hooked up for quicker acceleration.

SPARK PLUGS AND NITROUS OXIDE: WHAT WORKS, WHAT DOESN'T, AND WHY

Over the years there seems to have been a great amount of technical material written about the simple operation of a spark plug and what a set can do in relation to the way an engine runs. There are a few basic characteristics about spark plugs that you need to know to make an intelligent choice about the correct spark plug for your application.

The most important point to remember is that a spark plug must be designed correctly to operate within the environment of your engine, not the other way around. This means that modern spark plug design has virtually no influence on how the engine burns fuel or runs in general. The correct spark plug will simply survive the conditions present in your engine. A spark plug must maintain a certain temperature to keep itself clean. The wrong heat range can cause an overheated plug or a fouled plug. The heat range refers to the temperature of the ceramic material surrounding the center electrode.

Lean air/fuel ratios are more difficult to ignite because there are fewer fuel

The plug with the skinny long ground strap is the stock application for a late-model, fuel-injected engine. The other plug is an NGK unit with a shorter, thicker ground strap. The stock plug will cause detonation with any amount of nitrous. Do not use your stock spark plugs with your nitrous kit. Zex offers a performance plug designed to work with nitrous systems and even on turbocharged and supercharged combinations. Its short, multiple ground straps provide an efficient heat path.

molecules in the area of the plug gap when the plug is scheduled to fire. Projected-nose plugs were designed for late-model lean-burn engines as a solution to this condition and modern high-energy ignition systems also allowed larger plug gaps. Igniting a lean mixture to reduce emissions and improve fuel mileage is one thing. Making power with nitrous oxide is another.

Quite often, a factory-type, wide-gap projected nose plug will produce a misfire condition after only a few seconds of nitrous use. The misfire is not due to the heat range. The misfire occurs because the ground strap of the spark plug becomes a glowing ember since it takes too long to dissipate the extra heat produced by a nitrous-accelerated burn condition. The correct solution is to install plugs that have shorter ground straps. By doing this, you will shorten the heat path from the ground strap to the plug case. You can use the same heat range, you just have to use a non-projected nose plug.

NITROUS-TO-FUEL RATIOS

One of the most overlooked concepts of tuning a nitrous system is that even with healthy doses of nitrous, you're only increasing the oxygen content of the charge by just a few percent.

That's wild when you think about it. Just a scant few percent increase in the oxidizer content of the intake charge will give you incredible power output.

Check this out: Measured by volume, air is about 20.95% oxygen and 78.06% nitrogen with the remaining .99% taken up with trace elements like helium, hydrogen, carbon dioxide, etc. By weight, nitrogen makes up 75.5% of the atmosphere's mass with oxygen contributing 23% of the mass; the remaining 1.5% is contributed by the aforementioned trace elements.

Of course it's the oxygen content that reacts with fuel to make power so we're very interested in that portion of the atmosphere. According to Ken Dutweiller, a noted west-coast tuner and drag racer, those percentages may be accurate for a global average, but in the environment from which engines draw air, oxygen usually accounts for around 19% of the mass of the intake charge. It does fluctuate, but he said 19% is a good working number, so that's the one we'll use in this exercise.

Nitrous oxide, measured by volume is 33% oxygen; 66% nitrogen. Measured by weight 36% of its mass is oxygen with nitrogen making up the remaining 64% of mass. When you first hear the numbers you think you're going to get a big jump in the oxygen content of the intake

charge with nitrous oxide. However, you don't get the whole 17% increase (36% - 19% = 17%) because you're not running the engine solely on the nitrous system. You're augmenting the atmospheric charge with nitrous oxide, blending two oxygen sources, each with a different amount of oxygen. How much of a blend you end up with is what tuning the nitrous side of the system is all about.

Complicating the tuning process is the usual motor mayhem of pulsing flow, changing rates of volumetric efficiency through RPM range combined with the flat flow rate of nitrous systems. Put roughly, a nitrous system makes prodigious force at low RPM and at the torque peak because at such points in the RPM range, you get the highest percentage of nitrous oxide to air. At higher RPM, the engine still makes more horsepower, but as the air flow demands outpace the flat flow rate of the nitrous system you get a lower percentage of nitrous oxide to air and power falls off. Unless, of course, you have a staged system that increases nitrous flow as the engine demands increase.

Because of the rate and volumetric efficiency variations of piston engines, we will confine our discussion of the nitrous vs. air flow rates to those that occur at the torque peak and the horsepower peak. By looking at the differing nitrous-to-air ratios at these points, you'll understand that these ratios change dynamically as the engine runs through its RPM range. Presenting a simple model will make the math and the concept as plain as possible. Let's have a look at the torque peak first.

MODELING A NITROUS SYSTEM

The gear heads at SuperFlow, Inc., makers of some of the better dynos, flow benches, and other power and flow measuring equipment in the market, say that, in general, an engine flows approximately 1.25 SCFM per horsepower at peak torque and 1.4 SCFM per horsepower at peak power. We'll use these values throughout our discussions.

Assume you're making 200 hp at the torque peak without nitrous. Using the SuperFlow constant, that ciphers out to about 250 SCFM. When you hit the button, suddenly the engine thunders to 340 hp at the torque peak and the SuperFlow constant is no longer valid. The reason the constant (this goes for the peak power constant as well) is no longer valid, is simply that nitrous has a greater oxygen content than air. That being so, it takes less nitrous oxide to react to a given amount of fuel. If you've grabbed hold of the concept we've been repeating like a mantra, "fuel makes power, not the nitrous," then this should make sense to you.

If we just take the additional power gain, ordain its genesis as nitrous and calculate what it would take to make 140 extra hp at the torque peak, then we can estimate how much nitrous we need to run. This isn't a completely accurate model of the reality within our engine. Reality is always so much messier. The difficulty here is that not only do we have the ever-changing conditions of a pulse device running through its RPM range, but now we have an oxidizing agent that's active in two other ways. First, it cools the incoming atmosphere, increasing its density and thereby its oxygen content. Second, it also slightly pressurizes the intake reducing the flow through the carburetor. What's a tuner to do?

Well, the pros measure everything. They measure the air and the fuel going into the engine naturally aspirated; with savvy nitrous tuners doing the same with the nitrous and the enrichment fuel. That's the way to do it if you have a dyno and generate brake-specific consumption data. For the rest of us, we have to tune on the run, literally. However, if you understand the relationships of the data from the dyno, you'll be able to make better tuning decisions at the track.

FUEL/NITROUS/AIR FLOW AT PEAK TORQUE

Since air flow constants aren't practical when using nitrous, the only other constant we can use is brake specific fuel consumption (BSFC). BSFC is the ratio of fuel consumed to the power output. Typically a BSFC value of .50 is about average for a well-tuned engine with

roughly a 12.5:1 air/fuel ratio. It's a good value to use when working with nitrous because "fuel makes power, not the nitrous." So if you know the total rate of fuel flow, you know, based on a .50 BSFC, approximately how much power that fuel flow rate will support.

To use our BSFC standard we need to convert the other values into like units of measure. So going back to our model, 200 hp at peak torque is about 250 SCFM. If you reference the ratio and flow charts in the nitrous tuning reference chapter, we find 250 SCFM is about 19.05 lbs./min. That corresponds to a fuel flow at .50 BSFC of 100 lbs./hr. (To convert the lbs./hr. to lbs./min. simply divide it by 60.) This converts to 1.67 lbs./min. 19.05/1.67 = 11.4 air/fuel ratio. At the torque peak an 11.4:1 air/fuel ratio is not too far off for an engine tuned to accelerate. Most engines accelerate quicker if they're slightly rich. Peak steady-state power comes with a much leaner mixture, somewhere around 13.5:1 depending on the combination.

Now let's do the math to factor in nitrous mass flow. The extra 140 hp equates, at peak torque, to a naturally-aspirated flow rate of 175 SCFM or 13.34 lbs./min. of air. For nitrous, it's only 50 cfm or 5.83 lbs./min. at a N20/fuel ratio of 5:1 referenced to a BSFC of .50, which is 1.17 lbs./min. mass fuel flow.

We come by the 5:1 N20/fuel ratio through the NOS crew. They've found that 5:1 is a good, conservative, slightly fuel-rich beginning ratio. About the leanest mix they suggest is a 6:1 ratio, but you can go leaner if you've got the nerve.

Before we go on, let's take a look at how we arrived at the CFM values of the nitrous at lbs./min. flow rates. It's basically an estimate. If you check the index for the physical constants of nitrous, you see its specific volume at 1 atm. Let's use the specific volume factor at 70°F of 8.726 ft. 3/lb. We don't know exactly what temperature and therefore volume it reaches in the engine before the intake valve closes, but this figure is at least a good estimate. Also, keep in mind that as the engine heats during a power run or dyno pull, the intake temperature increases. As it does, the vol-

ume of the nitrous charge increases and its temperature increases as well.

To recap what we've done so far:

200 hp on air @ 11.4: a/f ratio = (250 SCFM = 19.05 lbs./min.) + 1.67 lbs./min. fuel

+

140 hp Nitrous @ 5:1 n/f ratio = (50 cfm = 5.83 lbs./min.) + 1.17 lbs./min. fuel

or

140 hp Nitrous @ 6:1 n/f ratio = (61 cfm = 7.00 lbs./min.) + 1.17 lbs./min. fuel

Next, add the flow rates together to get the total:
200 hp +140 hp = 340 hp
=
Naturally aspirated: 19.05 + 13.34 = 32.39 lbs./min. + 2.83 lbs./min.
N2O @ 5:1 ratio: 19.05 + 05.83 = 24.88 lbs./min. + 2.83 lbs./min.
N2O @ 6:1 ratio: 19.05 + 07.00 = 26.05 lbs./min. + 2.83 lbs./min.

MASS FLOW COMPARISON OF NITROUS TO NATURALLY ASPIRATED

If you compare the mass flow rate of a nitrous-enhanced engine with that of a naturally-aspirated engine of the same output, you'll see that the nitrous system generates much less mass flow on the intake side of the equation. We'll discuss the exhaust side of the equation later.

One of the great advantages of nitrous is that it packs in more oxygen in a smaller package than a naturally-aspirated engine. How much? Take a look at the chart located nearby comparing mass flow of a nitrous engine with that of a naturally-aspirated engine.

The point of this exercise is to show you that a nitrous system doesn't have to supply huge rates of oxygen and you don't need unreasonably large quantities of enrichment fuel to add impressive horsepower levels. Once again, it is the fuel that makes the power, and it takes X amount of fuel to make Y amount of power no matter how you introduce the oxidizer. It doesn't matter to the engine if the oxygen is supplied by a compressor or a bottle of compressed nitrous oxide.

FUEL/NITROUS/AIR FLOW AT PEAK POWER

We've just taken an in-depth look at the air, oxygen, nitrous oxide, and fuel flow demands of an engine at peak torque. Peak torque usually occurs at an RPM level well before the horsepower peak. At those air flow rates a nitrous system supplies a higher percentage of the O_2/fuel mixture. As the engine's RPM increases, so does the air flow rate, which reduces the percentage supplied by the nitrous system. Power falls off because of this. Friction increases with engine speed, and the volumetric efficiency of the engine falls off because there just isn't enough time to fill the cylinders.

After reviewing the charts, you can see how our theoretical numbers add up during peak power. Notice the nitrous flow didn't change nor did its enrichment fuel flow for the peak power model. Again, that's because a single-stage nitrous system is a constant flow system. Still, you can see that a moderate dose of nitrous raises power impressively.

OBSERVATIONS AND INTERPRETATIONS

These stats suggest a nitrous system increases mass flow from the torque peak to the power peak 12% more than an all-natural combination. The 60% increase in mass flow with nitrous compared to the 48% increase of a naturally-aspirated engine is consistent with the fixed flow of a single-stage nitrous system. This is explained as the natural consequence of the nitrous system supplying a greater percentage of the intake charge at peak torque, where air flow is also lower, than at the power peak.

Analyzing the percentages for the volume flow in CFM, the values are different because the volume and weight of nitrous oxide and the atmosphere have different values. However, the explanation for the percent increase is the same as the increase of mass just given. Remember that we aren't accounting for volume increases due to intake manifold temperature rise and therefore charge temperature rise during a power pull.

The increasing proportion of oxygen is where it gets interesting. We get a 48% increase, true; that has to occur to support the power level, i.e., the amount of fuel available to react with the oxygen. The question we need answered in our quest for nitrous expertise is, how much of the additional oxygen comes from the nitrous system and how much from the atmosphere? According to our calculations, at peak power with a 6:1 nitrous-to-fuel ratio, 28% of the oxygen comes from the nitrous system; at peak torque that value jumps to 41%. At peak power, 17% of the mass contributes to 28% of the oxygen.

The fuel and HP increases are purely for reference, though these exhibit an interesting trend. They show a larger increase in fuel consumption compared to the power output. This expresses the tendency of internal combustion engines to be more efficient at the torque peak.

That being so, some of the power generated by the additional fuel at the power peak is being consumed by a higher rate of friction caused by the engine spinning at a faster RPM.

EXHAUST NOTES

Even a mild nitrous system delivers more fuel and oxygen to the combustion chambers than a naturally-aspirated engine. Of course, if more goes in, then more has to come out. Traditionally this is accomplished by choosing a cam with an exaggerated exhaust lobe. Usually this has meant compromising engine performance when not on the bottle. Most "nitrous" cam combinations trade throttle response and low-end torque for high-end performance. This occurred because in order to provide a good exhaust duration, the cam had to open

Mass Flow Comparisons: Naturally Aspirated vs. Nitrous							

NATURALLY ASPIRATED

HP:	CFM	=	lb/min. air	x 0.19	=	lb/min O_2	+	lb/min fuel
326	456	=	34.74	x 0.19	=	6.60	+	2.70 (approx)

NITROUS: SUGGESTED BEGINNING RATIO OF 5:1

	CFM	=	lb/min. air	x 0.19	=	lb/min O_2	+	lb/min fuel
5:1 ratio:	050	=	5.83	x 0.36	=	2.09	+	1.17
Air Equivalent	144	=	11.00	x 0.19	=	2.09	+	1.17

428 HP naturally aspirated (air:fuel = 11.81:1)

	600	=	45.74	x 0.19	=	8.69	+	3.87

428 HP with N_2O (8.69/3.87 = 2.24 O_2/fuel ratio; 3.87/9.12 = .424 fuel/O_2 ratio)

	506	=	40.57		=	8.69

NITROUS: SUGGESTED MAXIMUM RATIO OF 6:1

	CFM	=	lb/min. air	x 0.19	=	lb/min O_2	+	lb/min fuel
6:1 ratio	61	=	7.050	x 0.36	=	2.52	+	1.17
Air Equivalent	174	=	13.26	x 0.19	=	2.52	+	1.17

450 HP naturally aspirated (air:fuel = 12.40:1)

	630	=	48.0	x 0.19	=	9.12

450 HP with N_2O (9.12/3.87 = 2.35 O_2/fuel ratio; 3.87/9.12 = .424 fuel/O_2 ratio)

	517	=	41.74		=	9.12

Comparative Flow Rates at Peak Torque and Horsepower

N$_2$O: FUEL RATIO OF 6:1

Flow Rates at Peak Torque	air		N$_2$O		fuel
450 hp @ peak torque:	19.05	+	7.00	=	26.05 lb/min + 2.83 lb/min
Percent nitrous in intake charge:	7.00/26.05 = 0.268, or 27 percent.				

Flow Rates at Peak Power:	air		N$_2$O		fuel
450 hp @ peak power:	34.74	+	7.00	=	41.74 lb/min + 3.87 lb/min
Percent nitrous in intake charge:	7.00/41.74 = 0.167, or 17 percent.				

Percent increases from Peak Torque to Peak Horsepower:

Percent increase in air mass:
With N$_2$O: ....60% (517/311 = 1.660)
 Naturally aspirated: ....41% (600/425 = 1.410)

Percent increase in O$_2$: ....48% (9.12/6.15 = 1.480)
Percent O$_2$ from nitrous at power peak: ....28% (2.52/9.12 = 0.276)
Percent O$_2$ from nitrous at torque peak: ....41% (2.52/6.15 = 0.409)

Percent increase in fuel...37% (3.87/2.83 = 1.370)
Percent increase in horsepower...32% (450/340 = 1.320)

That's how our theoretical numbers add up during peak power. Note that we didn't change the nitrous flow and its enrichment fuel flow for the peak power model. Again, that's because a single-stage nitrous system is a constant flow system. Still, you can see that even a moderate dose of nitrous raises power impressively.

the exhaust valve in such a way that the design had lots of overlap. For street cars, most enthusiasts opted for a cam that gave good performance without nitrous or just left it stock to pass emission testing, knowing that the nitrous system would make serious power anyway. If you want to keep your car legally streetable, keeping the cam stock is a good option.

Because of innovations in valve train design, cams makers such as Zex, Comp Cams, and others will be able to offer very powerful emissions-legal cam designs, and perhaps even emissions-legal nitrous specific designs as well.

A good nitrous cam profile will open the intake valve faster (resulting in more vacuum and more response) and close it sooner (resulting in more cylinder pressure and more torque.) The exhaust profiles are chosen to have enough area to scavenge the extra gases released from the combustion of oxygen-enhanced mixtures. The intake and

A good nitrous cam profile will open the intake valve faster (resulting in more vacuum and more response) and close it sooner (resulting in more cylinder pressure and more torque.) The exhaust profiles are chosen to have enough area to scavenge the extra gases released from the combustion of oxygen-enhanced mixtures.

exhaust centerlines are chosen to optimize responsiveness and power, while overlap area is maintained at the desired value. With this design strategy, any combustion pressure lost due to opening the exhaust valve early is more than compensated for by the improved intake profile. Cam choice is very specific to your engine combination. We could give you popular designs and leave it at that, but we'd prefer to have you call a reputable cam maker or consult your engine builder. At the very least, you should buy a dyno program such as that offered through Motion Software and "test" some combinations.

MORE NITROUS TUNING TIPS

Staged Systems

Each stage should have it's own optimum ignition settings. Remember, as you increase power with nitrous you always retard ignition timing. See the tuning reference section for a chart of suggested baseline tuning combinations.

Direct-port injection and plate systems can have different timing requirements. Take good notes on the ambient temp when you're tuning. A good racing weather station is ideal. Plates give the charge more time to absorb heat from the engine. Sometimes you can get the mixture so cold with a port injection flowing huge amounts of nitrous, that it slows the burn rate to a point where you lose power. This can happen with subtle changes in ambient temperatures, such as the difference in day and night time temperatures. An example of this is found in a staged plate and direct-port system that runs fast during the day but loses power at night.

The reason seems to be that the nitrous charge picks up heat from the intake manifold before being captured in the combustion chamber. The easy fix for this is to add timing depending on the temperature drop. If you track ambient temperatures with your tuning, then you'll have an advantage. Depending on your combination, a rule of thumb is to bump up the timing .5 to 1 degree for every 10-degrees drop in temperature from your baseline tune.

Heat Soak Changes Timing Requirements

Another factor influencing timing and one that further complicates tuning a system, is heat soak. As you approach the end of the track, the temperature in the cylinder increases, which reduces timing advance requirements. This phenomenon happens so fast that it doesn't show in EGT or coolant temps. These will remain virtually constant, but the timing requirements can vary a great deal. Be aware.

MSD's Multi-Step Retard (PN8972) unit works with MSD 6, 7, and 8 ignitions. It's a great device for drag racers employing multi-stage nitrous systems. Installation is easy by slicing into the 12V solenoid wires. Once installed, every time you activate a stage, a different retard stage is also activated. A versatile device, it also has a 20-degree retard start-up mode to make starting high compression with fixed timing a little easier (such as that used with crank triggers or locked out distributors).

One Bottle Per Stage

With multiple stage systems, using a separate bottle for each stage is ideal because it allows you to evaluate the tune of each stage by accurately gauging nitrous consumption. It also gives you a better idea of how much power each

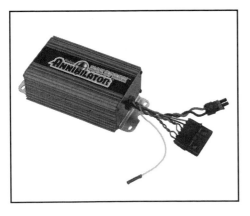

When installing a nitrous system, upgrading your ignition system is a must. Holley's Annihilator Max Spark DA for sport compacts is designed to fit the factory wiring harness. It is a great backup for a street dry-manifold setup. (Holley)

Holley designers state the Commander 950 ECU is good to manage up to 950 hp. It has the capacity to command and control nitrous systems, turbo boost and spark timing, fuel pump, cooling fan, idle quality, and more. (Holley)

stage is contributing. Using a separate bottle for each stage ensures that each starts with the correct bottle pressure. Consistent pressure equates to consistent flow. If you run two systems on the same bottle, the jetting will be corrupted because you can't know exactly how much pressure you'll have when you activate the second system.

Nitrous bottle temperature and pressure must also be constant. Also, don't forget that line length, diameter, distribution blocks, hard line length, and amount of bends in a circuit influence flow rate and hence nitrous fuel mixtures.

Use Separate Fuel Systems Per Stage

Fuel delivery must be as constant as possible. As we've already stated in a previous section, you should use one fuel system for nitrous and another for the carb or fuel injection. Concerning multi-stage systems, if you have a pump that will deliver the volume and pressure, you can use a bypass-type regulator for each stage of multi-stage systems.

Trade Ballast Bars for Batteries

This is a tip for the truly hardcore racer who's racing without an alternator. Think about this: A hot ignition is

going to pull 10 - 25 amps; a big fuel pump will pull up to 10 amps. If you're running one pump per each stage, those numbers add up quick. The bigger nitrous solenoids can pull 15 amps each. So that's 30 amps for one stage of port nozzles. Dual plate systems with two more nitrous solenoids add another 30 amps. As you add stages the current draw keeps going up. If you tax the battery on a run and voltage or amperage sag, the low resistance solenoids, usually the fuel, will close first. So racers without alternators and elaborate systems run a risk of leaning out quick and unexpectedly. The moral: If you have the room, trade the ballast bar for batteries.

Uneven Air/Fuel Distribution and Detonation

Making sure each cylinder receives the same amount of fuel is very important when you are trying to get the last bit of power from your engine. If an

The popularity of small-displacement, high-RPM, turbocharged racing engines has created a need for an even higher output ignition for distributorless ignition systems (DIS). Like the popular MSD DIS Ignitions, the DIS-HO models are designed for vehicles with distributorless ignition systems with two-, three-, or four-coil packs. (MSD)

engine has uneven distribution of the air/fuel mixture between cylinders, the leaner cylinders are more prone to detonate. That means you have to (or the computer has to) retard the timing for the mixture of the leanest cylinder. This most often occurs on carbureted cars,

Nozzles for Nitrous Systems

Nitrous nozzles mix fuel with the nitrous. Some do a better job of it than others but in general a mixer nozzle per cylinder is the most efficient way to ensure proper fuel ratios per cylinder. NOS offers several designs to meet your nitrous tuning needs.

Jet spray nozzles feature a compact size for space-restrictive installations, such as hidden systems. They come in fixed orifice sizes so you need to specify jet size when ordering. (NOS)

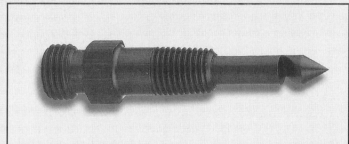

Fan Spray NOS Nozzles are smaller than Fogger nozzles to allow installation in tighter spaces. These nozzles are fully adjustable with jet change and spray in a fan pattern at a 90-degree angle. (NOS)

The annular discharge nozzle from NOS provides better fuel atomization and more even distribution within the nitrous flow. (NOS)

The soft plume nozzle from NOS produces a smooth, homogeneous fog 90-degrees to the nozzle. Its design is optimum for small-displacement engines. (NOS)

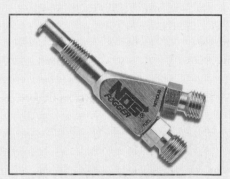

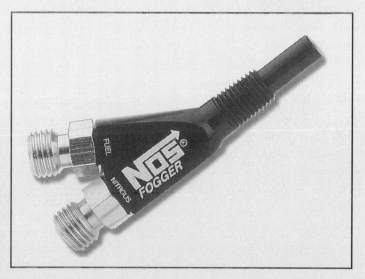

NOS Fogger nozzles come in standard and Fogger 2 configurations. The Fogger nozzle provides excellent performance and fuel into nitrous mixing at mid-range power levels. For very serious power levels and flow rates, the Fogger 2 is the proper solution. It has a specially-designed flow pattern and offers better atomization of fuel and more homogeneous fuel distribution in the nitrous plume. (NOS)

Nitrous at Work

Every facet of this RX-7 is well designed and executed. It's as fast as it is gorgeous. The monster rotary engine in Abel Ibarra's bad and nasty RX-7 makes a lot of noise even behind the big— make that very big—turbocharger. It pushes this tube-chassis version of Mazda's venerable sports car to 7-second blasts with nitrous-enhanced gusto.

Key to this car's quick combination is the super powerful rotary engine. Rotaries love to rev so they make killer top-end horsepower, but the small displacement of the engine means it needs help building quarter-mile conquering torque. That's where the NOS single Fogger nozzle system comes in. It gives the rotors an instant hit of high temperature and high pressure pumping up the torque to get the car moving. In addition, the exhaust is equally energetic and sends the turbo spinning. Once the turbo spins up, it's making all the air flow that's needed and the nitrous system can be shut down. Or, you can leave it on to help intercool the charge while adding additional fuel. It's all a matter of tuning your combination.

The key to winning a drag race is acceleration. Acceleration comes from a force (torque) applied to a mass (the car). Horsepower is a measure of acceleration, i.e., of the rate at which work is done. You have to have the torque, but it has to be applied at a very high rate, which is horsepower.

Here's the heart of the beast. This turbocharged rotary, burning nitrous and alcohol has to be putting out just over 900 horsepower. That's what it would take to push a car weighing in around 2000 lbs. to 180+ in the quarter-mile. You can see the NOS Fogger nozzle positioned before the throttle body. Notice the smooth radius bends in the intake manifold. There is no loss of air flow or unnecessary heating of the air. It comes to the throttle body in almost a straight shot from the turbo.

Abel Ibarra's Wet NOS System Turbocharged 7-second RX-7

Here's a chance to look into the air horn of Ibarra's turbo. Big turbos are called for to flow over 900 horsepower's worth of air without heating it up, but they need help to get spinning. They make awesome top-end power, but the flat flow characteristics of a nitrous system work wonders here.

This killer big turbine side is heat shielded to retain exhaust gas energy and velocity. Notice the huge waste gate. This is one extremely powerful drag racer.

Rotary engines use dual spark plugs to get the fire going in the narrow and long combustion chamber of this engine design. This is singularly difficult when you combine methanol and the high boost pressures involved.

In this shot you can see the big NOS Alcohol Cheater solenoid used to flow the fuel. When you use alcohol you essentially have to double the flow requirements so you need big components. Notice the purge set up.

Accurately monitoring engine functions and parameters is a fundamental part of tuning any race car.

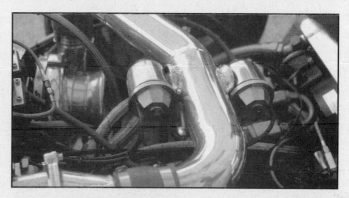

Because of the sheer volume and velocity of the air flow through this engine, Ibarra uses a pair of blow-off valves. Blow offs allow intake pressure to bleed off when the throttle snaps shut, allowing the turbo to keep spooled and also to avoid surge and turbulence that can damage a turbo.

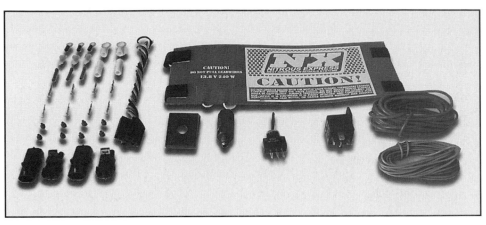

Tuning your nitrous system depends on the fuel pressure and nitrous bottle pressure. You have to control both: the fuel pressure at the injectors and the jets in a wet system's mixer nozzles, and the nitrous pressure at the injection/mixer nozzle. A bottle heater and blanket are the best combination for controlling bottle pressure. (Nitrous Express)

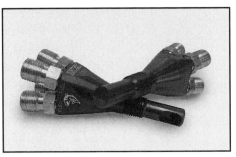

Nitrous Express's new Shark nozzles allow you to run a dual-stage system using only one nozzle.

Direct-port wet systems are still the most powerful nitrous systems. They require careful tuning and maintenance, but if you want to go really quick with nitrous, this is the way to do it.

but it also happens to throttle-body-injected engines or to port-fuel injected cars as the injectors get clogged or just weren't built right at the factory. Basically, if one cylinder is down on power, the rest of the cylinders are brought to that level by the computer as it retards timing.

A combination with poor distribution can easily turn into a broken engine once you hit it with nitrous. Be very careful about this. Dial up the power and always read the plugs; all of them. Don't just spot check. If one of the cylinders is going lean, you better know about it before putting more nitrous into the engine.

Aiming Nozzles and Spray Bar Orifices

Aiming nozzles and spray bar orifices are not nearly as crucial as has been marketed. As the plenum size increases, aiming become even less of a concern. The reason is the severe pulsing of the intake tract. With all the flow changes, the moving air carries the nitrous fog with it no matter which direction it's introduced. Don't forget an engine is not a linear device. It is a pulse flow device; the air is constantly changing direction in the intake.

TUNING HOW THE NITROUS HITS

The distance from release point (i.e. the solenoid) to the next restriction or orifice is a chamber the nitrous has to fill and pressurize. The greater the volume, the longer it takes to pressurize. So you can use this physical fact as a tuning aid. The longer it takes the nitrous to pressurize such a chamber, the softer the power comes on and the less you shock the tires. It's more of a roll-in feel. Adjust the nitrous side and leave the fuel side alone. This method is best for traction-limited cars if you can't adjust the clutch.

OPERATING NITROUS OXIDE SYSTEMS

There are several things to keep in mind when operating a nitrous system. We've already discussed some of these items in earlier chapters, but for safety's sake they bear repeating.

- Work safely. Always wear eye protection and gloves when working with lines or hoses that contain pressurized nitrous oxide or fuel. Never transport nitrous cylinders loose in a trunk or the back of a pick-up truck and especially NOT within a vehicle's interior whether the cylinder is full OR empty. Make sure the cylinder is secured so it won't get damaged from bouncing around. Always disconnect the GROUND side of the battery when working on any electrical components.
- Be realistic about the amount of additional power your engine can reliably handle. If you're in doubt, it's always better to guess less than more. The various nitrous companies can lend some very valuable information concerning particular engine and component strength and durability. They don't want you to reach the point of damage any more than you do.
- Consistency is everything. Fluctuating fuel pressure, different nitrous cylinder temperatures, worn or sticky mechanical advance mechanisms,

intermittent wiring problems, etc., can all lead to erratic system performance and possibly engine damage.
- Nitrous oxide won't fix problems you already have. Before you install your nitrous system, be sure your engine is in good mechanical condition. Ignition problems and carburetor or fuel-injection calibration problems become bigger problems when combined with nitrous oxide.
- Install as many safety devices as you can. Power relays, oil pressure safety switches, wide-open-throttle switches, RPM-activated switches, and low fuel pressure safety switches are just a few examples of things you can install to ensure that your system can only be activated when the engine is running and is at wide-open throttle.
- Never defeat the operation of the safety relief disc in the nitrous cylinder's valve stem. It's required by law and is there for your safety.
- Never drill, machine, weld, deform, scratch, drop, or modify a nitrous oxide tank in ANY way! Although some people have polished their

The Autometer Sportcomp Monster tach is accurate and easy to read, making shifting at the correct RPM that much easier. You must have a boost gauge if you have a turbo. it's most useful during the tuning process. You don't have much time to look at it when you're racing.

tanks to a chrome-like appearance, even this is not recommended because it removes a non-uniform layer of the tank's material that may or may not affect it's integrity. Certainly, never attempt to subject a nitrous tank to any type of plating process because this often affects the strength of the tank's material.

- Never overfill nitrous cylinders. That little extra amount will put you and others at great risk for injury. More often than not, when the cylinder warms up, the pressure goes above the limit of the safety relief disc and you lose all the nitrous you just paid for. If you are a retail dealer and you overfill a cylinder beyond its rated capacity in weight, whether intentional or not, you could be held liable for the consequences of any damages or injury. If your customer specifically requests an overfill, don't do it.

- All the power comes from the fuel, not the nitrous. Nitrous oxide is simply a tool that allows you to adjust how much and how quickly the engine burns the fuel. If the fuel isn't there, the power won't be either.

- Avoid detonation at all times. Nitrous-enhanced detonation is much more damaging than detonation that occurs when an engine is naturally-aspirated due to the increased amount of fuel available for releasing energy and the fact that more oxygen is present.

- When you check the spark plugs, check every plug. Don't just spot check the easiest plug you can get to. Due to the wide possibility of air/fuel mixture variations, you need to check every single plug for signs of detonation or other problems.

- Always start with the recommended calibration that came with your system. If your system is an adjustable type, begin with the lowest supplied level of calibration. The calibration is the combination of nitrous and fuel jets that determine how much nitrous and fuel will flow when the system is activated.

- At the first sign of detonation, backfire, or misfire, **always reduce the nitrous jet first!** Don't think that you will cool things down by adding more fuel. Since nitrous oxide is an oxidizer, the safest approach is to reduce the nitrous first, identity the problem, and go from there.

- Check the fuel and nitrous filter screens on a regular basis. Clogged screens are one of the most common problems that can lead you in circles for days. It doesn't take much to alter the calibration. Even a small scrap of pipe-sealing tape can cause big problems.

- When your system is activated, if something doesn't feel or sound right, BACK OFF. If you hear any detonation or feel anything unusual, get off the throttle. It's a lot easier to check everything over than it is to just try to drive through it and break a lot or expensive parts.

SYSTEM CHECKS

Before you take your nitrous-enhanced machine down the track, always take a few moments and perform a system check. The purpose of a system check is to verify that the nitrous circuit and the fuel circuit are both operating correctly. Make this procedure a habit before racing and you'll spend more time running and less time on the trailer.

There are two scenarios regarding system checks depending on whether you have a dry-manifold system or a wet-manifold system.

Dry-Manifold System Check

To check a dry-manifold system, first energize your car's ignition. Then check all your fuel and vacuum lines for leaks. It is pretty easy to spot fuel leaks but vacuum leaks are harder to spot. Generally a vacuum leak causes the engine to idle rough if it is bad enough.

Assuming the fuel and vacuum lines check out, start your engine. While the engine is running, open the nitrous bottle valve. Listen carefully to your engine as you open the valve. You should not hear a difference in idle speed or exhaust tone. If you notice either one of these changes or both, your system has a defective nitrous solenoid. That means you have to remove and inspect the solenoid and repair or replace as needed. For more information, see the sidebar located in this chapter on troubleshooting.

Hopefully you won't notice any change in idle speed or exhaust tone leaving you free to inspect the nitrous lines and fittings for leaks. Leaks in the nitrous supply line will be obvious because they'll be covered with frost. If you have no leaks in the nitrous supply line, you are cleared for takeoff.

Dry Manifold Check List

1. Energize ignition.
2. Check fuel and vacuum lines for leaks.
3. Start engine.
4. Open nitrous bottle valve, check for stable idle speed and exhaust tone.
5. Inspect nitrous lines and fittings for leaks.
6. Go faster.

Wet-Manifold System Check

To check a wet manifold system, first turn on the fuel pump then check the lines and fittings for leaks. Next, arm the system by switching the arming toggle switch to "ON." Rev the engine to 2000 rpm and hold it steady. Briefly activate the nitrous system by pushing or squeezing the button. You should notice a decrease in engine speed because, assuming the fuel system is working properly, the engine should be running extremely rich right now. If not, you have probably wired the system incorrectly, have a restrictive fuel line, or a malfunctioning fuel solenoid. See the trouble shooting sidebar in this chapter for more information.

If the fuel circuit checks out, open the nitrous bottle valve. At this point you don't want any changes in engine speed or tone. If you notice such, you have a broken or defective nitrous solenoid which needs replacing or repairing. If the system passes this system check, inspect the nitrous lines and fittings for leaks. Once again if the system passes this check, you're cleared for takeoff.

Wet Manifold Check List

1. Turn on fuel pump.
2. Check fuel lines and fittings for leaks.
3. Turn arming toggle switch to "ON."
4. Set engine speed at 2000 rpm.
5. Briefly push N2O activation button. Engine speed should decrease.
6. Open nitrous bottle valve. Engine speed to remain stable.
7. Inspect nitrous lines and fittings for leaks.
8. Go faster.

TRANSFER PUMP INSTRUCTIONS

Your NOS nitrous oxide transfer pump is designed for high-speed filling of NOS nitrous oxide bottles. For proper performance, it is necessary that all instructions be followed carefully. Please read through the instructions and safety tips thoroughly before attempting to use your transfer pump. If you have any questions about its operation or components, call the NOS Technical Department.

Safety Tips

- Never directly inhale nitrous oxide. When inhaled in large quantities, nitrous oxide can cause respiratory ailments or in extreme cases, death via suffocation.
- Never allow escaping nitrous oxide to contact skin. Nitrous oxide discharges at -130 degrees Fahrenheit. If allowed to contact skin, it will cause severe frostbite.
- Never overfill any compressed gas cylinder. Maximum weight that any NOS cylinder should weigh is clearly labeled on the side of the cylinder.
- Always wear hand and eye protection when performing nitrous oxide transfer operations.
- Always use an airline water trap.
- Never permit oil, grease, or any other readily-combustible substances to come in contact with cylinders, valves, solenoids, hoses, and fittings. Oil and certain gases (such as oxygen and nitrous oxide) may combine to produce a flammable condition.

- Never deface or remove any markings used for content identification on compressed gas cylinders.
- Nitrous bottle valves should be closed when transfer pump is not in use.
- Keep valves closed on all empty bottles to prevent accidental contamination.
- After storage, open nitrous bottle valve for an instant to clear opening of any possible dust or dirt.
- Notify supplier of any condition that might have permitted any foreign matter to enter valve or bottle.
- Never drop or violently strike bottle.
- Do not use an air-line oiler with this pump.
- Do not overtighten AN style fittings. They can easily be damaged.

System Requirements

The transfer pump is driven by compressed air. Your air compressor must be capable of producing a working line pressure of at least 50 psi. In general, the higher the line pressure, the more effective the pump. Maximum operating pressure should be limited to about 125 psi.

Transfer Pump Operation

1. Place the NOS cylinder you intend to fill on an accurate scale. Determine how much nitrous oxide is left in the cylinder. If there is only a small percentage left in the cylinder, open the valve and relieve all the pressure in the cylinder. If a cylinder is more than 1/3 full and is going to be "topped off," it may be necessary in hot climates to place it in a refrigerator or freezer for a short period of time to cool it off to approximately 45° F. Lowering the temperature will also lower the bottle pressure and allow a complete fill. In areas where daytime temperatures exceed 80°F, this method of cooling cylinders before filling may be necessary for all cylinders, regardless of whether they are full or empty.
2. Connect the N2O control valve assembly to the NOS cylinder to be refilled, using a 6AN bottle nut. Be

sure to use a Teflon washer between the NOS cylinder and the bottle nut. If the cylinder being refilled is equipped with a 4AN fitting, use a 4AN X 6AN adapter fitting and 1-ft. 4AN hose. If the cylinder is equipped with an old-style valve, use the standard valve adapter.

3. Place the NOS cylinder on the scale and note weight. There will be a slight weight increase due to the N20 control valve assembly. This additional "tare" weight must be added to the filled weight of the cylinder as stated on the cylinder label.
4. Close the shut-off valve on the N2O control valve assembly.
5. Fully open the valve on the nitrous oxide source bottle.
6. Fully open the valve on the NOS cylinder to be filled.
7. Open the shut-off valve on the N2O control valve assembly. Wait for the pressure in the source bottle and the NOS cylinder to equalize.
8. Slowly open the air pressure control valve on the compressed air on/off valve assembly. Watch the scale reading and close the air pressure control valve when the NOS cylinder reaches its full weight.

If the cylinder being refilled reaches 1100 psi before the full weight of the bottle is reached, stop the pump by turning off the compressed air valve. Invert, then right the NOS cylinder. Repeat several times until you feel the bottle temperature drop. You can then turn the pump back on and continue pumping.

9. Close the valve on the NOS cylinder.
10. Close the valve on the N2O control valve assembly.
11. Carefully disconnect the 6AN transfer line from the NOS cylinder.
12. Close the valve on the nitrous oxide source bottle. Slowly open the valve on the N2O control valve assembly.

Chapter Four contains a detailed discussion on nitrous bottles. Included in that discussion is a chart detailing weights of nitrous bottles – both filled and empty. Please refer to that chart for additional information.

Nitrous At Work

Zex™ doesn't just sell performance components. Zex designers constantly develop and test these components at the track. The Zex CRX drag car is used as the ultimate test bed for camshafts and nitrous systems. Matt Patrick, Zex's Product Manager, pilots the car. He attends all NIRA races throughout the country to not only race, but to provide technical support for loyal customers at the track. The car was purpose-built for NIRA's Power 4, heads-up category. The car weighs 2,290pounds with the driver. Its best e.t. is 11.47 at 129.65 mph.

D16A6 block with Hard Block filled water jacket (3/4 fill); O-ring receiver groove around cylinders that have a .010 over bore. It uses ARP head studs, Crower steel-billet rods, SRP 9:1 forged-aluminum pistons and a stock crankshaft, as well as the stock oil pump and oil pan. The cylinder head is D16Z6 SOHC V-TEC that has been ported and polished and runs stainless steel valves with Zex valve springs (912-16) and a Zex camshaft (59300). A copper head gasket and O-rings installed seal the combustion chamber and water passages. The engine, with 18 lbs. of boost and a 100 hp shot of nitrous, made 412 hp to the wheels at 6900 rpm and 365 ft./lb. torque to the wheels at 6500 rpm.

Induction setup consists of a 100 hp Zex™ nitrous system custom designed to work with a full T-04 turbo setup (60-1 Turbonetics compressor) and Spearco liquid intercooler.

The 550 cc/minute rated RC Engineering injectors required massaging the fuel pressure regulator to give 17 psi at idle. At stock idle pressure it would be too rich with these high-flow units and would not idle. At 17 psi across the injector, however, the engine idles at 10.5:1. Rich, but just rich enough to provide an 11.5:1 when the 100 horsepower shot of nitrous comes on.

The Zex 1989 Honda CRX Si Drag Car

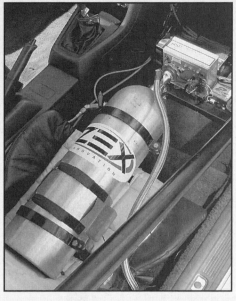

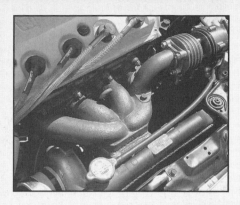

The fuel circuit is designed to deliver fuel with and without boost while using the stock computer. This is required by the "Power 4" rules. The Zex crew does this by using a heavy-duty version of the Zex street nitrous kit. The adjustable regulator reduces the 900 psi nitrous bottle pressure to 70 psi. The 70psi is the pressure signal to the fuel pressure riser.

A 25-lb. Zex nitrous bottle with temperature probe is properly mounted in the lightweight passenger seat. The valve is facing forward with the bottle oriented so the siphon tube picks up liquid nitrous even when the bottle is nearing depletion during a drag race. Notice the stainless, braided blow-down tube running to the floor.

This exhaust comprises an OTI International cast turbo manifold with a Tial waste gate, 3-inch down pipe, Borla 3.5-inch inlet and outlet stainless steel racing muffler with Borla 3.5-in. stainless steel turndown.

The Tial waste gate is an integral part of the turbo combination. It bleeds exhaust pressure off to regulate the amount of boost the turbo makes on the intake side.

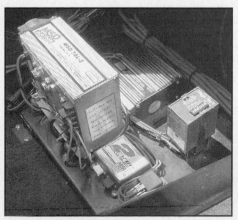

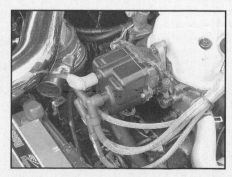

A boost pressure switch is set to activate the nitrous solenoid downstream of the nitrous pressure regulator at 1 psi of boost. This allows the fuel system to keep up with the turbocharger as it spools up and creates more boost. This occurs between .5 to 1 second after activating the system.

The total timing on this combination is set at 17 degrees. When the nitrous activates, the MSD box retards ignition timing 4 degrees. When the boost gets above 1 psi, the box retards timing another 9 degrees for a total of 30-degrees retard from the initial 17 degrees of timing advance.

The distributor is gutted save the rotor. All it has to do now is distribute the spark from the crank-triggered MSD ignition system.

Nitrous At Work (continued)
The Zex 1989 Honda CRX Si Drag Car

Some AN bulkhead fittings make a safe and secure path for the liquid nitrous in the bottle in an emergency. You never want to vent an oxidizer into the cockpit. A little fire can become a blow torch, so make sure you vent the nitrous valve's safety disc system properly.

Residual pressure that is generated when you close the throttle and the turbos still spooled up, can escape to the atmosphere with this blow off. It keeps the turbo from hurting itself and keeps it spooled up between shifts.

The Zex machine uses a Spearco liquid intercooler. When the intercooler's reservoir is filled with ice water, these units are extremely efficient. They cool the heated, compressed air coming off the turbo.

This shot details the intercooler reservoir system. It's filled with ice water and the pump circulates the water through the intercooler to remove the heat from the charged air. Notice the handy drain.

In addition to the Zex camshaft and valve springs, the car uses a Zex adjustable cam gear. As you can see, the grind on the Zex cam works best straight up—no retard or advance needed.

The Zex machine uses an MSD crank trigger for precise ignition timing. It's altered from a big-block Chevy kit and uses the a/c brackets to mount, which is a quick and relatively simple method of mounting.

All the switches to the various systems in the car are contained in a center-mounted control panel. Notice the purge button. Purging the system makes sure that the nitrous feed lines are filled with dense liquid nitrous instead of less-dense gas. The system hits harder when you do this.

Tuning your air-to-fuel ratio is critical, when you're using a turbo with nitrous. A wide-band oxygen sensor with high-resolution display is very accurate.

INSTALLATION TECH GUIDE

Installing a nitrous system is relatively easy compared with most other power adders. The approach is much like installing any other component system. First, decide where you are going to mount all the hard parts, bottle, solenoids, nozzles, switches, etc. Plan the positioning of these parts and install them. Next, if you're using a "wet" system, you need to place the nitrous and fuel lines from the bottle to the solenoids, and from the solenoids to the nozzle. Finally, you need to wire the system as appropriate. Of course, it is easier said than done. Before you start, read through the following to aid you in evaluating your particular system during the installation process.

INSTALLING THE BOTTLE

Accurately calibrating and tuning your NOS nitrous system depends on the temperature of the bottle remaining stable. Mount the bottle away from heat sources, such as the engine compartment or exhaust system, and away from windows, where the bottle is exposed to direct sunlight. In fastback-styled vehicles such as Camaros, Firebirds, 300ZXs, etc., it is impractical to mount the bottle away from direct sunlight. For cars such as these, the bottle should be covered or insulated with an NOS bottle blanket or an equivalent.

The professionals at NOS recommend that the bottle be environmentally separated from the driver's compartment. Again, fastback vehicles do not have separate trunk compartments, so kits designed for these cars include an external blow-down tube. The safety blow-down tube should be vented to the exterior of the vehicle (preferably under the vehicle). This procedure will prevent filling the driver's compartment with a cloud of nitrous oxide if, for any reason, the safety pressure relief cap raptures.

Bottle Orientation

Bottle placement is critical to the performance of your NOS nitrous sys-

Installing a nitrous system involves three distinct phases: First, plan the system and mount the components (bottle, solenoids, injectors, etc). Second, route and connect the nitrous lines and fuel lines for wet systems. Third, install the wiring. Now you're ready to energize the system and begin the tuning process.

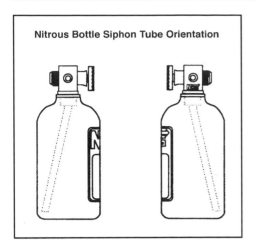

To allow the most latitude in bottle placement most nitrous manufacturers provide or have available offset internal siphon tubes. This lets you place the bottle at various angles and keep the nitrous pick up tube deep in the liquid nitrous. NOS orients its siphon tube opposite the label. (NOS)

tem. It is important to understand how the bottle valve and siphon tube are assembled to properly orient the bottle in your vehicle and ensure that it picks up liquid nitrous while undergoing acceleration. All NOS nitrous bottles are assembled so that the bottom of the siphon tube is at the bottom of the bottle and opposite the bottle label.

Whenever the bottle is mounted in a lay-down position, the valve handle

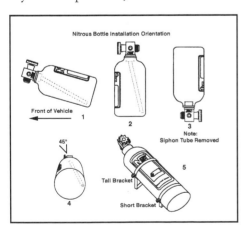

Orient your nitrous bottle to one of the positions shown. You want to have the siphon tube pickup positioned so it is submerged in liquid nitrous while the car is stationary as well as when under acceleration. (NOS)

must be towards the front of the vehicle with the label facing up (1). If the bottle is mounted vertically, the valve handle and label must face toward the front of the vehicle (2). This orientation will position the siphon tube at the back of the bottle where the liquid N20 will be during acceleration. DO NOT attempt to remove siphon tube without completely emptying bottle of all nitrous and pressure.

A bottle mounted upside down must have the siphon tube removed before use (3). Non-siphon bottles can be specially ordered from NOS and other manufacturers. If the bottle must be mounted parallel to the axles of the vehicle (sideways), the valve handle and label must be angled at approximately 45∞ toward the front of the vehicle (4). This orientation will properly position the siphon tube to capture liquid N_2O during acceleration.

This set up is still in progress. A blow-down tube using stainless braided line will soon be installed. Braided stainless lines coupled to AN bulkhead fittings make a very nice blow-down tube system.

When using a bottle with a siphon tube, the tall bracket should be at the valve end of the bottle and the short bracket at the bottom (5). The most efficient mounting is the lay-down position (1) with the valve handle toward the front of the vehicle. This position allows the greatest amount of liquid to be used before the siphon tube begins to pick up gaseous nitrous oxide.

Bottle Placement in Racing Vehicles

Before mounting a nitrous bottle in a racing vehicle intended for use in sanctioned events, check with the sanctioning association for any rules regarding this subject. Most associations require the bottle to be mounted inside the safety roll cage, with the safety pressure relief cap vented away from the driver's compartment.

This bottle is mounted in the cargo area of a late-model Toyota Supra. It's covered with a blanket as recommended, and it has a hard line blow-down tube installed.

Depending on the class you compete in, you may have to install a fuel cell. The Bullish Supra uses an ATL racing fuel cell. It is plumbed to allow a feed and return line for the fuel-injection system. Since the vehicle uses a dry nitrous system, additional nitrous enrichment fuel plumbing isn't necessary.

Installing Lines for Racing

Race cars usually have shorter nitrous supply lines. The shorter the line the more it flows and, in general, the system hits harder too. Racers put the bottle near the engine to shorten the nitrous feed line length. Usually this means mounting it in the front passenger area.

Always use grommets on fuel, nitrous, or electrical lines that pass through a firewall, even if they are braided steel. The nitrous feed line takes the shortest path to the nitrous solenoid. A small line coming off the main one goes to the purge valve.

INSTALLING HARD LINES AND NOZZLES

Plumbing the nitrous and fuel hard lines on a port-injection system isn't as easy as it looks. Designing a hard line plumbing job requires a little imagination and visualization skills. You have to visualize how all the elements of your plumbing (i.e. hard lines), distribution block, nozzles, solenoids, etc. will fit with the existing intake and fuel management components.

Before you can select the mounting location for the distribution block, you need to plan your design around the throttle linkage, TPS, and other devices that are physical obstacles. Once you've compensated for the throttle linkage and other devices on and around the intake, you can position the distribution block where there is adequate clearance to allow you to mount the solenoid(s).

If you are not experienced in tube bending, make a sample tube using either a piece of brake line or a coat hanger before you bend each solenoid extension tube. This practice will help you minimize errors and help you to produce an aesthetically-pleasing plumbing job.

Installing a Nitrous Feed Line on a Stock Vehicle

A typical nitrous feed line installation on a production car isn't what you'd call rocket science. With stock street-driven cars, it is usually best to follow the stock fuel line route. One more thing: Some nitrous enthusiasts like to insulate the supply line with water heater pipe insulation, available at most hardware stores. The following installation notes are typical for unibody construction, which covers most modern vehicles, domestic and import.

Before you attach the nitrous supply line to the nitrous solenoid inlet port, purge the nitrous supply line. To do this, wrap the end of the nitrous line with a rag and hold it securely. Point the opening away from people and briefly open the bottle valve. This will remove any debris the line collected on its journey through the undercarriage.

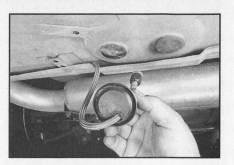

Often a body panel lip will provide a good place to lay the line up to the point where you can re-enter the interior. A drain plug is an easy access point. Just punch a hole in it and run the line through it. After reinstalling the drain plug and attaching it to the nitrous bottle, seal it with a liberal application of RTV. Sometimes attaching the nitrous supply line to the nitrous bottle valve adapter requires using an optional 4AN to 4AN 90° fitting.

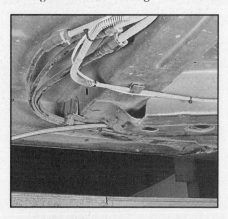

Generally you'll find a channel for the nitrous line inside the wheel house. If you bend back the fender liner, that will give you access to run the line inside the subframe rail. If it is necessary to support the nitrous supply line under the vehicle, use 1/2-inch Tinnerman clamps or nylon tie-wraps. Use a combination of clamps, tie-wraps, and body panels to place the nitrous line away from axles, exhaust, and other obstacles.

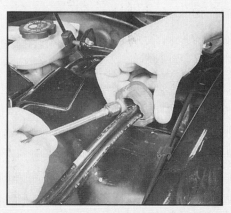

The safest route for the nitrous system fuel and nitrous lines is following the factory line. The factory has done crash studies and has determined the best route to keep the fuel line safe. So your first choice is always to follow the factory fuel line route if at all possible. You should start at the front and work your way toward the rear of the car, first working the line through the fuel line grommet in the firewall.

In dry-manifold nitrous systems, you need to direct a pressure signal to an adjustable fuel-pressure regulator. This allows you to raise the fuel pressure and, in turn, deliver more fuel to compensate for the nitrous. To do that you need to split the nitrous circuit with an additional solenoid that directs nitrous at bottle pressure to a nitrous pressure regulator. This will drop the line pressure to something the fuel pressure regulator can handle, such as 70 psi.

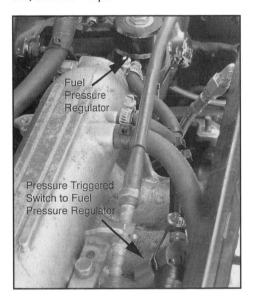

Fuel Pressure Regulator

Pressure Triggered Switch to Fuel Pressure Regulator

On turbo cars, you can have a switch sensitive to boost pressure that will deactivate the nitrous system, or just the nitrous pressure signal to the fuel pressure regulator. Since many tuners use nitrous to get the turbo spooled up, they'll deactivate the entire nitrous system and let the turbo take it from there. On more aggressive setups, you can keep the nitrous running to help produce even more power. Just be sure of your fuel curve tuning.

To position the nozzle in the manifold runner, use a straight edge to establish two reference lines: one to position the nozzle along the length of the intake runner, and one on the centerline of the runner. Repeat for each runner. Punch mark the position for each nozzle where your reference lines intersect.

With the nozzle positions marked, the next step is to drill the holes. Most installers prefer to use a drill press. This keeps all the holes on the same plane. You should also use the drill press to tap the holes. When tapping the holes, do not run the tap all the way through the hole. These are pipe threads and as such are tapered. If you run the tap all the way through, you won't have the taper to cause a bind and force an interference fit. When you install the nozzle, it will thread but it will be far too loose.

Adjust how far you put the nozzle into the runner by how far you run the tap into the hole. This is where you need to exercise judgment. The idea is to spray the nitrous and fuel into the port. If the nozzle is too shallow, it will hit the runner wall causing the fuel to stick to the wall and the nitrous to cool the metal instead of the intake charge. A workable approach is to determine how many "turns" it takes to position the nozzle to your desired distance from the intake wall. For example, if the nozzle has three threads showing, that places it .600-inch from the runner wall. Once you've installed the nozzles, check alignment with a straight edge. If one or two nozzles are low, correct by screwing the higher nozzles farther into the manifold.

Shaping the Hard Lines

Next, mock up your system. This step is done to make sure the all the components will work together, the bends will be where they should, etc. Most installers recommend dry fitting as much plumbing as you can, especially the center nozzle and distribution block. These form the reference point off which you build the rest of the system. When you're mocking it up, you can dry fit the plumbing but fit it loosely. Don't tighten. Otherwise you can gall the fittings and they won't seal correctly. Also, don't

over tighten during final assembly. Run it in until the fitting is tight, then give it one more turn. Be sure to use thread sealant with Teflon on final assembly.

If you're plumbing a V-6 or V-8, always start on the throttle linkage side. This allows you to set the height of the distribution block in relation to the throttle linkage. If you start on the other side, you may put the distribution block too low or too high.

Work from the inside nozzle outward to attach hard lines to the distribution block, connecting hard lines to the bottom inside port of the distribution block first. Keep in mind that double-flare fittings have a thicker flange than single-flare fittings. This means you have to adjust the length of the hard line depending on which flare configuration each connection requires. You may have to make a "down length" longer or shorter.

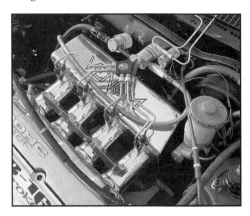

The trick to a great looking set of hard lines is to find the right place for the distribution block. You need to plan your design around the throttle linkage, TPS, and other devices that are physical obstacles. Be sure to position the distribution block where there is adequate clearance to allow you to mount the solenoid(s).

When bending a tube, remember that you have to allow some tube length to make the curve. For example, mark your reference point on the bender or tube about .050 - .075 inch further than your reference lines indicate. For professional-looking results, the following steps need to be performed with a quality tube-bending tool. One recommendation is the Imperial Eastman No.

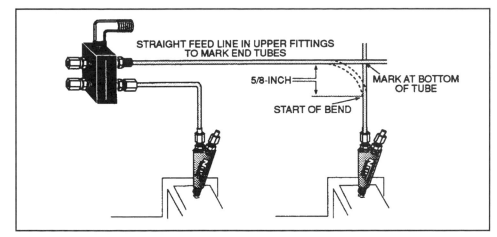

STRAIGHT FEED LINE IN UPPER FITTINGS
TO MARK END TUBES

5/8-INCH

MARK AT BOTTOM
OF TUBE

START OF BEND

Installing hard lines takes some practice. It take a few tries to get the right feel for the proper distance to begin bending the tube to have it arrive at the desired position with the desired shape. (NOS)

364FH tube-bending tool, which retails for about $40. You need a good tube bender, one with reference marks to do this job right.

When you have to make a bend near the connection hardware, install the blue sleeves and B-nuts over the flared ends. Mark the tubes at the desired height above the nozzle for the first bend. The mark should be a minimum of 1 inch from the end of the tube. The bend should start at the mark and proceed away from the flared end of tube.

Install two bent solenoid extension tubes, blue B-nuts, and sleeves on the Fogger nozzles closest to the distribution block with the two long legs of tubes crossing. Make sure the tubes are attached to the nitrous ports of Fogger nozzles. Measure between the insides of the tubes and place a center mark across the tubes. Position the distribution block centered between the two nozzles using the center mark you just made as a reference. Mark the tubes as shown using the block as a guide. See illustration below.

Put the top of the B-nut right on the first scribe mark. The top of the B-nut goes there and then you just bend it 90 degrees. Repeat, making two inside 90-degree tubes. These will be your standard.

Align the tubes side-by-side, then mark the spot in the middle of the scribe marks you just made referencing the distribution block. This gives you the length of the tube necessary to touch the

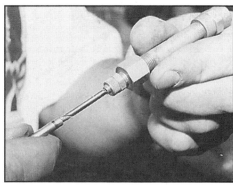

Be sure to deburr the cut ends of all tubes. Chamfering the inside edge with a drill bit tip removes burrs and loose metal from the saw cut. Such loose material can easily become dislodged and clog a jet.

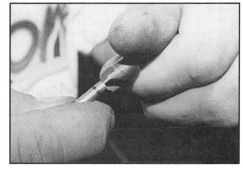

face of the compression fitting. Then you want to put it next to the compression fitting and mark it at the end of the threads on the inside, because that's where the end of the tube should butt against. Now make your cut in the tubes using a band saw or a hack saw.

With two tubes completed "dry-install" them on the nozzles and distribution block. At this point you may need to bend the tube out to allow room for linkage or other components. Doing so requires a "feel" for the metal you're bending. The best means to accomplish this is by fitting your tube bender to the tubes, adjusting the tool to place the bend

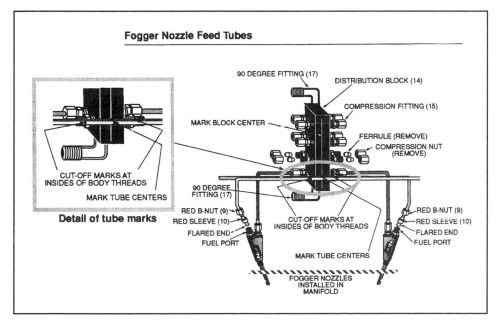

Fogger Nozzle Feed Tubes

90 DEGREE FITTING (17)
DISTRIBUTION BLOCK (14)
COMPRESSION FITTING (15)
MARK BLOCK CENTER
FERRULE (REMOVE)
COMPRESSION NUT (REMOVE)
90 DEGREE FITTING (17)
RED B-NUT (9)
RED SLEEVE (10)
FLARED END
FUEL PORT
CUT-OFF MARKS AT INSIDES OF BODY THREADS
RED B-NUT (9)
RED SLEEVE (10)
FLARED END
FUEL PORT
MARK TUBE CENTERS
FOGGER NOZZLES INSTALLED IN MANIFOLD

CUT-OFF MARKS AT INSIDES OF BODY THREADS
MARK TUBE CENTERS
Detail of tube marks

When sizing lines that terminate at the distribution block, be sure to make the cut mark at the seat of the port. That is past the threads. Doing so will hold the shape and position of your line while providing proper sealing when fastened.

Other Threads

National Pipe Threads (N.P.T.) are the next most popular thread size used in Competition Plumbing. We can actually find a resemblance between the size call outs and the I.D. (inside diameter) of the fitting as shown in the chart. Some of the most popular adapter fittings shown in Earl's catalog are AN to NPT adapters. While many variations are offered, column three in the AN Spec Chart shows which AN size corresponds to each NPT size when inside diameters (flow dimensions) are considered.

All Earl's Swivel-Seal™ hose ends are designed to provide little or no restriction when used with the corresponding AN fitting size. They also offer a number of Metric and British Standard Pipe threads to AN fitting adapters.

exactly where you want it, then smoothly applying force to bend the tube.

Now that you have your base line bends, your next task is to finish the tubes for the remaining ports. A quick-

AN Spec Chart

AN Size	Metal Tube O.D.	Thread Size
-2	1/8	5/16 - 24 SAE
-3	3/16	3/8 - 24 SAE
-4	1/4	7/16 - 20 SAE
-5	5/16	1/2 - 20 SAE
-6	3/8	9/16 - 18 SAE
-8	1/2	3/4 - 16 SAE
-10	5/8	7/8 - 14 SAE
-12	3/4	1 1/16 - 12 SAE
-24	1 1/2	1 7/8 - 12 SAE
-28	1 3/4	2 1/4 - 12 SAE
-32	2"	2 1/2 - 12 SAE

and-easy tip is to use a modified distribution block to help set the plumbing. Such a block is drilled allowing uncut tubes to run through. This makes marking the correct cut lines easy since the block serves as a guide.

How to Run Lines & Install Fittings

Running nitrous lines and fuel lines is simple in concept. There is not a lot that can go wrong. Still, there is a right way and a wrong way to install and lay out your fluid transport system, be it nitrous or fuel or whatever. For a nitrous system, it's important to avoid running these lines near the exhaust system. Heating the nitrous line can boil it, reducing the amount of nitrous delivered to the engine. If you look at the drawing from Aeroquip, you can see the most common mistakes and how to correct them. To these we should add several more conditions to be aware of and avoid.

The most important of these is to be aware not to install a line so that it gets hit or gets tangled up in some dynamic situation. Remember the suspension is usually at full droop on the jacks, and what looks like a handy avenue for the nitrous lines, may not be so free flowing once the suspension begins working in its normal space. This is just one of many scenarios you need to anticipate when you route your nitrous and fuel hoses.

Carroll Smith in *Nuts, Bolts, Fasteners and Plumbing Handbook* lists several situations to avoid. First, leave sufficient clearance between each hose end and any other fixed objects. You don't want the hose ends to contact anything or vibrate against anything. While the hose is flexible, the hose ends are not.

Second, don't allow a hose to come in contact with a sharp corner, a nut, a bolt, a rivet stem or anything else that might abrade the hose. You also need to install a grommet wherever a hose passes through a panel.

Third, do not allow a hose to rub against anything — even flat, smooth surfaces. The stainless braid makes a very efficient file and will abrade through anything that it moves against.

AN Basics

AN (Army-Navy) Sizes were established by the Aerospace industry years ago and were designated as the outside diameter (O.D.) of the rigid metal tube with which each size fitting is used. The sizes are designated by a dash followed by a number : -6, -8, and so on.

The numbers assigned equate to the O.D. of the tubing in 1/16-inch increments that is considered equal in flow to the hard line it replaces. Since tubing and hoses are available with assorted wall thicknesses, we can now understand that the designated size number does not necessarily tell you how large the inside diameter will be. (For example, the inside diameter of an Earl's size -6 hose end is nearly as large as the inside diameter of some other manufacturers' -8 hose ends.)

Each AN size number has its own standard thread size which can be seen in column three of the AN Spec Chart located nearby. Again, these are the same thread sizes that have been used in aircraft and industrial applications for many years.

AN and MS (Military Spec) specify a 37-degree cone angle. Industrial hose ends and adaptors are designed to JIC (Joint Industrial council) specs with a 45-degree cone angle. The two do not mix, so be careful.

This is particularly true in where brake and clutch lines pass through the fuel cell compartment. In this instance, encase the hoses in a thin-walled aluminum tube. Spiral wrap is a neat and convenient way to prevent chafe damage under normal conditions.

Fourth, do not kink the hose — either by bending it too tightly (both Earl's and Aeroquip include minimum bend radii tables in their catalog) or by placing the hose in a torsional bind.

Fifth, avoid over tightening the hose ends onto their adapter fittings or into their ports. Both the seal and the self-locking feature are provided by the design, not by force. It helps a lot to use the wrenches made for the job. Their handles are short enough to make over tightening difficult.

Sixth, do not stretch the hose, and allow enough room for flex. There is a right way and a wrong way to run hoses. The right way mainly calls for common sense.

Finally, flex hose and hard lines are not designed to carry weight, they are designed to transport fluids. As such they need to be supported. Current design practices suggest a clamp or tie wrap at 18-inch intervals.

Keep in mind the above are general rules. You'll find out more as you get into your own installation.

ZEX NITROUS SYSTEM ACTIVATION/CONTROL

What makes the Zex dry-manifold nitrous system once of the smoothest, easiest to use systems on the market is how the firm designed the activation and enrichment fuel circuits. Most current nitrous systems use a throttle-arm-actuated micro switch. That means you have to fabricate a mounting bracket for the switch, and adjust the placement of the switch to make it work right. The Zex nitrous kit uses a wire that you simply clip on the throttle position sensor (TPS) output voltage wire. The TPS

The interior of this nitrous-enhanced turbo Supra is state-of-the-art, high-tech race car. The nitrous system controls blend seamlessly. Once armed, it all happens automatically.

The big hanging turbos need nitrous to help them spool up quickly for drag racing. Turbos are great, but big turbos that flow lots of air and make killer top-end horsepower need some help to get spinning in order to create boost and power down low. A shot of nitrous is the tactic of choice for most tuners and racers.

voltage signal is sent to an electronic switch that engages and disengages the system at a predetermined voltage threshold. Above the threshold determined for wide-open throttle the system activates, below it, it remains dormant.

The Zex system automatically tunes the amount of enrichment fuel to the amount of nitrous the system is delivering. It does so by a feedback loop between the pressure of the nitrous circuit and the fuel-pressure regulator.

The nitrous oxide that is delivered to the engine's air inlet is conveyed via a delivery hose to an injection nozzle. The amount of nitrous oxide is adjustable by means of a metering jet installed in the injection nozzle itself. The nitrous oxide circuit communicates to the fuel-control circuit through a small bleed orifice. This bleed orifice provides a reference source of bottle pressure and a controllable source of pressure to perform the needed function of fuel enrichment. Fuel enrichment occurs by conveying this source of pressure through a delivery hose to a vacuum-ported, fuel-pressure regulator. This source of pressure on the rubber diaphragm of the fuel pressure regulator causes an increase in inlet pressure. This increase in inlet pressure performs the function of adding fuel volume through the engine's own fuel injectors. The amount of addi-

tional fuel that is added can be changed by an adjustable metering jet in the fuel-control circuit. This jet accomplishes the task by controlling the amount of pressure allowed to build in the delivery hose to the fuel-pressure regulator. The jet bleeds off excess pressure in the fuel-control circuit and vents it through a delivery tube, back to the intake manifold plenum.

Installing a Zex Nitrous System

Before you drill a hole in your car, make sure you know where you're going to install the various components of this kit. You'll have to discover the best positions for each component by trial and error, there's just no other way. We can give you a few tips that should help.

First, the nitrous line that attaches within the engine air intake is about 2-feet long. That means where you choose to install the nitrous nozzle decides, within a 2-feet radius, where you have to mount the head unit. Also, you need to connect the vacuum circuit for the fuel regulator to the control head, so be aware of the distance between these components.

Keeping in mind the length restrictions of the nitrous nozzle feed line, mount the head unit in a suitable location. Use the four screw holes provided for this purpose. The head unit is a rugged piece of equipment built to withstand underhood temperatures as well as exposure to weather. It is not

Installing and using the Zex nitrous systems is easy. The kit comes with everything you need. It's about as close to plug and play as a nitrous system gets.

The Zex system comes with brackets, fasteners, and nitrous line. Mount the nitrous supply bottle so that it is separated from the passenger cabin. If you have a trunk, the bottle should go there. Fastback-style cars that do not have separate trunk compartments have to be equipped with a vent tube. Route the vent tube from the safety pressure relief cap to the exterior of the car, preferably under the car. Doing so will prevent your car from filling with a cloud of nitrous oxide should the safety pressure relief cap rupture.

designed to support loads or withstand huge force shocks.

You'll also have to decide where to install the arming switch and nitrous bottle. The arming switch should be installed in a position convenient to the driver but not in an area that increases the chance of unintentionally arming the system. Then you'll have to run a wire

through the firewall to the head unit. Run this wire just like you would run a lead for your stereo system. In fact, if you have a stereo system installed, you can probably run the arming lead through the same grommet. If not, try to use a wire loom hole that is grommeted. If you have to drill a hole in the fire wall to run this lead to the head unit, drill a 3/8-inch (.375-inch) hole in the fire wall and use the grommets provided in the kit to protect against shorting the lead.

Adjusting Power Levels

The Zex Nitrous Kit is designed for two power stages: 55 hp and 65 hp. These stages are controlled by a meter jet installed in the nitrous nozzle. To change the power output, all you need to do is install the appropriate jet. You do this by first unscrewing the nitrous feed line. Then remove the metering jet as shown, and replace it with the jet of the power level you desire.

Since a crucial part of the system is its active-fuel adjustment, you need to trim fuel adjustment with meter jets as well. Remove and install the jets as you did when first installing your system. For a 55-horse power stage, use a #32 Nitrous jet and a #36 fuel jet. For a 65-horse power stage, use a #35 nitrous jet and a #34 fuel jet.

When routing the nitrous line under the car, try to use the subframe as a conduit, if possible. This protects the line as well as eliminates the need to use clamps. The supplied cable ties work if you can run the line higher in the under-body so that it's safe from road-level obstacles such as speed bumps. For the pro-race look you can use steel loom clamps with rubber sheathing to fasten the line to the body.

After you determine where you'll mount the nitrous nozzle in the intake, make sure this location won't interfere with other components. If your engine uses a mass airflow sensor, mount the nozzle after the sensor but before the throttle body. After you've found the spot, mark it and remove the rubber air inlet duct from your engine. Drill a 7/16-inch (.4375) mounting hole and install the bulkhead fitting. Be sure to remove any drill shavings since they can severely damage your engine.

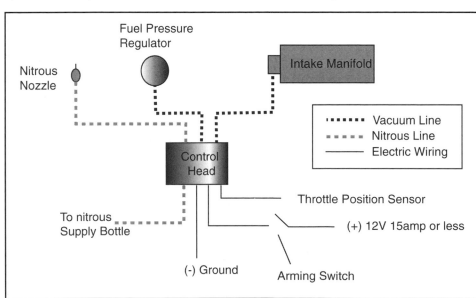

Once you've mounted all the components, you're ready to wire it up. This is very simple. All the hardware and connectors are provided in the kit.

Plumbing the Zex system is a no-brainer. Connect the circuits as shown.

NITROUS ENGINE BUILDING TECH

Building a good nitrous combination is not that much different from building any other high-performance engine. There are tuning considerations, and that's where the combination of components comes into play. Do you want a high-revving, high-horsepower combo, or one that makes good low- to mid-range torque? Depending on which is more important to you, you will choose different components, right down to the size and style of engine.

Small four-cylinder engines are good at making high-end horsepower, but no so good at producing low-end torque. Larger six- and eight-cylinder engines are good at both and can be designed and tuned to deliver what is required. This stems from one of the major factors of performance of an engine called Mean Effective Pressure (MEP). MEP is a theoretical constant pressure exerted on the piston top during the power stroke. MEP is equal to torque divided by the cubic capacity of your engine, multiplied by a factor of 150.8. In short, the more piston top area (bore size and number of pistons), the more torque your engine makes and, therefore, more horsepower.

Nitrous oxide is a good choice for high-revving, multi-valved, four-cylinder engines. Since you're limited by the piston area to increase torque and horsepower, simply increase the MEP per cylinder to achieve those goals. This is particularly true since nitrous is a very good system to build low-end torque. You can build a naturally-aspirated combo that makes great top-end power, or feed it with a turbo, and use nitrous to inflate low-end power. The important thing to remember is that a powerful engine combination, one that makes good power naturally aspirated no matter how large, will make better power with properly administered nitrous oxide and enrichment fuel.

Of course you can't neglect the reliability of your engine because it has to contain the additional MEP. That's why you have to begin your build from the bottom end. The bottom end of your engine consists of the block, crankshaft, connecting rods, pistons, and lubricating

Automotive Racing Products (ARP®) has a catalog filled with top-quality fasteners — like these head studs — for racers, engine builders, and street-performance enthusiasts (domestic and import). You can depend upon each of these fasteners to be the absolute best product possible for its application. (ARP)

system. In general terms, the function of the bottom end is to turn the heat energy released in the combustion chambers into the mechanical energy that drives your wheels. Ideally, you want it to do this as efficiently as possible while being as reliable and long-lived as possible. How you prepare these assemblies has a great impact in these areas. Keep in mind, our discussion here is intentionally brief. Whole books have been written on this subject alone, so we can't address all the pertinent issues here. We'll touch the highlights and encourage you to talk to industry experts to fine tune your requirements.

CRANKSHAFTS

Let's start at the bottom end and work our way up. Aftermarket crankshafts such as those offered by Crower and others, are very expensive and are required equipment once you pass a certain power output. They are always good insurance, and a custom crankshaft lets you choose your rod ratios. They are stronger and more efficient as they move through the oil bath and air in the crankcase. Ideally, you want a longer rod because it gives you more piston dwell at the top, keeping compression high while the crank rotates to get the rod at a good angle, and slows peak piston speed, reducing friction.

CONNECTING RODS

Let's talk about the rods. A lot of historic work has been done by hot rodders, but the fact of the matter is, today's metallurgy is much better and the factories now make excellent parts. Factory rods and crankshafts of current manufacturing methods are reliable products.

In hard-core racing, if the rod shows any weakness, pro teams replace it with a good rod and you should too. Install a good stock rod making sure to use new bolts and nuts, as they are the weakest link. If you assemble it correctly, if the engine's at a power and RPM level that the rod can hold, and if the engine's tuned properly, then the stock rod should be okay without the traditional massages. By the time you get into grinding the beams and removing stress risers, you're spending a lot of money, and you might as well buy an aftermarket rod. You'll spend $75 per rod anyway on shot peening, grinding, heat treating, etc. Just put that money toward a good set of rods.

Some drivers believe in heat treating stock rods, in order to get rid of the flex in the top of the connecting rods. Ron Hasse, one of Jackson Racing's sponsored racers, and others in ITC and ITA who dominate their road racing classes are allowed to run aftermarket or massaged stock rods, but they don't. Some tuners, such as Oscar Jackson, don't find it necessary to mess with the stock rods. Jackson's opinion is that when you heat treat a rod, you make it hard and brittle, so it can snap. When you get to the point where you need to massage the stock rods, you should just toss them and get a good set of aftermarket rods.

"I've been involved in extreme applications," says Jackson, "such as the 4AG motors Jackson Racing built for Class 10 desert racing, which have totally different requirements. We never did race in the desert, but we were hired by an off-road team. I looked at the situation and found we were going to build a 13:1 compression engine running in 100 degrees at 8,000 to 9,000 rpm. In these conditions you can't even think about using the stock rods; we had to use Carrillo rods. We started with a 4AGZ motor with bigger journals, got Carrillo rods for it and ran it 12.5 13:1. We won the Mint, the Baja 1,000, and the Championship and never had a failure. The outfit we had built this engine for went on to another engine builder who thought you didn't need to change parts as often. They broke five motors in a row and never finished a race. There's a point where you have to be realistic about what you're asking the engine to do.

"For example, Jackson Racing had been approached to build a Mazda Miata engine. The owner wanted to run a lot of compression, and the first thing I told him is he that needs to use Carrillo rods. He didn't want to put that kind of money in it, so I had to tell him he didn't want us to build it. I told him, from an educated point of view, the stock rods won't last in this application — high RPM, high compression.

"Now, let's look at the Honda blocks. The metallurgy of these blocks is pretty good. Even though the siamesed cylinders float in the water jacket, it's been my observation that they don't start moving around until you reach 15 pounds of boost. The Honda block is really sound for its light weight.

"As for bearing tolerances, I'll give you an example. Dan Paramore Racing is doing the cylinder head for Ron Hasse's motor, so it should be very powerful. Still, on the bottom end we stay pretty close to the factory bearing tolerances. I've heard all the stories about running loose tolerances, but the fact of the matter is, the factory isn't stupid. We try to stick with exactly what the factory does and make it just absolutely right. If you go too loose on any of the bearing tolerances, you trade improved oil flow for a loss in pressure. I'm not saying pressure's better than flow, you have to have both in the proper proportions. If I had a motor with a dry sump system that could run more volume and more pressure, yeah, I'd go a little looser on the clearances. In a stock class application, though, you're not going to go real loose on the motor."

When choosing an aftermarket rod, choose on the gives a rod ratio to make power at some efficient point; somewhere between 6000 and 7000 rpm for engines with two valves per cylinder; and up to 8000 or so for engines with four valves per cylinder. Most engines breathe well at these engine speeds and with nitrous there is no reason to twist it real tight and tear it up. When using nitrous, you don't have to rely on high rpm to do more work in less time. Instead, add more nitrous and fuel into the engine and it will make as much power as your bottom end and the seal between the block and head will take. Even the Pro Mod creatures don't spend much time past 7000 rpm. They've found they don't have to. Just put more nitrous and fuel into the engine, choose the right gear, and put as many gears in the transmission as you can, then go racing. Keep the engine in a very narrow power band and you can go very, very fast.

PROPERLY TORQUE ROD BOLTS

Rod bolts break from the inertial loading at overlap, the highest loading the rod bolts ever see. On the compression stroke they see pressure, helping to slow the rod down. On the power stroke the rod sees compression, but the rod bolts aren't stressed since the load on the big end is on the rod side of the bearing. The rod bolt could fall out here and it wouldn't make a difference.

When the piston comes up on the exhaust stroke, there's still a little pressure as it pushes the exhaust gas out until it gets to top dead center. Then the intake valves open as the exhaust valves are closing, releasing cylinder pressure that was cushioning the piston by absorbing some of the inertial energy. Now the only thing holding the rod and piston to the crank is, you guessed it, the rod bolts.

When you snap off the power at the end of a long straight or the quarter mile, the butterfly is closed. That means there is no pressure coming through the intake. In fact, on a naturally-aspirated car, there's a slight vacuum. So in addition to the piston and rod wanting to continue in a straight line through the head, as the crankshaft starts pulling the rod and piston back down the bore, the inertia of the rod and piston combine with the opposing force of the crank rotation. The rod bolt gets stretched. A few cycles of this and crunch — there goes your motor. If you're going to stretch a rod bolt, you can only stretch it at overlap.

This problem is accentuated by a motor with a short rod ratio. The shorter the rod, the faster the piston has to slow down and the faster the crank throw will re-accelerate it. On a real long rod ratio motor, the piston seems to hang around top dead center forever. So the inertial energy of the piston and rod can dissipate before changing directions.

If a rod breaks in the middle of the beam just under the pin, it is called a compression break and is indicative of too much power for that rod. Severe detonation can also bend the rod.

Russ Collins of RC Engineering, says he's seen broken rods and rod bolts from an army of race engines. With the new Preludes, or the new B-series VTEC, they are torquing the rod bolts at 30-32 ft-lbs. The only failure I've seen is where the rod bolt was missing or bent. It was bent because the other bolt went away. It didn't break; instead it stripped the last four threads off the rod bolt and the nut came loose. The rod was either over torqued and lost its tensile, or the nut wasn't tightened and it just backed off before the failure. What is the moral? Properly torque your engine's rod bolts.

PISTONS & RINGS

The engine component most impacted by nitrous is the piston/ring assembly. The piston and rings, among other functions, have to contain cylinder pressure and keep oil out. If you get oil in the combustion chamber, it lowers the octane of the fuel mixture leading to detonation. Even though this is a concern, you don't need to order special oil rings as long as you use quality components. Regarding the viability of rings and pistons in a nitrous-enhanced engine, we have a few tips from the engineers at Federal-Mogul and JE Pistons, maker of the SRP piston line.

With high-horsepower engines, whether nitrous enhanced, turbocharged or both, you need to be concerned with sinking the heat out of the crown of the piston. If you're using a high flow of nitrous to make power in the normal RPM power band, then you shouldn't use a thin ring. If you do, you are asking for trouble because a thin ring holds the heat in the crown.

The heat in the piston crown has to go somewhere, and much of it will travel through the side of the piston and through the rings into the cylinder case. Most people think the piston is cooled by oil splashing on the bottom of it. It is true this provides some cooling, but not nearly as much as is commonly supposed. In fact, most cooling of the piston top comes from the heat path through the rings into the cylinder case. This explains the fact that when you start losing ring seal, you start losing pistons.

Unfortunately losing ring seal tends to be a common problem for nitrous users. When you get into detonation with nitrous, the piston is really hot and the pressure in the combustion chamber will bend the ring land down, pinching the ring.

One of the more common solutions to this problem is to move the top ring down away from the crown of the piston. However, a better solution can be found in putting more space between the rings. Moving the second ring down puts more land material between the top and second ring, providing more support for the top ring. This is important because the top ring is under tremendous pressure to bend down over the land. In severe cases, you'll be able to see a shiny ring on the bottom of the top ring that develops from the distortion, a tell-tale sign that the ring has been bent over from the pressure and has ridden on the sharp edge of the ring land.

If that happens, the ring loses its seal because the ring face is at an angle to the cylinder wall instead of sitting flush. The ring is still sealing, but it is not transferring the heat from the piston crown to the cylinder case as effectively as before. The reason is less surface area is now available to transfer heat. This causes the piston to heat to a point that it softens, and the pressure forces the ring land to collapse on the second ring. The second ring is usually the one that binds; the top ring remains free with apparently no problem.

So, if you are not spinning your motor past 7000 to 8000 rpm, use a wide ring. Even a ring as wide as 5\64 inch (1.9 mm) would not be detrimental to performance. With nitrous you don't have to run thin rings in an effort to get that last few horsepower. Go wide and build reliability, and avoid wasting pistons and rings.

A nitrous motor and a pro stock engine are two very different animals. In a nitrous motor you don't have the cooling cycle like that of a naturally-aspirated, pro-stock engine. Nitrous Motors have a longer burn time and more thermal loading of the pistons. The technique of moving the whole ring pack down is a tactic to control the long burn/high thermal load of nitrous and turbo/supercharged combinations. Here's the theory: The cylinder pressure acts hydrostatically. In other words, the pressure will still be as great no matter how far down the piston you put the ring pack. It isn't necessarily a pressure problem — it is a heat problem.

If you were to design a stronger piston, one of the things you'd want is more material behind the rings. With most current designs, as you move the ring package down you get into an area where the piston is thinner than it is at the top. In such an area, the heat flows through the small cross section of piston skirt and through the rings. These thin areas of the piston really take a high-thermal load, which tends to soften these areas allowing them to bend. It's like a bottle neck and pretty soon, as these areas soften, the whole top of the

piston wants to come off. Placing more material between the ring land helps the piston structure manage high-thermal loads in order to remain stable.

You should also have a little larger ring gap on the second ring than on the top ring. This results in a better seal under high-thermal loads. How hot is too hot? You know the engine is too hot when the rings butt together. Should that occur, the top ring closes more than the second ring. So even if you set the end gaps of both rings at .025-inch, the top ring gap will be smaller than the second ring gap.

It is important that the ring gaps retain these dimensions. You want the pressure between the top ring and the second ring to go out the gap of the sec-

ond ring faster and easier than it gets past the top ring gap. You do not want the pressure to equalize before and after the top ring. If that happens, there is no pressure to force the top ring against the cylinder wall and seal the bore. If the pressure is equal here, then all that's sealing the cylinder is the ring tension, which isn't nearly enough. You have to have a pressure difference above and below the top ring for it to work properly.

This type of problem happens often to drivers running zero-gap rings on nitrous engines. Zero-gap tactics don't make sense because the pressure is taken off the top ring, which causes the cylinder to lose pressure. What's really happening when you observe horsepower gains with zero-gap rings is the friction of the top ring is eliminated, which shows up on the dyno as more power at the flywheel. However, the top ring is no longer sealing. Now the second ring has to do all the sealing and heat transfer work.

Should you use Hypereutectic Pistons?

Hypereutectic pistons will take a lot of pressure. You can stand a mountain on them and they won't break under the weight. However, the minute you ring them with the frequency that nitrous causes when it detonates, they shatter like glass. They don't melt; they break. Don't use them in a nitrous engine.

IMPROVING AIR FLOW

Anything you do to increase the air flow through the engine will help you make horsepower. That's true with or without the nitrous system. So installing a good free flowing intake, head work and headers are always recommended. Just be sure you tune the fuel curve to match the increased flow.

There are some tuning choices with manifold selection. You choose the manifold design to make power in the rpm range that matches the rest of your combination. For street engines you want a manifold that produces power over a wide rpm range. These will typically have longer and narrower runners than full race intakes. The longer narrower

Venom Intake Manifolds have a CNC-machined, billet-aluminum head flange, and an intake runner surface with CNC-machined runners to reduce turbulence, thus increasing the speed and volumetric efficiency of the intake manifold. The manifold accepts up to 66 mm throttle body and can be used on naturally aspirated or forced induction engines. Increased volumetric efficiency by 70% over stock intake. Ideal for forced-induction applications or heavily modified, naturally aspirated motors.

This is an example of Coast Performance's competition valve job. The valve seats get the treat to help low-lift flow and improved seal.

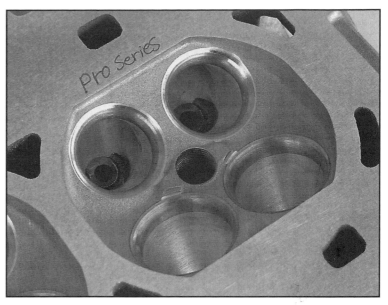

The Coast Performance Pro Race setup features more port work to allow increased flow volume and high-RPM power. The increased volume comes at a loss of charge velocity and low-end power.

runners help the engine's volumetric efficiency at low to mid rpm but restrict the efficiency at higher rpm. The racing intake is tuned to enhance volumetric efficiency at higher rpm at the expense of low end power and torque.

There are a few considerations on placement of the nitrous injection nozzles. For example, dry systems work better if you install the nozzle farther away from the throttle body. In addition on wet systems, aiming and positioning port injection nozzles will influence air flow through the manifold. You want to point the nozzle so the nitrous

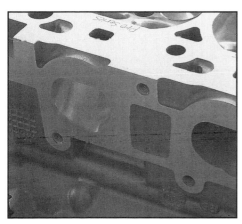

This detailed view of the intake shows the larger diameter of the Pro Race treatment and the stock intake port.

and fuel are aimed at the port, but don't worry about the precision in doing this as it is not going to help or hinder power all that much. Whether the nozzle is angled 45 degrees off the flow path or shooting straight down the port, it won't make much difference in a direct-port system. If you look at the air flow through the runner at any particular time it is starting and stopping, you will see it pulsing as the valve opens and closes. So there is always going to be a period of time in which the nozzle is flowing with the valve closed and no air going down the runner.

Since the intake and exhaust ports in the head are part of the air flow path, again improving this area is beneficial to over all power output with and without nitrous. The key is always matching the components properly to your combination. For street cars, the biggest polished ports possible, will hurt overall performance. You want the ports sized and flowed correctly to match the intake manifold that is designed to produce power in the rpm range for the street. If your building a track only combo that's burning alcohol and spinning at 10,000 rpm then you need huge ports that flow lots of air.

And of course the exhaust system is important to any engine combina-

tion. Exhaust tuning is very sensitive to small changes in tube length, diameter, distance from the port where the tubes merge, etc. Though it's true that exhaust tuning finds horsepower, once you've reached a certain efficiency, you have to work very hard to find power and then it is in very specific and narrow rpm ranges. Still it is power so it's worth going after it'll give you an advantage. For most performance enthusiasts a good set of aftermarket headers will suffice. Just plan the engine combination with the headers, intake, head work and cam.

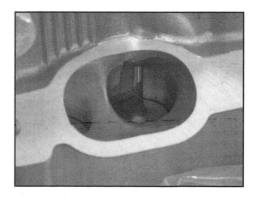

Looking into a race-prepped intake port of a full race Toyota V-8, you can see the large cross section of the exposed back of the valve. This combo should flow mega CFM and generate awesome horsepower.

Nitrous Engine Component Buyer's Guide

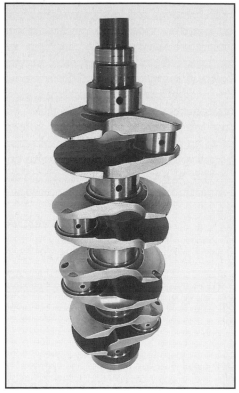

This pair of JE Pistons show the differences between a naturally aspirated combination and a boosted one. The 12:1 CR piston on the right has additional material and large valve reliefs to bump the compression. The turbo piston is dished to give it a static 8:1 CR. However, once boosted, the dynamic CR will be much higher and more fuel and oxygen will be forced into the chamber. It's difficult to tell from the photo, but the ring pack of the turbo piston is positioned further down with more material between the ring lands and a larger oil control ring land.

Crower billet stroker crank or reworked factory crank 95mm for B18 or 89mm for B16. Custom billet crankshafts are available for any make (Nissan, Toyota, Mitsubishi, Porsche, etc.), however lead times are 2-3 months for delivery. Prices start at $2000. (Crower)

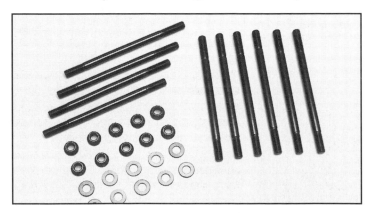

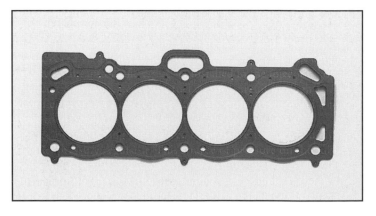

With nitrous you don't have to rely on high RPM to do more work in less time. Just add more nitrous and fuel into the engine and it will make as much power as your bottom end and the seal between the block and head will take. Stud Kits and metal gaskets, such as the AEM kit and Greddy Honda piece shown, are examples of products that will help contain the pressure of nitrous-boosted combustion. (AEM) (Greddy)

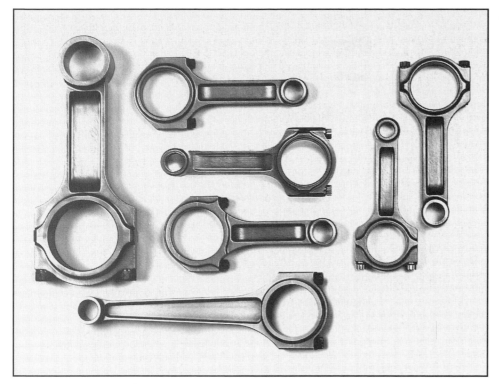

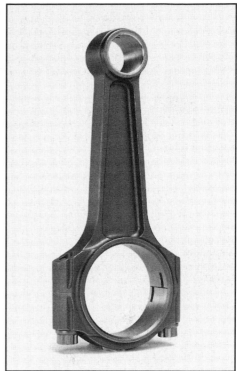

When your engine combination makes substantially more power than stock, you have to step up to aftermarket rods, such as these from Crower. (Crower)

Crower offers rods in custom lengths to help you get the rod ratio you're looking for. (Crower)

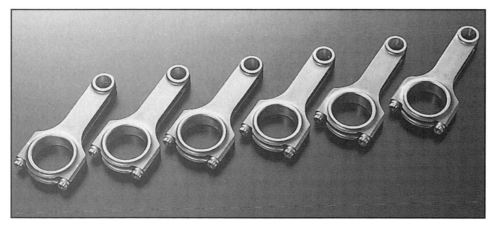

Greddy forged connecting rods are available for Toyota Supras and for Nissan 300 ZX motors. (Greddy)

Crower is the industry leader in high-performance connecting rods. Choose from the largest selection of import makes available including Honda/Acura, Mitsubishi, Toyota, Porsche, Nissan, Saturn, Neon, and Volkswagen. CNC machined from premium-quality 4340 chrome-moly steel, Crower billet rods are the only choice when running nitrous oxide, high boost or high RPM in your "all motor" application. They're insurance for your block. (Crower)

These AEM high-performance pulley kits are made from 6061 T-6 billet aluminum, each is CNC machined for perfect balance, lightweight, and precise function. Tru-Power Pulley Kits come complete and ready to install with correctly engineered performance belts. AEM Tru-Power pulleys increase horsepower and engine response without the need to remove the torsional vibration damper or emission-control devices. The larger diameter pulleys slow down the power steering pump and alternator, reducing the amount of energy needed to drive them. (AEM)

Buyer's Guide
Crower Cams

Part #	Description	Duration	Gross Lift w/1.55	HP/RPM Range @ 1mm (at valve)
#63400	Stock replacement, similar to ITR spec	Int-257 mid Exh-245 mid	Int-10.82 mid Exh-09.72 mid	5-7 hp/9200 rpm
#63401	Street/Strip, similar to CTR (JDM) spec	Int-259 mid Exh-251 mid	Int-11.37 mid Exh-10.69 mid	8-10 hp/9500 rpm
#63402	Road/Rally race, mild drag race	Int-265 mid Exh-260 mid	Int-11.37 mid Exh-11.37 mid	10-15 hp/9700+ rpm
#63403	Top end drag profile, perf built heads	Int-274 mid Exh-268 mid	Int-11.98 mid Exh-11.40 mid	15-25 hp/9900+ rpm
#00063	Custom ground, contact factory for specs			

- Specs are as of press time. Check with manufacturer for latest info.

Crower is in the R&D stages of its new DOHC VTEC cam cores available for the Honda B16A and the Integra B18C. Crower, with over 50 years of camshaft experience, offers a wide variety of designs, from stock replacement to road race to fully prepared, all-out drag race. These are premium Crower cores, not regrinds. Custom, proprietary grinds also available. (Crower)

If you're really on the fringe, you may want to have a totally custom cam profile made up for your engine combination. You can have the factory cam welded and reground. With this process, if it is done absolutely right, it's nearly as good as using a billet.

Crower Camshaft Hard Facing and Regrinds

When you send your stock cam to Crower, it draws on 50 years of camshaft experience to grind the exact profile required for your application. Whether it's cruising (lope at idle) or full race with full NOS shot, Crower has the profile you need. Here are the options available:

1. Hard facing — Welding up stock lobes (if VTEC, mid only) to allow unlimited spec while maintaining stock base circle. Cost $20 per lobe plus $100 per cam for the grinding. VTEC weld is only on mid lobe (8 lobes + grinding = $360 total). You supply stock cores. VTEC specs listed above are available on hard-faced cores. Full drag race, road race, turbo, or nitrous. No wear or compatibility issues.

2. Straight regrind — Reduced base circle allows more lobe lift. Limited spec, emphasis on top end power. Typical specs are .005" to .010" more lift, 5 to 10 degrees more duration at .050" and an increase of 5-10 hp depending on other engine modifications. $100 per cam for the grinding. You supply stock cores.

Part #	Description
65000	SOHC, Custom ground, any make, contact factory for specs
65014	DOHC, Custom ground, any make, contact factory for specs
65020	VTEC (DOHC), Custom ground, contact factory for specs

Buyer's Guide
Crower Springs and Retainers

Part #	Description	O.D./I.D.	(Seat Pressure)	(Open Pressure)	Coil Bind Wire Dia.
68180	Single Spring	(B18A/B) 1.081/0.805	(1.320=77#; 1.425=65#)	(0.954=123#; 1.079=106#).810	.134
68181	Dual Spring	(B18A/B) 1.105/0.815/.630	(1.320=66#; 1.425=42#)	(0.908=153#; 1.010=136#).710	.141 / .086
68185	New VTEC Dual Spring	1.175/0.890/.628	(1.400=37#; 1.300=60#)	(1.000=138#; 0.900=170#).830	.146 / .097

Crower's spring and retainer kits are available for the VTEC (B16A/B18C) as well as the LS/RS (B18A/B). Premium Crower dual spring with Crower titanium retainers are intended for use up to 10,000+ rpm for VTEC engines. These kits are designed for high-lift, high-rpm camshafts, and work well with stock valves and keepers. Installation is basically drop-in, with no machine work required. (Crower)

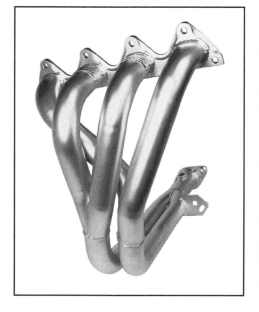

Buyer's Guide
New Crower Titanium Retainers

Part #	Description	Weight
87080	Aluminum Retainers for B18A/B18B fits #68180 spring	5.5 grams
87092	Titanium Retainers for B18A/B18B fits #68181 spring	6.0 grams
87091	Titanium Retainers for B18C/B16A fits Type R spring	6.0 grams
87093	Titanium Retainers for B18C/B16A fits #68185 spring	5.5 grams
87095	Titanium Retainers for Mits/DSM 2.0L fits stock spring	8.0 grams

Note: Stock Honda/Acura retainers weigh 11.5 grams.

This DC Sports header not only offers great looks, it also offers the durability of T-304 stainless steel. Mandrel bent tubing, CNC-machined flanges, and hand-welded construction ensure that you're getting the best header available. Some models will be changed to a new single-piece design, which offers a more powerful (1-2 hp over the two-piece model) and lighter header. (DC Sports)

DC Sports 4-1 Header is designed to optimize top-end performance. This 4-1 header features dyno-tested, equal-length header tubes to provide the most power of any 4-1 header. DC Sports uses a high-flow, merge-style collector to help evacuate exhaust gasses and increase horsepower. Designed for top-end performance with merge-style collector and lightweight flanges. (DC Sports)

Inside Craig Paisley's 1000-plus Horsepower

By now you've seen Craig Paisley's factory-backed Toyota Tundra drag truck in action. Paisley is taking import drag racing to the next level with a professional drag racing effort using nitrous and the latest electronic engine management systems, in NHRA competition no less.

We had the chance to get a behind-the-scenes look at the engine combination while it was in development at Toyota Racing Development's HQ in southern California. This was the perfect opportunity to pick the brains of TRD's engine guy, Larry Slutter, regarding his tactics, thinking and strategy for building and tuning a nitrous-enhanced, DOHC four-valve per cylinder iron block V8 for drag racing.

Q: What are some the technical challenges facing the modern performance enthusiast?

LS: "The first thing to recognize is that there is not a lot of easy horsepower left on the table with most modern engines. They're all very efficient and if you make changes without really thinking it out, you're more likely to lose than gain power. For most aluminum block engines, if you bore more than 2 mm, the cylinder walls get very thin so you're limited there. You can add stroke, though usually not a lot, before you get the wall of the block interfering with the rod. But when you add stroke the piston speed goes up, so you have to slow the engine down. So you have to be very thoughtful when making changes. "

Q: What was your thinking on the Tundra V8 combination? And why this engine?

LS: "The reason we used the Tundra block as opposed to the Lexus block is because it offered more room to play, even though it has the weight disadvantage of an iron block compared with an aluminum block. But with the Tundra block we can bore and stroke it out to almost 5.7 Liters. In drag racing, bigger is definitely better.

"We've had to build special parts such as cams, the crankshaft, titanium rods and a few other parts, but that's were we are in the R&D cycle. We added 6 mm to the bore to put it at 97 mm (3.8-in) ,with a 95 mm (3.7-in) stroke for 342 cid; round that to 5.7 liters.

"The heads are very good for a passenger car or truck motor. Unbelievably good. They have a straight intake port, nice small chamber, not very shrouded at all, and a very efficient exhaust port.

"The engine produces good torque on its own, and with the power adder we're hoping it'll be competitive and reliable — if there is such a thing in racing. Anyway we don't want to be replacing this after every run. The combination is very reliable now.

The Tundra V-8 heads are very good for a passenger car or truck motor. The intake port is straight, the combustion chamber is small and not very shrouded, and the exhaust port is efficient.

Toyota Racing Development Tundra V8

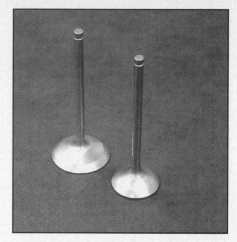

Titanium valves offer several performance advantages. For example, they reduce parasitic power loss by allowing lower valve spring seat pressures than a steel valve, while still giving a higher rev limit. The valves shown are blanks.

"The goal is to make 1000 hp for the beginning of the season. We're very close to that. You know with nitrous it's not a lot different than running a blower. If you want more power, just add boost and fuel. With nitrous you just flow more nitrous and fuel and watch the tuning for any signs of detonation. So we're very confident this motor will do the number."

Q: So you're going to make 1000 hp with a single stage of nitrous?

LS: "Yes."

Q: How did you tune the nitrous?

LS: "We ran the engine naturally aspirated first, without nitrous. We have a combustion analyzer that reads the cylinder pressure and where it happens (in crankshaft degrees). We follow those two metrics religiously. When we know where the best spark is for the naturally aspirated combination, we have a benchmark. When we add nitrous you generally have take some lead out and you have to add more fuel because you're going to make more power. We do that pretty conservatively [taking more timing out and adding more fuel than needed] so we're not rebuilding the engine after every test session. That was our approach on the hill car when we ran Pike's Peak. We ran a bit of nitrous in the hill car and that's how we approached that engine tune.

"The hill car took us quite a bit of running to figure out where we wanted to be with the nitrous and the turbo.

"The Tundra is only one stage at this point, though we're projecting to add a second stage mid year, probably have to have three stages by year's end. We'll just keep adding nitrous as our R&D and competitive environment indicates.

Notice that the ring pack is protected by a fairly thick lip of the dish-topped piston. Making this area strong keeps occasional and brief detonation from destroying the engine. The ports at the top of the compression ring direct cylinder pressure behind the ring to ensure a tight seal.

Paisley's engine is using titanium rods and special alloy pins and forged pistons. Though the rod ratio wasn't specified, most likely they're using a long rod, 152-mm (6.0-in) or so. That length is inferred from what is very successful with other race engine combinations of the same capacity. A long rod will keep the mean piston speed lower and tends to make more power on the top end.

"The engine management system is made by Pactel. It's pretty simple, hit the nitrous button it adds fuel and takes spark away. Getting it all mapped out will take some time. We added a lot of fuel and took a lot of spark out in the very beginning, but we found we didn't have to pull the spark back as much as we thought. We only take maybe 4-degrees lead out of it but we add a lot of fuel. A lot of fuel.

"We're planning on leaving at 6,500 rpm on the bottle and spin the engine up to 8,200 or 8,500 rpm.

"Bottle pressure is key to this combination. In testing if we didn't have the bottle temperature controlled with a heater and blanket, we'd lose bottle pressure and wonder where the power went. It's very critical. With the heater and blanket, the pressure drop during a seven second hit is only about 100 psi which isn't too bad.
(continued)

Inside Craig Paisley's 1000-plus Horsepower
Toyota Racing Development Tundra V8 *(continued)*

"The current ECU is only set up for two stages. The next ECU we build will have capability for more stages. But the motor has to be compatible with the truck. Maybe the truck doesn't like all the power. That is probably not the case since the truck has a good adjustable clutch, the chassis is well designed, so it'll probably take the hit of a single stage and maybe more. It all depends on how quick we have to go to stay competitive and win.

"It'll be interesting to see how it does against the 1400 hp turbo engines. We're the rookies this season, so if we're competitive out of the box that'll be great. This is new for us. We've done turbos, turbos and nitrous; this nitrous only effort should be very fun. And we won't have to deal with all the added heat of the turbo, since the energy of the nitrous is all inside."

Before we leave this subject we like to make a few comments on that last point. The TRD/Paisley effort stands a better chance than the reference to 1400 horsepower competition suggests. Here's why we think so.

The engine is very stout on it own. So it's putting out around 500 lb/ft at 6500 rpm off the launch. When the nitrous hits that will instantly jump up since nitrous is a flat flow system. So instead of waiting for the turbo to spool up the power is already there. While it's true the power falls off with a single stage of nitrous as the rpm climbs as opposed to the power rising as it does with a turbo, still the average power output in the rpm range could be higher with the nitrous engine than with a turbo, depending on the combo. In racing, especially drag racing, it is more important to have higher average output as opposed to higher peak output. Nitrous has the advantage of an instant on power adder.

TRD's piston choice is instructive because it demonstrates the "compression compromise" needed in building a strong nitrous combination. The piston is dished to lower compression and provide more "compressed volume" as is done on super/turbocharged engines. But the cylinder head chamber area is relatively small and the choice of a longer rod length allows the engine builder to raise the compression in order to increase mean effective cylinder pressure. In addition the dished piston top helps shape the charge which also increases efficiency and power.

The plan is to make 1000 horsepower from 5.7 liters. The TRD crew has elected to make this a dry system in that 1000hp worth of fuel is controlled and delivered by the injectors. The motor is good for around 650 horsepower worth of air flow, leaving the last 350 horsepower for the nitrous system to deliver. The two Cheater nitrous solenoids are each capable of delivering 250 horsepower of nitrous flow.

The intake velocity stack length can be adjusted to tune the power curve. Shorter stacks moved the power curve at higher engine speeds; longer stacks move it lower.

HOW TO WIRE IT

To operate a nitrous system, your vehicle has to have some sort of electrical system. It can be as simple as a dry-cell battery with no alternator or generator to recharge it, just as long as it has the appropriate voltage and amperage capacity. You need an electrical system to support the fuel pump, injectors/engine management system, and nitrous system. In addition, the electrical system has to be designed to reduce the potential for RF interference and minor failures leading to major system failures.

You should be aware that the electrical current draw, measured in amps, is a concern when wiring your nitrous system. Especially if it is dual stage (or more) with a heap of electronic controls. Remember that the nitrous solenoid must generate a magnetic field strong enough to open the plunger against 850 psi. As a result, the nitrous-solenoid coil windings require 4 to 6 amps in the smaller solenoids and upwards of 16 to 18 amps in the largest solenoids currently available. Therefore it is always good practice to use a power relay for the high-amperage circuit that feeds the voltage from the battery to the solenoids. The switches, the micro switches, the electronic boxes, and the connections could easily be damaged by the high-amperage draw of the solenoids. A power relay isolates the switch circuitry from the high-amperage circuits.

If you're connecting your high-capacity, high-pressure fuel pump to the accessory power supply, make sure that circuit will support the additional amperage draw required by your fuel pump. Fuel pumps are notorious guzzlers of amperage.

With automotive electrical systems, although a portion is lost in heat, what goes in has to be returned to the battery. So it is best to err on the high side and build in reserve current capacity on the return side by using a heavy-gauge ground strap. It's safer and your system will be more reliable and perform as designed.

DESIGNING A WIRING SYSTEM

Wiring is simply a fact of high-performance life. You have to have it, and there is no easy way to lace a car chassis with all the cables and wires necessary for a modern high-performance car. Of course, lacing and running the cable is only half of the work. You also have to properly connect several separate components not only so they will function, but so they will continue to function in the demanding automotive environment.

Fortunately, most systems come with all of the wiring components and accessories you need to let the juice flow. In addition, a host of companies from the auto sound industry cater to this aspect of electrical and electronic component installation. Firms such as Scosche, Esoteric Audio, Metra, and even manufacturers of high-end mobile audio equipment have designed and supply a full range of specialty cables, fasteners, and connections for the auto sound enthusiast.

The first rule of wiring your nitrous system is to use the best quality cables, wires, and connectors you can afford. If you have to make budget adjustments, use the wiring kit that came with your system, but upgrade as soon as you can afford to.

The second rule is to decide where you will mount each component before you lace a single strand of wire. This positions the component, which allows you to establish wiring routes and distances.

The third rule is to keep your wires and cables as short as possible. You need to have a cable that is slightly longer than the pure physical distance between components, but exercise judgment when deciding how much excess you have. Longer cables use more energy than shorter ones. If you want to get the same voltage and amperage at the end of a long cable that you have at the end of a short cable, then you need to start out with more power.

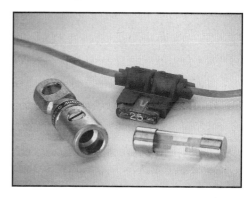

Solderless connections offer a wide variety of wiring solutions. From inline blade fuse holders and trick heavy-gauge power connections, to fuse solutions.

The fourth rule is to work with wiring in the following sequence: 1) Disconnect the negative terminal of the battery. 2) Route the main power cables and ready the fuses for each component. Be sure to leave excess at each end for adjustment and working slack. 3) Make the final connections as you work your way toward the control unit (if you're using electronic system controls) beginning at the component that is furthest away.

The last rule is to learn all the rules, including the ones that we left out, misplaced, or forgotten, so that you can break the rules when the situation calls for it. In other words, be prepared to change designs once you begin the wiring process.

Matching Power Cable Gauge To Power Demand

A direct-current electrical system, such as that in your car, behaves similar to a hydraulic system under pressure. In this metaphorical system, pounds per square inch (PSI) is to hydraulics what volts are to an electrical system — namely electrical pressure or force. The wires and cables are as tubes and pipes. A battery is a chemical reservoir of voltage just as a water tower is a reservoir of water pressure. In auto electrical systems, the pressure standard is 13.8 volts although everybody calls them "12 volt systems." The next concept is current flow.

Current flow in electrical systems and hydraulic systems are directly analogous. It is the amount of water or electricity that passes through a given point in a given amount of time. In electrical systems, the current flow is measured in amperes, or amps for short.

There are two ways to get more amperes (current) flowing through a circuit. You can increase voltage or you can reduce resistance. The limitation to current flow in a circuit is resistance. Resistance is friction within the circuit or wire that resists the flow of electricity. That is the source of the heat that sometimes melts your wires and blows your fuses. Resistance is measured in Ohms.

Ohm's law states that the ratio of the potential (voltage) difference between the ends of a metallic conductor and the electron current flowing through it is a constant. Expressed mathematically:

1 ohm = 1 volt/1 ampere

Ohm's law rules electronics and it's just as important to power delivery cabling. In a perfect world you'd have 0.00 Ohms — no resistance in all of your circuits. Unfortunately we can't reach that theoretical ideal, but we can get close.

The fundamental import of Ohm's law as it affects power cables is this: Given a constant gauge of cable, the longer a cable is, the more resistance it will generate. Hence, a longer cable will show lower voltage and amp values than a shorter one. The way around this resistance limitation is to use larger gauge cables because larger gauge cables have less resistance for a given length. So large gauge wires are in order for 12V systems. That's why it's important to choose and use the right gauge of power cable when you're designing your system.

Of course to do this you need to know the current demands that will be placed on the cables. The nitrous solenoids are the most current-hungry devices in a basic nitrous system. For example, the NOS Cheater and Pro Shot nitrous solenoids pull between 12 and 16 amps each; the Power Shot and Super Power Shot pull about 4 or 5 amps each. Other manufacturers' units should be near the same for equivalent power levels, but be sure to check or measure the amperage draw of each of your system's solenoids.

Fuel solenoids demand far less amperage, somewhere on the order of 1 to 1.5 amps each, because they don't have to overcome the high pressures of the nitrous line. That doesn't mean you can ignore their amperage draw. You have to design the system to provide power to all components. If you have a bottle warmer, remote valve controller, and/or other electronic components added to a staged nitrous system, the total current draw can be substantial. Determining the power draw for your nitrous system can be an

Cable Gauge Guide

This chart gives the minimum cable gauge required for a given length and amperage.

Current	0-4 ft.	4-7 ft.	7-10 ft.	10-13 ft.	13-16 ft.	16-19 ft.	19-22 ft.
0-20 amp	10-ga.	10-ga.	8 ga.	8 ga.	8 ga.	8 ga.	8 ga.
20-35 amp	8-ga.	8-ga.	8-ga.	8-ga.	8-ga.	4 ga.	4 ga.
35-50 amp	8-ga.	8-ga.	8-ga.	4-ga.	4-ga.	4-ga.	4-ga.
50-65 amp	8-ga.	8-ga.	4-ga.	4-ga.	4-ga.	4-ga.	4-ga.
65-85 amp	4-ga.	4-ga.	4-ga.	4-ga.	2-ga.	2-ga.	2-ga.
85-105 amp	4-ga.	4-ga.	4-ga.	2-ga.	2-ga.	2-ga.	2-ga.
105-125 amp	4-ga.	4-ga.	4-ga.	2-ga.	2-ga.	2-ga.	1/0-ga.
125-150 amp	2-ga.	2-ga.	2-ga.	2-ga.	1/0-ga.	1/0-ga.	1/0-ga.
150-225 amp	2-ga.	1/0-ga.	1/0-ga.	1/0-ga.	1/0-ga.	1/0-ga.	1/0-ga.
225-300 amp	1/0-ga.	1/0-ga.	1/0-ga.	1/0-ga.	1/0-ga.	1/0-ga.	1/0-ga.

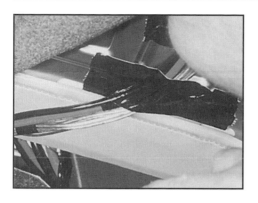

As you run cable along, around, and through the structures of the vehicle body, tape it into place to keep it from moving. By keeping it stationary, you reduce the chance of abrading the insulation and causing a short. Besides, it just plain looks cleaner.

There is one more thing to keep in mind. Always use the same gauge ground cable as for the positive power cable. With an automotive electrical system, although a portion is lost in heat, what goes in has to be returned to the battery. So it is best to err on the high side and build in reserve current capacity including a heavy-gauge ground strap. It's not only safer, your system will be more reliable and perform as designed.

Routing Power Cables

Routing power cable correctly is one of the secrets that keeps your system trouble free. Routing along the perimeter of the body or along the transmission tunnel is also acceptable. Occasionally, it is necessary to route the cable underneath the vehicle. Be sure to provide adequate protection for the cable. One method is to use split loom covering and route the cable above the frame or sub frame members. Another form of protection is to use a grommet whenever a cable is run through a wall or bulkhead to protect the cable from being cut and grounding out. In addition, be aware of potential snags or other obstacles in the path of the cable that could cut through the insulation forcing a short circuit.

Reliable Electrical System Connections

Good wiring habits keep your system performing better longer. Planning and designing your system before you install it is a good habit to get into. First, decide where you're going to mount all your new components. Then, make a sketch of the wiring system. This gives you a map to guide you and helps you determine cable gauge and lengths, as well as what types of connections you'll have to make.

The two primary methods of making connections are soldered and solderless. In addition, there are the mechanical means manufactures use for power, input, and output connections to their components. There are many opinions about whether it is better to solder a connection or to use solderless connec-

Good installers use grommets whenever they have to drill a hole to run cable through a panel to protect the cable from the sharp metal edges of the car body.

tors. The consensus seems to be that it depends on the connection. Both methods are used and each has benefits.

There are a couple of common soldering techniques that are easy to learn and use. The first one is standard soldering. You heat the ends of the wires you wish to join until they are hot enough to melt the solder. When the joint wires reach the right temperature, the solder melds them together. Remove the solder

The most misunderstood connection is the ground connection. Improperly grounded equipment is the cause of at least 90% of all problems in your system. The best way to ground your equipment is to have a single ground path to the negative side of your vehicle's electrical system for all your equipment. Then you have to route that common heavy-gauge ground wire to a point on the vehicle body or frame that you're certain is part of the negative side of the car's electrical system. The best ground point of all is the battery's negative terminal.

exact science, but we don't really need to go to those lengths, an approximation should do fine.

As we said, the nitrous solenoids are the most power-hungry components in the system, along with high-capacity/pressure fuel pumps. We've provided a chart with the peak current draw of several popular solenoid sizes. You'll have to measure the current demand of other components with a multi-meter. To do this, add up the amperage values of all the components on a circuit. For example, if you have a pair of Pro Shot solenoids on a circuit, you have to have a cable that will carry 32 amps before it splits off to each unit, where the cable only has to carry 16 amps. By breaking down your system in such a way and adding up the amperage draw, you can arrive at the total current your main power cable will have to carry.

If you have components in the circuit that are rated in watts, you can convert watts to amps by dividing the wattage by the volts of the system. In this case it's watts/13 = volts. Once you have your amperage figured out, you can measure or estimate the length of power cable needed to reach from the battery to the distribution block and from the fuse block to each device needing power. Then refer to the Power Cable Calculator chart located nearby and it will guide you to the proper gauge of cable.

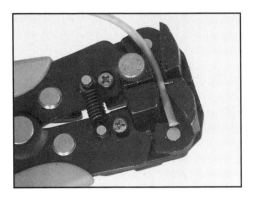

To make connections, strip the ends of the cable, just enough to fit into the solderless connector. The exact length depends on the gauge of wire, so you'll have to use your judgment.

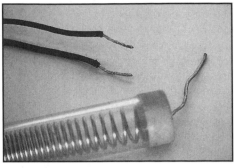

Tinning involves flowing solder into each side of the joint separately. Then place the two sides together, holding the soldering iron to them until the solder melts. Remove the soldering iron and hold until the solder freezes.

Heat the ends of the wires you wish to join until they are hot enough to melt the solder. When the joint reaches such temperature, the solder flows into it. Remove the solder iron from the joint while holding the joint still until it cools enough to become rigid again, and you have your joint. Then use heat shrink to seal and insulate the connection. You can use electrician's friction tape, but it will unravel quickly in areas with high heat, such as the engine compartment.

iron from the joint wires as you hold them steady until the solder cools slightly. Once cold, the solder becomes rigid again and you have your joint. The next step is to slip a shrink tube around the joint. With a heat gun, apply heat until the tube shrinks, sealing and insulating the joint. That's it.

The second soldering method is a modification of the first and is known as tinning the joint. This just means that you heat and flow solder into each side of the joint separately. Then to join the two ends, place them together, holding the soldering iron to them until the solder melts. Remove the soldering iron and hold until the solder freezes. As always, use a shrink tube to insulate the joint. One advantage to this method is the solder melts quicker. Use on tricky joints, or

on devices that are heat sensitive, such as speakers and crossover components.

If you terminate your wires with solder, use heat-shrink tubing to insulate the joint. Heat shrink tube is the right way to insulate a joint. Friction tape will work if you're in a jam, but the hold will only last a short time. It's best just to use a heat shrink tube.

Solderless connectors are the quick alternative to soldering every connection. Solderless connectors come in all forms. From the common butt connector, which connects the ends of two wires, to the heavy-duty, high-current battery ring-terminals.

Solderless connectors work by forcing a mechanical grip on the wire end. This is done by squeezing the connector, with the wire in place, with a special pair

of pliers nicknamed "crimps." The crimps have a curved area that puts pressure on the seam in the shaft of the connector, bending and clamping the wire in place. It only sounds complicated when you have to write it out. Doing it is simple. In fact you've probably used solderless connectors before.

The other type of connection is the screw type. You strip the wire back a bit, insert it, and tighten a screw. Simple, effective and usually nice looking as well.

This is how the solderless connection should look before crimping. The wire should come right to the end of the clamp area. The plastic coating should be tight against the clamp area beneath the insulating sheathing.

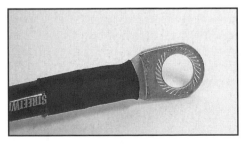

Heavy-gauge power cable ring terminals offer improved performance for your electrical system. It is best to use shrink wrap to seal and insulate the joint, though electrical tape is acceptable. Use these terminals for ground connections. Remove paint from the area of the ground to ensure optimum electricity flow.

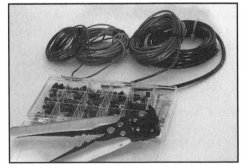

Working with solderless connectors is a quick and easy way to wire your vehicle. It's best to have a good supply of various styles and sizes of connectors to fit all the different gauges of cable you're using on your machine. A good wire stripper and crimper also help the job go smoother.

ENGINE TUNING REFERENCE

To properly tune a nitrous system, you first have to properly tune your engine. Further, you have to know how to respond to changing track and atmospheric conditions. If the air is becoming more dense, you need to know how that affects your tune and nitrous combination. Of course the reverse is also true. Even though you're most likely to have an electronically fuel-injected engine that automatically adjusts to the change in local atmospheric conditions, chances are your nitrous system is a simple mechanical device that delivers a constant flow rate unless you physically change the jetting. So when the air is better, what should you do? Increase the nitrous jet, or the fuel jetting? Maybe you should decrease the nitrous jetting only? Both? We'll help answer those questions here.

Fuel is a critical factor in tuning so we'll focus our discussion on gasoline. Gasoline is a volatile liquid petroleum distillation that when atomized and heated to a high temperature wants to rapidly combine its atoms with oxygen atoms. A huge amount of heat is released during such a chemical reaction. The heat causes the gases in the combustion chamber to expand thereby forcing the piston down the cylinder. This linear force of the piston is turned to a rotational force by the piston rods connected to the crankshaft.

When more oxygen is present, gasoline tends to react and generate higher temperatures (and thus higher cylinder pressure) quicker and it reacts slower with less oxygen in the cylinder. It is through the mechanism of this observed behavior of gasoline that superchargers, turbochargers, and nitrous oxide make power. All three of these techniques put more oxygen and more fuel in the combustion chamber. The first two by mechanically forcing more fuel and atmosphere, and therefore more oxygen, into the chambers.

Nitrous, in contrast, uses chemistry and stored mechanical energy to insert more oxygen and fuel into an engine's combustion chambers. The mechanical energy is stored by compressing the nitrous gas until it takes liquid form.

A fabricated aluminum intake hosts the Edelbrock Performer RPM nitrous and fuel solenoids. Just a hint of the power potential of this combination.

When released from the bottle it expands and is able to absorb heat, thus super-cooling the intake charge. Super-cooling the intake charge increases its density, and therefore its oxygen content.

You might think if oxygen is so chock full of power potential, why not inject pure oxygen into an engine?

Dumping pure oxygen into your engine's combustion chambers without controlling the ratio, and then lighting it off, would just burn a hole through the pistons. Pure oxygen can react with just about anything but it's really fond of aluminum. You know about the solid rocket boosters on the space shuttle? The solid part is powdered aluminum to which oxygen is added to create a very hot fire. More oxygen in an engine's combustion chambers means a hotter, as well as faster, burn. So you must add more fuel to control the rate and temperature, which of course, when properly controlled allows the engine to generate more horsepower.

For maximum performance you have to precisely control the burn rate and the temperature. Here's why.

It has to do with two things: the optimum timing, in crankshaft degrees, of peak cylinder pressure, and detona-tion. Detonation occurs when the fuel in the chamber develops one or more flame fronts and burns in an uncontrolled fashion. The rattling you sometimes hear during severe detonation is the flame fronts colliding and the resulting pressure spikes.

The timing and control of peak pressure during the power stroke is one of the most important elements of engine tuning. Get the timing and burn rate right, and the pressure will build gradually to force the piston down the cylinder with great intensity for as long as practical. The longer and more intense you can make cylinder pressure at the right time, the more power an engine will produce.

Detonation destroys engines and while it is doing so does not create much power. A four-cycle, gasoline-fueled engine cannot capture much energy from detonation-generated pressure spikes. All the energy of the intake charge is released too quickly, focusing the force on the top of the piston. It's sort of like the difference between driving a stake into the ground with a sledge hammer and shooting the end of the stake with a hunting rifle. There is so much force generated so quickly during detonation that it can crush the top of the piston, collapse the upper ring lands, punch holes through the pistons, destroy rod and main bearings...the list goes on and on. So it is very important to control how the fuel burns as well as the timing of the ignition.

CONTROLLING MAX CYLINDER PRESSURE TIMING

Basically you have four techniques at your disposal to control burn rate (to avoid detonation) and peak pressure timing: the compression ratio of the engine, the octane rating and chemistry of the fuel you choose, the amount and ratio of oxygen to fuel present in the combustion chamber, and ignition timing. Balancing these four factors is really the essence of tuning an engine.

Compression Ratio

You have to decide on a compression ratio before you build your engine. If you're installing a nitrous system on a stock engine, or one that's already assembled, you have to at least know what the compression ratio is. An engine's compression ratio is equal to the cylinder and combustion chamber volume, divided by the combustion chamber volume. For example an engine with a combined cylinder and chamber volume of 100cc at Bottom Dead Center (BDC) and only 10cc at Top Dead Center (TDC) has a compression ratio of 10 to 1.

Static vs. Dynamic Compression

We need to discriminate between static compression and dynamic compression ratios. Static is just that. The volumes of the cylinder and combustion chambers mentioned above. Dynamic compression ratio is the real compression ratio achieved in the chambers with the engine running and making power.

Once you get air moving in columns as it is in an intake manifold and in the exhaust headers, the air's inertia forces more air in the cylinder than the physical volume of the cylinder. In other words, charge air density is increased. So if there's more air in the cylinder at the

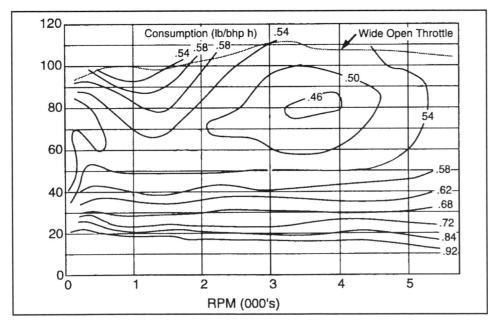

Brake specific fuel consumption isn't a static value. As the engine sweeps through it rev range under various loads and throttle openings, it goes through "efficiency islands." Most engine make best us of fuel at peak torque. That is, they make the most power for the fuel used.

start of the compression stroke, all other things being equal, you'll get a slightly higher compression ratio. Factors affecting volumetric efficiency and therefore the dynamic compression ratio of an engine include the intake runner design, head porting, and camshaft profile. Turbo and superchargers also change the dynamic compression ratio. With more boost, you get high compression.

You might as well consider the dynamic compression ratio as *the* compression ratio since the static ratio is just a reference. You're more concerned with the state of the fuel mixture with the engine running than when it's stopped, right? How do you find the dynamic compression ratio?

There are so many variables that it is nearly impossible to identify the dynamic compression ratio precisely, and it changes as the volumetric efficiency changes through the RPM range of the engine. It is more important to control the range of the dynamic compression ratio with cam choice. A cam that closes the intake valve early tends to increase dynamic compression and therefore low-end torque.

While we can't give a recommendation for every combination, we can give a general baseline for a naturally-aspirated, street-driven engine combination using pump gas. Assuming 92 octane premium, 10:1 static compression ratio is about as high a compression ratio you should run. This should put the dynamic compression ratio (assuming a real world street cam) right around 9.5:1 at the best VE point, which is approximately 85-90%.

Cam Lift/Duration Choice

Nitrous engines respond to different cam profiles than naturally-aspirated engines. Choosing the right cam is one of your more important decisions to get the most from your engine combination.

Nitrous engines are very sensitive to dynamic compression ratio changes, so you have to be aware how certain cam grinds affect this parameter. In general, a cam with a shorter duration will yield a higher compression ratio than a cam with a longer duration. For a race engine with

a static compression ratio of 12:1, using a cam with less than about 240 degrees of duration measured at .050 lift can get you into detonation rather quickly.

Another consideration is exhaust duration. Nitrous engines receive a lot of fuel and oxygen due to the super-cooled, high-density charge. Once it is burned and expanded it needs to come out of the engine. Because of this a cam with ample exhaust duration consistently makes more horsepower. Bear in mind, however, that simply increasing exhaust duration, i.e., opening the valve earlier and closing it later, will change the overlap. This in turn will affect and the dynamic compression ratio, as well as the amount of time the intake and exhaust tracts communicate. Most engine tuners agree that nitrous engines respond better if the increased exhaust duration is gained by opening the valve earlier in the cycle.

Octane Rating

The reason we're concerned with compression ratio is because the charge, fuel mixed with air, can only be compressed so much before the mixture ignites prematurely, or detonates. Fuels are rated by their resistance to compression-caused ignition or detonation. That's what an octane rating is. A higher octane number corresponds to a fuel's greater resistance to reacting with oxygen from compression-induced heat. High-octane fuels are more resistant to detonation than low-octane fuels. As we discussed, detonation is detrimental to your engine's health and horsepower. Choosing an appropriate compression ratio and fuel octane is a way to avoid detonation.

Air/Fuel Ratio

Assuming that you understand the affects of compression ratio and fuel octane on burn rate, let's move on. The next item is controlling the oxygen to fuel ratio. With a normally-aspirated engine, you control the oxygen to fuel ratio by mixing more or less fuel with the atmosphere as it travels down the intake manifold. Carburetor jetting, or changing the pulse duration for fuel-injection motors, is the usual channel for such adjustments. The key here is that fuel is added or subtracted from the mixture since the oxygen content of the atmosphere is stable at 20 percent.

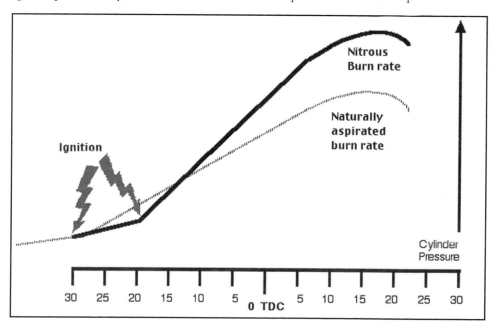

Because fuel reacts quicker with the oxygen-rich mixture of nitrous oxide, it raises cylinder pressure faster. Instead of wasting the cylinder pressure with "naturally aspirated" timing, reducing it slightly will put the pressure on the piston when it begins to travel down the bore.

When you're tuning your carburetor or fuel-injection system, the idea is to find the right amount of fuel that, depending on atmospheric conditions, will use the available oxygen to produce the most power. On most naturally-aspirated engines, 12.5 to 13 to 1 air-to-fuel ratio is where they make the most power. Any leaner (less fuel, higher oxygen ratio) the mixture burns hotter, quicker, and it's difficult to ignite. That means peak pressure is difficult to control and usually displays as a loss of power.

Controlling Ignition Timing

Controlling the timing and duration of cylinder pressure is where all your engine's power is generated. Timing peak pressure correctly is a function of ignition timing and burn rate. Since it takes time for fuel to burn and the piston is traveling at a very high speed, you have to ignite the fuel before you want peak pressure. The Burn Rate chart located nearby illustrates why your engine needs some advanced ignition timing. Notice the accelerated burn rate of fuel with additional oxygen supplied by injecting nitrous. With the burn rate accelerated, you have to retard the ignition timing to keep peak pressure in the engine's "sweet spot" around the 12 to 14 crankshaft degree mark.

TUNE YOUR ENGINE WITHOUT NITROUS FIRST

You should get your engine running right without the nitrous system first, because 90% of the time you'll be running on the motor alone. You don't want to jet the carburetor super rich or install super-oversized injectors to add fuel or anything like that. You want all the additional fuel to come through the nitrous system. Next, start tuning the nitrous system with the fuel jets to bring it back to a better state of tune. Typically you should start with a conservative jetting combination and tune toward higher output. You don't want to start at the leanest jetting and break your engine right at the gate. If you don't have a reference point, then you're much better off starting conservative. It's just much

more fun installing larger jets than sweeping up your engine.

Just keep putting in larger jet sizes, fuel and nitrous, or alternate between the two until the plugs read about like they would naturally aspirated. If you have the jetting correct, the plugs should read almost exactly like a naturally-aspirated engine, only you're running nitrous and they see a lot more fuel. You don't have to run a nitrous system so rich the plugs are black. It is true that it's safer to run the mixture rich and some engines will make more power on the rich side than on the lean side. However, these observations come about from distribution problems not so much from the characteristics of the chemical reaction of fuel and nitrous.

Regarding spark plugs: the ground strap on spark plugs is usually longer on stock engines because the combustion temperatures aren't that hot. The problem with running these types of plugs with nitrous is that the heat path is so long that the ground strap becomes red hot, the plug turns into a glow plug, and then you get detonation.

Even if you use a plug a few steps cooler, like the nitrous kit manufacturers instruct, you can still run into this problem. Again, it is the style of plug with a long ground strap that causes the problem, not necessarily the heat range.

What you really need is a plug with a short, wide, and thick ground strap. You can even trim the ground strap back to where it isn't over the electrode, forcing the spark to jump from the corner of the electrode. This maintains the same gap, but because the strap is shorter it dissipates heat quicker and is less likely to force detonation. You'll find this same approach on racing plugs that have a very short ground strap mounted to the side of the electrode. On these plugs the ground strap is very short, thick, and wide so it more effectively transfers the heat to the cylinder head.

You choose the heat range of the plug for the type of duty the engine sees. If you go too cold, then the plug won't clean itself and the cylinder won't fire. If you go too hot, then you can get into detonation and even melt and crack the plug. With nitrous you don't have to use

a non-projected style plug, such as a racing plug, but you do have to tune your choice of ground strap.

HOW AIR DENSITY AFFECTS AIR/FUEL RATIO AND POWER

In general, the power output of a naturally-aspirated engine is at the mercy of the prevailing atmospheric conditions. With denser air (the lower the altitude) and lower humidity and temperature, an engine can generate more power — with or without an electronically-controlled engine management system. Air density changes with altitude and temperature and is a major factor in tuning your carburetion and wet manifold nitrous system to meet weather and track conditions.

To clarify this sometimes cloudy subject, we talked to Bruce Huggard of B&G Racing Computers. B&G Racing Computers manufacture a racing weather station. Such weather stations and computers have become an essential tool for the serious racer. To be consistently quick, a racer needs to understand how air density affects performance and be able to measure air density and make appropriate adjustments to the carburetor.

Says Huggard, "The aeronautics industry has described a standard column of air as one that, at sea level has a barometric pressure of 29.92-inches of mercury and is 59 degrees Fahrenheit and which loses 1 inch of mercury, or barometric pressure and 3.5 degrees per 100 feet of altitude gain. What that means to the racer," Huggard continues, "is that elevation and temperature are the main factors determining air density. Therefore, if you are at a track elevation of 1000 feet the relative air density could be similar to that found at 4500 feet in a standard column of air, if the temperature happens to be very high.

"If you go to a different track with a big difference in elevation, you will notice a change in the performance of your equipment because of the large change in barometric pressure. But once there you'll find that the barometric pressure will remain nearly the same except when the temperature changes.

Density Altitude

If you're a pilot, you've probably seen this chart. It shows the relationship between pressure altitude and density altitude. This is a subject that's confusing for pilots as well as performance enthusiasts, so pay attention. It'll help you fine tune your combination so you'll go quicker when your uninformed opponents slow down or hurt their engines. The crucial thing to understand however, is that density altitude is just one way of looking at the air. It doesn't take into consideration the water vapor content. The water vapor content is important to you because it, along with the temperature and barometric pressure, tell you how much oxygen is available to your engine.

There are three important factors that affect air density: ALTITUDE, TEMPERATURE, and HUMIDITY. As you increase altitude, air density decreases. As temperature increases, density decreases. Humidity is also important because it influences engine power output and aerodynamic lift. At high ambient temperatures, the atmosphere can retain a high water vapor content. For example, at 96 degrees F, the water vapor content of the air can be eight (8) times as great as at 42 degrees F. However, high density altitude and high humidity do not often go hand-in-hand.

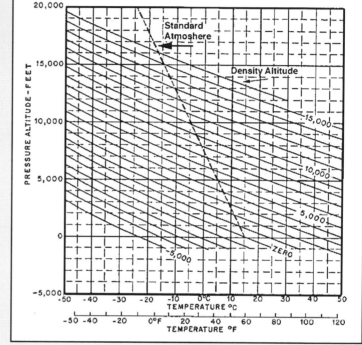

As density altitude increases, the molecules of air decrease which means there will be less air flowing over your car and into the engine. The further effects of high temperature and high humidity are cumulative, resulting in an increasingly high density altitude which reduces all performance parameters. Don't confuse density altitude with pressure altitude, indicated altitude, true altitude or absolute altitude.

The published performance criteria in the Pilot's Operating Handbook is generally based on standard atmospheric conditions at sea level (59 degrees F and 29.92 inches of mercury, dry air). When the temperature rises above the standard temperature for the locality, the density of the air in that locality is reduced and the density altitude increases. This decreases aerodynamic drag and downforce as well as decreasing horsepower output of the engine.

The graph shows density altitude for most temperature/ barometric pressure combinations. If you're using an aircraft altimeter set it at 29.92 inches; it now indicates pressure altitude. Read outside air temperature. Enter the graph at your pressure altitude and move horizontally to the temperature. Read density altitude from the sloping lines.

Example 1: Pressure altitude is 4,950 feet; and temperature, 97 degrees F. Enter the graph at 4,950 feet and move across to 97 degrees F. Density altitude is 8,200 feet. Note that in the warm air, density altitude is considerably higher, indicating less dense air, than pressure altitude. As you can see, this gets you close to knowing how much oxygen is available to your engine, but doesn't factor in the increasingly important effects of humidity as the temperature rises.

Humidity will affect performance but not as much as elevation and temperature. The exception is when you get an increase in humidity at a very high temperature. This is because the relative air density is low to begin with and with more water in the air to displace the oxygen content of a given volume of air and

the amount of fuel that can be suspended, then the power potential of your engine is reduced under such conditions."

Now let's learn a little about fuel mixture and its effect on performance. The chart located nearby illustrates a fuel mixture curve for horsepower. As you can see the slope on the left, or rich

side, is closer to horizontal than the right, or lean, side of the curve. This means horsepower drops off more rapidly when slightly lean than when slightly rich. In addition, engine damage is most likely to occur when running lean.

"Most stock or mild engines are set on the rich side so they can run all year round and travel from a higher altitude to a lower altitude without running too lean. This is why during a race, performance will usually pick up as the air gets cooler at night. Cooler air means a lower density altitude and thicker air. If the fuel remains the same, the mixture will be getting leaner. As the mixture gets leaner the engine will develop more power because it is approaching the maximum horsepower point from the rich side of the curve. It is desirable to stay slightly on the rich side for two reasons. First, there is only a minimal loss of power, second, you can hurt your engine if the air-to-fuel ratio is just slightly on the lean side. If you are already operating on the lean side, and the air gets better, your vehicle will slow way down and the probability of hurting your engine goes way up. If this happens immediately go up four jet sizes to improve performance and get a safety margin."

BASELINE YOUR FUEL CURVE

The purpose of baselining your fuel curve is to establish a standard that you can refer to under varying weather conditions. Though this is more important for carbureted engines, it is still impor-

tant to tuners using aftermarket fuel injection systems on their cars, even if they have a barometric sensor. Your baseline is a reference point to help you regain your bearings and proper tune for your car under the various condition you'll have to tune.

Baselining the fuel curve is a simple but time-intensive task. The goal is to find the best jetting combination or injector fuel pressure/duty cycle for your car at a specific air density. Start with a properly-adjusted fuel system. For carburetors, check that the throttle opens 100 percent, the linkage is satisfactory, float levels and fuel pressure are correct, etc. On fuel injection systems you want to make sure the throttle body is opening 100%, that the sensors are all working, and that you know your fuel pressure and duty cycle. Set the jetting or the duty cycle/fuel pressure so that it is too rich for the altitude and temperature at the test site. The reason you start from the rich side, is because it's safer and because the power levels are not affected as much coming from a rich condition as coming from a lean condition. So when in doubt go rich, not lean.

If you're not sure of the current jetting and whether or not it is too rich,

physically inspect the system. Write down on the carb, firewall, even a piece of paper, the number or orifice size of the jets; or the fuel pressure and duty cycle of the injectors, then ask some of the faster racers at the track for guidance. For carbureted combinations, the stock jetting is on the rich side but if you're running a high-RPM combination, heads ported with a massaged manifold, big cam and headers, then you need to be at least two jet sizes up from what is considered stock.

For fuel injected combinations, the stock ECU will usually be right on the tune unless you've altered the combination as mentioned above. Then you'll need to raise fuel pressure to match the additional fuel requirements of the high flowing components you've added. If you've got a tunable aftermarket fuel injection you can alter the duty cycle as well as the fuel pressure to achieve the best ratios.

Run your car down the track, changing jets and adjusting the fuel curve until you get the fastest MPH. It is best to stay in the same lane for your test runs in order to reduce variations in traction, even though the MPH at the end of the quarter mile is the significant figure. While you are establishing a baseline remember to only make one change at a time. Do not change timing, or adjust the lash, or perform any other tuning procedures. Simply change jets or tune the fuel pressure/duty cycle of the injectors until you get the fastest speed in the quarter mile. The MPH at the end of the quarter mile indicates horsepower generated.

Once you find the fastest MPH in the quarter, note which jet sizes are installed and the fuel injection metrics, injector size, fuel pressure and for aftermarket systems duty cycle. Take a temperature reading, in the shade with open air and make a note of it. Also note the altitude of the test track.

While the physical altitude is good to know what is more important is the density altitude. To find that you need a properly calibrated pressure altimeter, such as one used in an aircraft or a full weather station kit used for tuning. The check the density altitude chart which

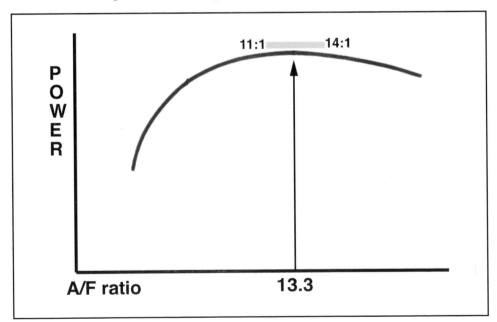

This fuel mixture to horsepower curve illustrates a basic engine-tuning concept. The slope on the left, or rich side, is closer to horizontal than the right, or lean, side of the curve indicating that horsepower drops off more rapidly when slightly lean than when slightly rich. In addition, engine damage is most likely to occur when running lean.

will correlate the pressure altitude, i.e., the one on the altimeter with the temperature reading to give you the density altitude.

Keep a log of the best jets for the altitude and temperatures and it'll help you tune for various conditions. Of course buying a weather station and racing computer is the best scenario, but good record keeping can create a firm data base from which to make tuning decisions if you're on a tight budget.

FUEL FUNDAMENTALS

A proper engine fuel provides quick starts, fast warm up, rapid acceleration, smooth performance, good mileage in various driving conditions and climates, and minimizes engine maintenance. That's a hefty shopping list, but for the most part pump gas provides all of these benefits. Yet for high-performance applications, you need to use a racing gasoline. These are specially blended to resist detonation, so you can run higher compression ratios than possible with pump gas. Racing gasolines also have more British Thermal Units (BTU) per unit of measure, about 1200 BTU more on average, than pump gas. The BTU content of a fuel is a measure of the potential heat a given unit of fuel can produce. Heat is what makes the pressure in the cylinder and that's where you get more power from racing gasoline.

We won't be able to tell you everything about pump and racing gasolines here. The purpose is really to get you acquainted with some of the basic concepts that will let you educate yourself more quickly and accurately as you start tuning your nitrous system to take advantage of racing gasolines.

Let's start with the engine factors that shape the properties needed in a good gasoline. The first is compression ratio. All the compression ratio does is heat things up. In effect, compressing the air/fuel mix heats it, thus getting it ready to be ignited by the spark plug.

So what is the advantage of a higher compression ratio? That's your control over the heat in the combustion chamber before you ignite it which influences burn rate. With lower compression you

can run more timing advance. This is because at lower compression ratio when you start the mixture burning it takes longer to heat and raise the pressure in the chamber. Basically it's a tuning tool. Instead of lighting it off too early, as with a lower compression combination, you can fire the cylinder closer to the dead center with a higher compression combination. Ultimately you have to get peak cylinder pressure at the same crankshaft degree for peak performance. So whether you use the pistons to heat the mix or burn it early to make heat is of little consequence. The real limitation is the fuel's resistance to detonation, which is called its octane rating.

The rule of thumb that raising compression makes horsepower is only partly true. The average engine is compromised in a lot of ways. It has to do a lot of different things in a variety of situations, particularly street engines. So if you ran it at the highest compression that the fuel would support, the number of situations in which the engine would function properly would be very few. About the only time you could drive such an engine would be on the coldest winter days. On hot summer days, forget it. You'd rattle the heads off the block.

So you can optimize an engine for track conditions, for the type of racing, or sometimes you may have cubic-capacity limitations by class rules. If you have a cubic-capacity limitation, you know you can't get power by making the engine bigger. The only way you can make more power is by doing more work in the same period of time. That means the engine will have to rev higher and make peak power at higher RPM. For example a 1.8-liter revving to 10,000 rpm. The problem with running at 10,000 rpm is that pump gas won't burn that fast and remain stable because it's not that good of a fuel. If you use a good racing fuel that has the appropriate energy content and octane rating, you still have the problem of burning it at a rate that makes power at 10,000 rpm.

To get racing fuel to burn fast you have to get it very close to its auto-ignition point, then light it off with a spark plug. With an engine combination design to make power at very high

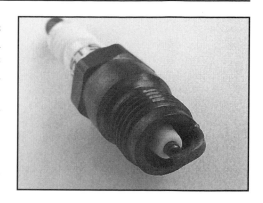

When base lining or tuning your engine, get in the habit of always reading the plugs. To get a correct reading however you need to snap off the throttle at the end of an acceleration run — even shut the engine off, if it's safe to do so. This will let you see the conditions in the combustion chamber at the point you closed the throttle. You're looking for an even, light brown fuel ring around the base of the ceramic insulator. If you see bluish colors or flakes of aluminum you're way too lean. Detonation will melt electrodes.

RPM, there just isn't any other sound way to put a predictable amount of heat in the chamber before igniting the mix. The heat goes up in direct proportion to how much the gas is compressed. So compression ratio is simply part of the overall combination.

If you're burning alcohol, which takes a different temperature curve, and has a slower burn rate compared to gasoline, then the compression ratio of that engine will be higher for most combinations. Most enthusiasts get excited by the thought that they can make all sorts of power with alcohol, but it's not all that simple. On one hand alcohol stays stable, it doesn't self ignite, in conditions that gasoline does. The advantage of alcohol is that for the same amount of air flow more energy is released.

There is a limit, both mechanically and chemically, as to how much you can raise compression ratios to get more efficiency from an engine. First of all, you need some clearance between the piston and the head, so that's the mechanical limit. More relevant to our topic is the limitation of the fuel. At some level of compression, an air and gasoline mixture will self-ignite, that's

Nitrous at Work

The Venom Civic uses Venom intake and fuel rails to demonstrate the effectiveness of both.

The Venom drag civic is powered by the famed B18C1 with turbo and nitrous. In an early dyno test with 25 lbs. of boost and 40% nitrous injection, the engine put to the wheels 725 hp at 8200 rpm and 476 lb./ft. of torque at 7000 rpm.

The Venom adjustable cam gears allow the cam timing to be retarded for maximum top-end performance.

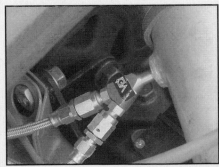

Turbo combinations respond well to single-nozzle wet systems. This system uses the Venom 2000 nitrous controller to adjust the amount of nitrous and enrichment fuel coming into the engine.

A huge water-to-air intercooler brings the charge temperature down to increase density after the turbo compressor heats it up while compressing it.

Venom Drag Civic

Wheelie bars reduce weight transfer off the front during launch to give the car more traction and quicker 60 ft. times. The webbing between the bars keeps the parachute from getting tangled. Most of the time the car stops with its brakes, keeping the chute as a safety device.

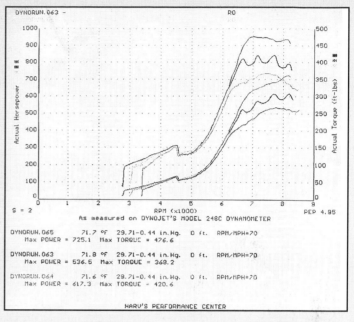

Smooth radius turns of the intake are important to an efficient intake. Notice the blow-off valve.

Dyno testing was done on this Venom drag Civic in March of 2000. The motor used in the Venom drag Civic is the famed B18C1. Take a look at the results gained under turbo apps. The middle dyno pull was the baseline on 25 lbs. of boost making 536 hp and 368 tq to the wheels. The bottom pull # 64 is 25 lbs. of boost and 20% nitrous injection, a gain of 81 hp and 42 tq at the wheels. The top dyno pull # 65 is 25 lbs. of boost and 40% nitrous injection, a gain of 189 hp and 108 tq at the wheels.

A Garrett turbo provides over 25 psi of boost. Notice the temperature probes in the turbo exhaust system. Tracking individual cylinder temps is a smart way to tune the engine, especially at this level of performance.

The Venom turbo/nitrous Civic getting ready for a 9-second quarter-mile blast. The tires are shielded from the sun to ensure even tire pressures across the front axle. This is important as it gives equal traction for the launch, enhancing control and e.t.

the chemical limit. When that happens, you have detonation.

In the broadest terms you can get into detonation in two ways. One we've just discussed: a compression ratio that raises the pressure in the combustion chamber beyond the fuel's ability to resist self ignition. The other occurs when the pressure in the combustion chamber rises to that point after the spark plug fires the charge. In this case the main flame front travels across the combustion chamber and pressure begins to rise in the cylinder. Next, a second flame front is generated by an area in the combustion chamber with raised temperature and pressures high enough where it self ignites in little pockets within the combustion chamber. The rattle you hear in severe detonation is the flame fronts colliding.

Let's call this condition dynamic detonation. The most common cause is too much ignition advance and/or a hot spot in the combustion chamber. Obviously if you light off the fuel too early, the piston isn't going to be heading down the bore soon enough to keep the pressure in chamber from reaching self-ignition levels. A hot spot can cause this condition to occur in the chamber even if the timing is set properly for the fuel.

A gasoline's resistance to detonation is known as its antiknock rating or its octane value. The octane rating on most pump and racing gas is an average of two laboratory tests using a single-cylinder engine with sensors to detect detonation. Research Octane Number (RON) is decided at 600 rpm and determines the fuel's resistance to detonation from compression. Motor Octane Number (MON) is determined at 900 rpm with the intake air heated and ignition advanced to get the fuel to detonate. A mixture of reference fuels, isooctane and heptane, are used in the tests from which we get a relative value to rate the test fuel. Add the Motor Octane value to the Research Octane value and divide the sum by two (R+M/2) to get the average value. This is the octane rating you see on pump and racing gas, although racing fuel usually has both listed in the literature.

A high octane number does not indicate a more powerful fuel. It indicates that, for example, your 10:1 compression ratio aluminum-headed engine won't detonate on (R+M/2 =) 92 octane-premium fuel. That's assuming you haven't advanced the timing to get the two or three horsepower you can find at the expense of significantly higher cylinder pressures and a high risk of detonation.

Most modern fuel-injected stock engines, have sensors that allow you to use middle-grade fuel, such as 89 octane or lower. The sensors detect detonation and the computer retards the timing or adds fuel or a combination of both. Since the timing is retarded, the power stroke is shortened and therefore the engine loses some power. A high-octane fuel lets the engine operate the way it was designed, in so far as compression ratio and efficiency is concerned.

For example, Unocal 100 Octane Unleaded Racing gas is advertised for use in engines with up to 11:1 compression ratios. That means an engine in good operating condition and tuned, i.e. timed correctly with proper fuel curves, shouldn't start detonating with this fuel. Therefore you won't have to back off the timing or fatten up the mixture to compensate for a problem. The engine takes advantage of the high compression, has a powerful air/fuel mixture, and is timed for a long power stroke. That's really what an appropriate octane number is all about.

COLD START CONDITIONS

Pump gas also needs to be designed to help your engine start when it's cold. Most of this work is done by the chemists who refine pump gasoline and racing gasoline by blending certain elements that vaporize easily at low temperatures. These are usually called the front ends or light ends or volatiles. The petroleum companies actually blend various ratio of these volatile compounds into pump gas to compensate for seasonal changes in average temperature. For example, they put more volatiles in gasoline in the winter when it's cold, to help cars start in the morning.

Most pump gas runs around 10 to 15 psi on the Reid Vapor Pressure test. This indicates how much of the gas is comprised of these light compounds. Racing gas on the other hand has a much lower RVP, around 6 psi, and isn't seasonally adjusted so you don't have to go chasing jet sizes or pulse widths to compensate for the fuel. That is why it's difficult to start engines using racing gas in cool weather. However, the payoff to hard starting is that since the gas has less light ends or volatiles, it has more of the dense, high BTU content compounds.

Of course these dense, high BTU content compounds have to vaporize to burn too, so they can't be too dense. A compound can have all the BTUs in England but if it doesn't vaporize in the cylinder it won't turn them into heat. It also has to vaporize enough to give you good throttle response. That is perhaps the trickiest configuration the chemists perform — blending compound to have a certain rate of vaporization for a given temperature rise.

That trick gives fuel its distillation curve. Most racing gasolines have an advertised distillation curve in the product literature. When it comes to choosing a racing gas for your combination, this is one of your most valuable guides. (You might think the BTU content is the most important reason to choose a fuel, but most racing gasolines are so close in BTU content it doesn't really matter.) What matters is how quickly and at what temperatures the gasoline turns to vapor.

Here's how it works: Trick 108 (R+M/2) Octane racing fuel has an advertised distillation curve beginning with an initial boiling point (IBP) of 97 F. At 137 F, 10 percent of the gas has turned to vapor; at 202 F, 50 percent has turned to vapor; at 243 F, 90 percent has vaporized; and when it hits 295 F, all of the fuel is vaporized. This indicates how quickly the heat in the engine will help turn the fuel to vapor so it can burn to make power. While you want as cool and as dense an intake charge as possible, as the distillation curve indicates, a little heat doesn't hurt. As the intake air travels through the manifold it picks up heat. Then the fuel uses the heat to vaporize, cooling the air back down. Then the charge gets compressed. Next, heat from friction of the compression, as well as from the engine surfaces, raise the temperature of the charge and the fuel hopefully vaporizes completely to make some heat of its own.

Most people think that octane is an indication of how quickly or slowly the fuel burns. That is not correct. According to the chemists at Phillips Petroleum, the hydrocarbons used to make gasoline oxidize, or burn at virtually the same rate, given the same conditions. The rate of burn, or the speed of the flame front, is basically the same for all gasolines as long as it's not detonating. The controlling mechanism of burn rate or flame front travel is the amount of oxygen in the combustion chamber available to react with the fuel. More oxygen means a faster flame front, at least to the natural limits of the fuel, and vise versa.

Another confusing concept about making power with gasoline is its energy or heat content. We've already talked about the BTU content of gasolines so we won't rehash it here. What we need to talk about is releasing all the energy in a specific amount of gas. Actually we're already talking about this concept, since the primary method of releasing the BTU content of gasoline is to vaporize it first.

Here's a key tuning concept: Use a gasoline with the highest calorie or BTU content per unit of measure that will vaporize in your engine in the ambient temperatures on race day. You don't necessarily want the most dense gas or fuel with the highest BTU content. Straight toluene is loaded with BTUs but getting it to vaporize and react with oxygen is another story.

Energy Density and A/F Ratio

Around the pits you'll hear about adjusting the carburetor jetting or setting injector pulse widths in accordance with the specific gravity of the fuel. Specific gravity is a measure of the density of the fuel at a certain temperature. As the temperature of the fuel rises, it becomes less dense. If it's less dense, then for given pulse width or jet size, you're introducing less BTUs. Assuming the air density is unchanged, the engine will run lean. This is a valid tuning concept.

An invalid tuning concept is using the most dense fuel, thinking that will have the highest BTU content. The specific gravity of a fuel and its energy density do not have a direct correlation. When choosing a fuel to tune your engine, you need to look at its BTU content per pound or gallon. Most of this information comes with the fuel's literature. In addition, as we've said earlier, select a fuel with a realistic distillation curve. Once again, if the fuel will not vaporize, it will not oxidize. It will not burn to make heat.

Still, it is very important to compensate for the energy density and the specific gravity of a fuel. If you're running a finely-tuned engine just on the edge of detonation, and you get a substantial decrease in the specific gravity of your fuel, you'll go lean and quickly get detonation. On the other hand, if the specific gravity increases then you'll run rich. A slightly rich condition does not result in a substantial loss of power, so this is seldom a concern. (See Air/Fuel Ratio to MEP to BSFC curve chart located nearby.)

Using Alcohol Fuels

Alcohol, specifically methanol, can make more power and with more of a detonation safety margin than gasoline.

The reason methanol is the racer's choice over ethanol is primarily one of cost, but also because methanol's chemistry is such that it releases more heat, in BTUs, compared to ethanol and gasoline per pound of air consumed. Ethanol and methanol have research octane ratings of 106, but ethanol has almost the same BTU content as gasoline (see BTU Comparison Gasoline vs. Alcohol chart). As you can see from the chart on a BTU per pound of fuel basis, methanol doesn't seem to be the fuel of choice. It has far less BTU per pound than either gasoline or ethanol. What gives?

The difference is that the stoichiometry of methanol requires 6.4 pounds of fuel to burn with one pound of air. This means that with perfect combustion, per pound of air flowing through your engine, methanol releases 9800 Btu per lb. Fuel. Now 9800 Btu/6.4 lbs. Air = 1531.25 Btu. Contrast this with gasoline's 20,700 Btu per lb. fuel/14.7 lbs. air = 1408 Btu. (Ethanol releases 1422.22 Btu/lb. air.)

So methanol releases close to 9 percent more Btu content per pound of air flowing through the engine. More heat means more cylinder pressure, and that means more force on the crankshaft and ultimately more power at the wheels. Of course to use methanol or ethanol you have to change the engine combination. Bigger ports, higher compression, and you have to calibrate your fuel system to deliver the appropriate ratios of fuel to mix with the air. When you're talking methanol or ethanol, you're talking about having larger jets, and longer injector pulse widths as well as increasing the capacity of the fuel lines and pump. If you decide to go for it, you will definitely make more power with methanol than with gasoline or ethanol.

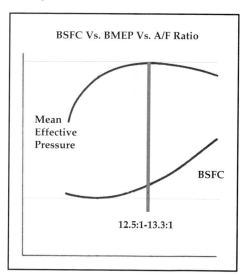

A low brake specific fuel consumption doesn't necessarily lead to more power. As the chart shows, an air:fuel ratio from 12.5:1 to 13.3:1 will produce the highest MEP. To be able to tune to that ideal you need to make sure that the specific gravity of the fuel your using is consistent and that the energy density is consistent as well.

High Performance Fuel Buyer's Guide

Turbo Blue Racing Gasoline Summary

	TBlue Ldd	TBlue Xtreme	TBlue Unldd	Method
Specific Gravity:	0.74	0.70	0.76	ASTM D287
Antiknock Index (R&M)/2:	110	116	100	
Reid Vapor Pressure:	6.6	6	8	ASTM D323
Distillation, °F:	114	114		ASTM D86
Initial Boiling Point:	90	100	90	ASTM D86
10% Evap.:	157	150	150	ASTM
50% Evap.:	210	220	210	ASTM
90% Evap.:	230	230	230	ASTM
Final Boiling Point:	260	260	260	ASTM
Oxidation Stability, Min.:	1440+	1440+	1440+	ASTM D525
Copper Strip Corrosion:	No. 1	No. 1	No. 1	ASTM D130
Existent Gum, mg/100ml:	1	1	1	ASTM D381
Color:	Blue	Orange	Clear	Visual
RON, Typical:	115	118	105	ASTM D2693
MON, Typical:	105	114	95	ASTM D2700
Lead, gm/gal.:	114	114	UL	ASTM D3237
Oxygen, Vol. %:	114	114	2.7	GC

Turbo Blue Racing Gasoline

Turbo Blue has the high energy content, smooth distillation range, and low vapor pressure necessary for carbureted, fuel-injected, supercharged and turbo-charged racing engines to safely produce the consistent high torque and horsepower demanded in all-out competition. Turbo Blue contains Tetraethyl lead and is not legal for use on public thoroughfares.

Turbo Blue Extreme

Turbo Blue Extreme is refined for race engines that demand an extremely high octane gasoline. Turbo Blue Extreme can be used in Pro Stock drag, Sprint car, cycle, NTPA pulling tractor, and offshore powerboat race applications utilizing compression ratios in excess of 14.5:1.

Turbo Blue Unleaded

Turbo Blue Unleaded is a refinery-produced, high-performance, street-legal, competition gasoline manufactured to perform in carbureted, fuel-injected, or turbo-charged performance engines. In addition, Turbo Blue Unleaded contains no manganese or alcohols and complies with regulations governing most major race sanctioning organizations.

VP Red®

Designed for the performance enthusiast and racers who need a racing gasoline but don't require C12 or C14 fuels. Used in any low-compression race engine under 12.5:1, off-road racing, marine engines, motor cross, karts, and personal water craft. Recommended for compression ratios up to 12.5:1.

Color: Red. Lead: 4.23 grams per gallon. Specific gravity: .742 at 60° F. Motor octane: 105.

C11®

Used in circle track racing, NHRA Stock and Super Stock, SCCA, karting, snowmobiles, and motorcycles. Recommended for 12:1 CR and under with restrictor plates and standard flow heads. With unrestricted heads and manifolds and carburetors, C11 works very well to 11:1. Anticipate significant HP and torque increases using this NASCAR- and NHRA-legal fuel.

Color: Purple (Also available in Green, Blue or Orange to satisfy color requirements). Lead: 4.23 grams per gallon. Specific gravity: .710 at 60° F. Motor octane: 104.

C-921®

Big Brother to C11. For use in low-compression applications, Drag Race, Oval Track, and Road Race Engines. Big HP and torque increases.

C12®

Used in oval track, drag race, and endurance competition. Race cars, race boats, motorcycles, PWC, and karts. Has won Modified Tour, GNN, D.I.R.T., Indy Lights, NHRA, MX and other local and national championships from coast to coast and around the world. Recommended for compression ratios up to: 14:1. Will satisfy 75 to 80% of today's racing engines.

Color: Green (Can be custom dyed Purple or Blue depending on the dress code). Lead: 4.23 grams per gallon. Specific gravity: .717 at 60° F. Motor octane: 108.

Late Model®

Recommended for use on circle tracks with long straights, using steel heads with less than 55cc combustion chambers, 358 CI and above high-compression engines. Chevy Vortech heads. Low compression with nitrous oxide.

Color: Aqua. Lead: 4.23 grams per gallon. Specific Gravity: .720 at 60° F. Motor octane: 110.

Late Model Plus®

Recommended for +15:1, +430 CI circle tracks with long straights. Use for low compression with two-stage nitrous oxide.

Color: Aqua. Lead: 4.23 grams per gallon. Specific gravity: .720 at 60° F. Motor octane: 113.

C14®

Used in NHRA Pro Stock and Competition Eliminator, 4-stroke motorcycle racing, and other normally-aspirated engines operating over 8500 rpm or with compression ratios of 14:1 and over. The fuel of choice in establishing VPs record 23 consecutive years of NHRA Pro Stock World Championships. Recommended in high-compression engines and high RPM.

Color: Yellow. Lead: 4.23 grams per gallon. Specific gravity: .690 at 60° F. Motor octane: 114. Aromatic hydrocarbon: 0%.

C14 Plus®

Used in ultra-high compression engines over 14:1 when additional octane is required while maintaining the same burn rate and specific gravity of

High Performance Fuel Buyer's Guide *(continued)*

C14, NHRA Pro Stock and Competition Eliminator. NHRA Legal for Comp Eliminator; National & FMDRS events. Easier to tune than C18.

Color: Clear. Lead: 6 grams per gallon. Specific gravity: .690 at 60° F. Motor octane: 115.

C15®

Used in normally-aspirated, ultra-high compression applications, some competition eliminator, circle track, and road race applications. Over 14:1 compression.

Color: Green / Lead: 4.23 Grams per gallon / Specific gravity: .713 at 60°F / Motor octane: 115 / Aromatic hydrocarbon content: 10%.

C16®

Used in turbocharged engines, blown engines, nitrous oxide and air-plane racing/pylon aircraft racers. NHRA Legal for Comp Eliminator; National & FMDRS events. Recommended for blown or turbocharged applications. See C23.

Color: Blue. Lead: 6 grams per gallon. Specific gravity: .730 at 60° F. Motor octane: 117. Aromatic hydrocarbon content: 10%.

C18®

Used in 500 C.I. NHRA Pro-Stock and Competition Eliminator. Recommended for high RPM and high compression ratios.

Color: Yellow. Lead: 4.23 grams per gallon. Specific gravity: .696 at 60° F. Motor octane: 116.

C19®

Used in Pro-Stock engines in NHRA drag racing. Easier to tune than C18. NHRA Legal for Comp Eliminator; National & FMDRS events. Recommended for high RPM and high compression ratios.

Color: Yellow. Lead: 6 grams per gallon. Specific gravity: .6952 at 60° F. Motor octane: 116.

C21®

Used in normally-aspirated engines operating over a wide range of RPM. Recommended for high RPM and high compression ratios.

Color: Yellow. Lead: 6 grams per gallon. Specific gravity: .7096 at 60° F. Motor octane: 118.

C23®

Used in engines with nitrous; 800 cid IHRA-style drag race engines. Recommended for ultimate performance in nitrous oxide applications.

Color: Blue. Lead: 6 grams per gallon. Specific gravity: .7096 at 60° F. Motor octane: 119.

C25®

Spec Fuel for NHRA Pro Stock, Pro Stock Truck, and Pro Stock Motorcycle for 2000. NHRA Legal for Comp Eliminator Class; National and FMDRS events. Recommended for winning races and championships, NHRA Style.

Color: Yellow. Lead: 8 grams per gallon. Specific gravity: .6947 at 60° F. Motor octane: 113.

VP Air Race®

Color: Blue. Leaded. Specific gravity: .710 at 60° F. Aromatic hydrocarbon content: 5%. Manganese: .2 g/gallon. Lean Knock F-3 (Method: 120.3). Rich Knock F-4 (Method: 157.2).

A5® and A7®

Meets FIA Rules; normally aspirated and turbocharged formulas.

CSP®

CSP is one of the highest octane unleaded fuels available. Spec fuel for Toyota-Atlantic North America Series in 1996, 1997, and 1998. Recom-mended for compression ratios up to 12:1.

Color: Yellow. Unleaded. Specific gravity: .7865 at 60° F. Motor octane: 96.6. Research octane: 107.9. R+M by 2: 102.3.

C10®

C10 is the best unleaded racing gasoline available. It meets ASTM D-439 standard specifications for auto-motive gasoline and is legal for use on the streets. C10 does not contain any metal compounds and will not harm catalytic converters or oxygen sensors. C10 has been used by the national champions in SCCA and IMSA stock classes.

Color: Clear. Unleaded. Specific gravity: .760 at 60° F. Motor Octane: 96. Research Octane: 104. R+M by 2: 100.

Performance Unleaded®

Performance unleaded is well suited for high-performance, street-legal cars. It meets ASTM D-439 standards and does not contain any metal compounds. Performance Unleaded will not harm catalytic converters or oxygen sensors. Performance Unleaded will typically allow turbo engines to *(continued)* raise the boost from the stock 8 - 10 lbs. to 20 - 25 lbs. Works well on the latest generation of electronically-controlled turbo engines.

Color: Light Yellow. Unleaded. Specific gravity: .760 at 60° F. Octane: R+M by 2: 100.

M7®

Used in FIM competition. Designed and specifically formulated to maximize power and performance. Conforms to 1999 FIM Fuel Regulations for 2- and 4-stroke motor-cycle competition. Used in MX, super bike, and road racing.

Color: Blue. Unleaded. Specific gravity: .761 at 60° F. Motor octane: 89.3.

Motorsport 103®

Motorsport 103 is VP's name for its street-legal gasoline, designed for maximum power and throttle response. Motorsport 103 is an unleaded fuel of high octane that provides the power and protection equal to some racing fuels. Meets California RFG requirements. Recommended for high-performance street cars, boats, snowmobiles, personal water craft, motorcycles, and high-performance import cars.

Color: Clear. Unleaded. Specific gravity: .728 at 60° F. Motor octane: 99.

Nitro Methane

VP Racing Fuels is the North American distributor for Angus Nitro fuel. Highest purity and consistency. Used by top teams in drag racing around the world. Mixes with methanol for drag, oval track, and hobby applications. Available in 1 gallon , 4-gallon case, 5-gallon pail, 30-gallon or 500-pound drums.

M-1 Methanol®

M-1 Racing Methanol has a 99.95% minimum purity. M-1 supersedes all ASTM specifications for pharmaceutical use. Due to extremely high purity, engines run cooler, and M-1 is less corrosive. Only lined drums are used which prohibit rust, corrosion, and metal deposits that can contaminate fuel-delivery systems. Recommended for all racing applications.

Nitrous at Work

Area 51's tube-chassis Toyota Supra shows the high-tech direction sport compact drag racing is headed. When complete, this nitrous-enhanced twin turbo should easily run in the nines and maybe into the eights.

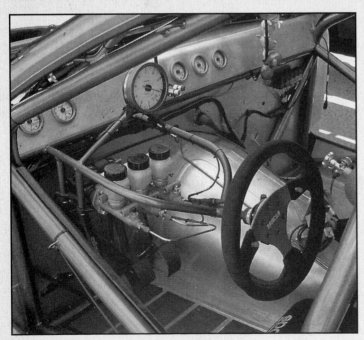

Area 51's tube-chassis Toyota Supra looks great from every angle and has wonderful fabrication throughout. It should be very, very quick.

A very stylish nitrous bottle mounting job. Edelbrock nitrous system components look great and will make any car quicker with a properly installed system.

Area 51's Tube-Chassis Supra

With a fuel solenoid in the combination, the engine builder is probably thinking of installing a direct-port system. That way the nitrous-to-fuel ratios can be controlled more precisely, giving the combination a performance and safety edge.

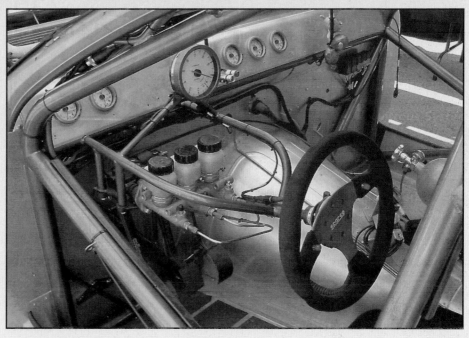

This new car looks great from every angle and has wonderful fabrication throughout. It should be very, very quick.

Two big turbos ready to pump up the power. These feed into an air-to-water intercooler to give the engine a dense, power charge of air. The beauty of nitrous is you can run huge turbos to make power on the top end while the nitrous system builds torque in the low and mi- range at the same time helping the turbos spool up.

A fabricated aluminum intake hosts the Edelbrock Performer RPM nitrous and fuel solenoids. Just a hint of the power potential of this combination.

F&L Racing Fuels Guide to Understanding Fuel and Octane Ratings

Octane Rating

This is an anti-knock scale developed in the 1920s to rate the quality of a gasoline's ability to resist detonation (knock or ping). Samples of any gasoline are placed in a laboratory Knock Engine (a small, one-cylinder variable compression engine). While the engine is running, the compression ratio is increased until the engine begins knocking. The gasoline is replaced with N-Heptane with an octane of zero and is mixed with the 100 octane ISO-Octane at various ratios until the motor "knocks." If you end up with 10% N-Heptane and 90% ISO-Octane ratio, your test sample has an octane of 90.

Octane

Is the reference fuel (ISO-octane) with the value of 100 used in testing to determine the octane rating of a gasoline. To determine octane rating two reference fuels are used. The other one is N-Heptane which has an octane value of zero.

Fuel Density

This is the weight of gasoline in relation to the weight of water. For example, F&L Fuel has a density of .721 lb./gal. Indicating it is lighter than water which is why gas and oil float on water. What is important for tuning your engine is to always use the same density fuel. Changing to fuels with a different density can richen or lean an engine. Good race fuels never change their density. Fuel density is an important tuning measurement. If you change fuel density you can flow less or more through the same carburetor jet or injector duty cycle.

Knock, Detonation, or Ping

This is an intense pressure wave within the cylinder and the sound you hear is the actual vibration of the cylinder wall.

Pre-Ignition

This is premature ignition before the plug fires, usually caused by something glowing inside the cylinder. Do not confuse this with detonation. It is not the same.

Octane Requirement

The sum total of all the factors in your motor's equation is the octane requirement. If you change the spark plug location, valve timing or valve clearance, compression ignition advance, thermostat, the air cleaner loads up, etc., then any one of these will affect the requirement. Put it all together, test it, and the engine will tell you what it needs. Add one more octane than it requires and it won't go any faster. Higher octane does not equate to more horsepower.

Modern Formula One engines in Europe run on octane around 100. As modern racing engines are developed, particularly with electronic-fuel management systems, the octane requirement will go down due to the electronic management system's ability to instantaneously monitor air/fuel ratio, outside ambient temperature and altitude, and engine running condition.

Flash Point

The lowest temperature at which the fuel vapors will burn is the flash point. Gasoline's flash point is usually around minus 20° F.

Freezing Point

The freezing point occurs when hydrocarbons start to form crystals. Then they fill in the venturi of the carte and the motor quits. To retard this problem, add less than one percent of Isopropyl alcohol.

Reid Vapor Pressure (RVP)

This measures the tendency of a gasoline to evaporate. Too high an RVP and fuel might boil or evaporate in the pump or fuel lines, and a fuel pump won't pump vapors. Too low and the engine won't start when cold. Racing fuels have an RVP of approximately 5.0 psi.

Stochiometric Air/Fuel Ratio

This is the exact air/fuel ratio required to completely combust a fuel to water and carbon dioxide. You get all the energy out of the fuel at this point and is considered to 14.7 air to one part of gasoline.

Storing Racing Fuel

Store racing fuel in its drum, not in your fuel tank or fuel cell. Anytime you wash your racer or get it wet you get water in the vented fuel cell. Don't race with old fuel, and put ethyl or isopropyl alcohol in the fuel cell before reuse, about 5 - 8 oz. Do not use rubbing alcohol because it already contains 25% water. Direct sunlight exposure to plastic fuel containers can harm gasoline. Gasoline can be stored for months without deterioration if it is absolutely closed to the atmosphere. F&L Fuel is packaged in 55 gallon drums with a nitrogen blanket over the gasoline to increase the storage life.

FUELS & LUBRICANTS COMPANY'S RACING FUEL SPECIFICATIONS

F&L SP-1
108 Octane R+M/2 Leaded
Specific Gravity: .720 @ 60°F
DISTILLATION IBP: 104° F, ENDPOINT: 305° F
Color: Green

F&L SP-3
110 Octane R+M/2 Leaded
Specific Gravity: .722 @ 60°F
Distillation IBP: 112° F, Endpoint: 290° F
Color: Amarillo

F&L SP-S/T Super/Turbo Charged
115 Octane R+M/2 Leaded
Specific Gravity: .750 @ 60° F
Distillation IBP: 180° F, Endpoint 290° F
Color: Blue

F&L Unleaded 100 Carb-2
100 Octane
California Carb Legal R+M/2 No Lead
Specific Gravity: .720 @ 60° F
Distillation IBP: 104° F, Endpoint 305° F
Color: Blue

NITROUS TUNING REFERENCE

USING RATIO & FLOW EQUIVALENT TABLES

When tuning your nitrous system, the key concept is mass flow. Just as the engine management system controls the air and fuel on the basis of mass, so you can control and calibrate the nitrous on the same basis. The difference is in the amount of oxygen contained in a given mass of nitrous oxide. That is what the tables are for. We've done the math and have approximate flow equivalents of nitrous in lb./min and CFM. So given that information you can get a pretty good idea of the mass flow rates given the nitrous jet size.

Ratio and Equivalent Flow tables display fuel flow and corresponding nitrous flow rates of 5:1 and 6:1 at a Brake Specific Fuel Consumption rate (BSFC) of 1/2 pound of fuel per hour for each HP. We express this in decimal form

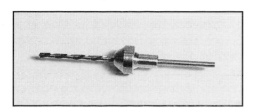

It's easy to check jet sizes, just fit them with a drill bit of known diameter. You can also drill out a smaller diameter jet to fine tune the jetting.

as .5 (i.e. 5/10ths or 50/100ths which are simply other ways of expressing 1/2). For example, to make 100 hp at a .5 BSFC means that the engine uses 50 lbs. of fuel per hour to generate 100 horsepower.

Why do we use .5 BSFC? This value has been found to be a good average number of fuel consumption in gasoline-fueled, internal-combustion engines. An engine doesn't really operate at .5BSFC all the time. The amount of power produced per unit of fuel consumed varies as the engine sweeps through its RPM range. This observation is displayed graphically in the chart on *Brake Specific Fuel Consumption*. As you can see in the chart, the BSFC varies a great deal, but the average consumption is right near .5 lbs of gasoline per hour per horsepower. It's just a convenient number that lets you calculate safe fuel needs for a given power output.

It may not be obvious, but you need a dynamometer to get BSFC numbers. We use these numbers here mostly out of convenience, since we'll have to assume a power output level. For nitrous oxide users, a BSFC number is okay since most kits are rated at a specific power output and using that number gives us a starting point.

Another concept we need to discuss is the relationship of air/fuel ratios to BSFC. The BSFC value is not the air/fuel ratio, but its magnitude is influ-

enced by air/fuel ratios. The chart on *BSFC vs. Brake Mean Effective Pressure vs. Air Fuel Ratio* shows the relationship of air/fuel ratio to BSFC. Engine tuners have found through experience that for gasoline-fueled engines, air/fuel ratios in the range of 12.5:1 to 13.3:1 make the most power but not the lowest BSFC.

Essentially these curves and the power/fuel consumption relationships hold true for each individual cylinder. The goal of an engine builder/tuner is to construct a combination that gives

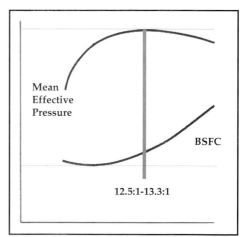

This chart shows the relationship of air/fuel ratio to BSFC. Engine tuners have found through experience that for gasoline-fueled engines, air/fuel ratios in the range of 12.5:1 to 13.3:1 make the most power but not the lowest BSFC.

each cylinder the same air/fuel ratio. In practice, however, this is almost impossible. Port fuel-injected cars get very close, because the computer regulates the fuel injectors at each cylinder to deliver precise amounts of fuel. Any unequal fuel distribution is usually the result of varying flow rates between individual injectors.

Carbureted engines, especially ones with centrally located carburetors can have quite poor distribution. In fact, one of the reasons a dual-plane manifold doesn't respond to a plate as well as a single-plane manifold is because the dual-plane manifold generally gives less equal fuel distribution.

What happens then is that instead of each cylinder performing at the point in the illustration, each cylinder gets a different air/fuel ratio and so produces more or less power as it consumes more or less fuel. So you can have one, two, or more cylinders getting the proper 12:5:1 to 13.3:1 ratio; two or three slightly rich; and two or three slightly lean.

The cylinders on the rich side aren't as great a problem as the lean cylinders, and here's why. If you look at the mean effective pressure curve, you'll notice that it doesn't drop off as quickly on the rich side as it does on the lean side. This means that a slightly rich cylinder still makes good power but at a cost of consuming extra fuel. The lean cylinder, on the other hand, produces much less power, a trend that is aggravated as the cylinder gets leaner. On a port fuel-injected engine, you can just increase fuel delivery to that cylinder to bring it up to power. However, on a single-carbureted system, you have to enrich all the cylinders to get the individual cylinder to perform properly. That scenario usually puts more of the cylinders on the overly-rich side, which increases fuel consumption and reduces power output. Still you have to do it because the lean cylinder is most likely to experience detonation before the richer cylinders. Remember, with a multi-cylinder engine the sum of each cylinder's output is what moves the flywheel.

It's interesting to see how interdependent all of these measurements are. The air/fuel ratio directly influences mean effective pressure which determines the torque for a given engine displacement. Torque influences how much horsepower is produced, which in turn affects BSFC, which is dependent on the air/fuel ratio. It's what tuning is all about.

These tables are here to help you dial in your nitrous combination. If you get totally lost then you can use these tables as a map to get back to where you want to be. You can also use them to figure your next tuning move or in designing your next stage or nitrous system.

The tables are keyed from the horsepower level in the far left column. The next column is a theoretical BSFC of .50 at that horsepower level. BSFC is calculated as the mass of the fuel flow divided by the horsepower. So if you're flowing 50 lbs./hr. of fuel and making 100 hp, you have a BSFC of .50. To convert that figure into lbs./min., we divide it by 60.

Next we get the nitrous mass flow per minute at a 6:1 nitrous-to-fuel ratio by multiplying the BSFC/min. figure by 6. In the next column we list the oxygen content of the nitrous flow rate by weight. This is done by multiplying the mass flow number in the preceding column by .36. (Nitrous is 36% oxygen by weight.) To convert our nitrous mass flow into a CFM rate, we use the specific volume of the gas at 70° F @ sea leveler 8.726 cubic ft/lb. Multiplying the lbs./min. figure by 8.726 gives an approximate expanded volume of that flow rate.

To get equivalent atmosphere flow rates, we chose an oxygen content slightly less than that most commonly presumed. According to basic encyclopedia listings, the atmosphere runs about 23% oxygen. We tend to overestimate the actual oxygen in the air that the engine ingests. We chose 19% because legendary engine guru Ken Dutweiller told us that's a more realistic number. The great average oxygen content of the atmosphere may be almost 24 percent, but under most conditions it only contains around 19% oxygen. So multiplying the lb./min. @ 6:1 figure by .19 gives us an approximate equivalent rate. Then we take this figure and divide it by .0762 to convert the lbs./min. rate to CFM.

That's how we arrived at the values chosen for the tables. The reason we chose them can best be explained by an example.

Assume you have a nitrous kit that's calibrated to make 100 hp. The jetting guide says use X nitrous jet and Y fuel jet, each at a specified pressure. You can take the suggested jetting on faith since the manufacturers are pretty accurate, but what if the combination doesn't perform as expected? What do you do then? What changes should you make in order to tune the system?

These tables are designed to give you reference points. Continuing our example, we know the kit is jetted to make 100 hp. That means at a BSFC of .5 it needs to deliver 50 lbs./hr. of fuel or .83 lbs./min. of fuel. With the formula we discussed, you can verify if in fact the nitrous kit's fuel side is delivering the required fuel. You know X-jet at 7 psi doesn't tell you that. The same is true of the nitrous flow rate. You can weigh the

N₂O Bottle Temp to Pressure

Bottle Temp. °F	Bottle Pressure (psi)
-30	67
-20	203
-10	240
0	283
10	335
20	387
32	460
40	520
50	590
60	675
70	760
80	865
97	1,069

NOTE: As ambient temperature drops, so will bottle pressure which can cause a potentially fuel rich condition. Although usually not harmful to the engine, loss of optimal power can occur. On the other hand, very high ambient temperatures can lead to leaner burning conditions and possible engine damage.

Nitrous Oxide Flow Rates at 5:1 Nitrous-to-Fuel Ratio with a .5 BSFC

Equivalent air/fuel ratio = 9.45:1

Horse power	Gasoline lbs./hr @ BSFC=.50 HP*.5	Gasoline lbs./min @ BSFC=.50 BSFC/60	Nitrous lbs/min @5/1 BSFC*5	Oxygen lbs/min @ 5/1 Nitrous lbs/min * .36	CFM @ 70°F Nitrous lbs/min * 8.726	Equivalent Atmosphere lbs/min Oxygen lbs/min / .19	Equivalent Atmosphere CFM Atmosphere lbs/min / .0762
50.00	25.00	0.42	2.08	0.75	18.18	3.95	51.80
45.00	22.50	0.38	1.88	0.68	16.36	3.55	46.62
40.00	20.00	0.33	1.67	0.60	14.54	3.16	41.44
35.00	17.50	0.29	1.46	0.53	12.73	2.76	36.26
30.00	15.00	0.25	1.25	0.45	10.91	2.37	31.08
25.00	12.50	0.21	1.04	0.38	9.09	1.97	25.90
20.00	10.00	0.17	0.83	0.30	7.27	1.58	20.72
15.00	7.50	0.13	0.63	0.23	5.45	1.18	15.54
10.00	5.00	0.08	0.42	0.15	3.64	0.79	10.36
5.00	2.50	0.04	0.21	0.08	1.82	0.39	5.18

A nitrous system tuned to flow 5:1 nitrous to fuel will be on the rich side. 9.45:1 air/fuel ratio is rich but it is safe. The chart shows the flow rate of nitrous required for that air/fuel ratio at BFSC of .5 lbs/hr. The chart converts pounds per hour to pounds per minute to make it more convenient for you to test flow your system. In addition this chart (and the ones that follow) convert the mass flow of nitrous at this rate into the equivalents CFM flow of nitrous as well as atmospheric equivalent flow rates in pounds per minute and CFM. The CFM flow rate of nitrous gives you some idea of how the gas displaces the atmosphere and influences the volumetric efficiency of a naturally aspirated engine.

Nitrous Oxide Flow Rates at 6:1 Nitrous-to-Fuel Ratio with a .5 BSFC

Equivalent air/fuel ratio = 11.40:1

Horse power	Gasoline lbs./hr. @ BSFC =.50 HP*.5	Gasoline lbs./min. @ BSFC =.50 BSFC/60	Nitrous lbs./min. @ 6/1 BSFC*6	Oxygen lbs./min. @ 6/1 Nitrous lbs./min. * .36	CFM @ 70°F Nitrous lbs./min. * 8.726	Equivalent Atmosphere lbs./min. Oxygen lbs./min. /.19	Equivalent Atmosphere CFM Atmosphere lbs./min./.0762
50	25.00	0.42	2.50	0.90	21.82	4.74	62.16
45	22.50	0.38	2.25	0.81	19.63	4.26	55.95
40	20.00	0.33	2.00	0.72	17.45	3.79	49.73
35	17.50	0.29	1.75	0.63	15.27	3.32	43.51
30	15.00	0.25	1.50	0.54	13.09	2.84	37.30
25	12.50	0.21	1.25	0.45	10.91	2.37	31.08
20	10.00	0.17	1.00	0.36	8.73	1.89	24.87
15	7.50	0.12	0.75	0.27	6.54	1.42	18.65
10	5.00	0.08	0.50	0.18	4.36	0.95	12.43
5	2.50	0.04	0.25	0.09	2.18	0.47	6.22

This chart shows the flow rates of a nitrous system jetted to achieve a 6:1 nitrous-to-fuel ratio with an equivalent air/fuel ratio of 11.40:1. These flow rates will produce more power that the rates shown in the 5:1 chart. These flow rates are produced by increasing the jet size of the nitrous circuit or increasing the bottle pressure. The preferred method is to increase jet size while maintaining a bottle pressure of approximately 900 psi.

Nitrous Oxide Flow Rates at 7:1 Nitrous-to-Fuel Ratio with a .5 BSFC

Equivalent air/fuel ratio = 13.25:1

Horse power	Gasoline lbs./hr. @ BSFC =.50 HP*.5	Gasoline lbs./min. @ BSFC =.50 BSFC/60	Nitrous lbs./min. @ 7/1 BSFC*7	Oxygen lbs./min. @ 7/1 Nitrous lbs./min. * .36	CFM @ 70°F Nitrous lbs./min. * 8.726	Equivalent Atmosphere lbs./min. Oxygen lbs./min. /.19	Equivalent Atmosphere CFM Atmosphere lbs./min./.0762
50	25.00	0.42	2.92	1.05	25.45	5.53	72.52
45	22.50	0.38	2.62	0.94	22.91	4.97	65.20
40	20.00	0.33	2.33	0.84	20.36	4.42	58.02
35	17.50	0.29	2.04	0.74	17.82	3.87	50.77
30	15.00	0.25	1.75	0.63	15.27	3.32	43.51
25	12.50	0.21	1.46	0.53	12.73	2.76	36.26
20	10.00	0.17	1.17	0.42	10.18	2.21	29.01
15	7.50	0.12	0.88	0.32	7.64	1.66	21.70
10	5.00	0.08	0.58	0.21	5.09	1.11	14.50
5	2.50	0.04	0.29	0.10	2.55	0.55	7.25

This chart shows the flow rates for a 7:1 nitrous-to-fuel ratio which is produced by increasing the nitrous flow from that of the 6:1 ratio rates in the chart above. This ratio is lean but if everything is right it could be a very powerful tune. If not, it could be a new set of pistons …

bottle, verify bottle pressure, turn on the system for a specific length of time, and calculate the nitrous flow. If the system isn't delivering the required amount of nitrous, you'll know that too.

The atmospheric equivalents were included to show the relationship between air and nitrous. Because when you get to the core, fuel makes the power not the nitrous. It also lets you establish an approximately equivalent air/fuel ratio. Just divide the equivalent atmosphere in lbs./min. by the BSFC in lbs./min. For example, at 100 hp the BSFC/min is .83 and the equivalent atmosphere is 9.47 lbs./min. Therefore, the equivalent air/fuel ratio is 9.47/.83 = 11.40:1. This puts the tuning in a more familiar format. From this you know you can put in a little more nitrous or take away some fuel if the plugs look like they need it.

TROUBLESHOOTING DETONATION

If you experience detonation, you could have a lean fuel mixture or too much nitrous. A lean mix may burn slower than a fat mixture, but the heat of combustion is higher. When you raise temperature, you also raise the pressure. It is then that you generate a second flame front and detonate your main bearings away.

Detonation can also be caused by too much ignition timing. Firing the cylinder too much before TDC means the piston is going to be dwelling at TDC when the cylinder reaches peak pressure. Because the piston isn't traveling down the bore yet to relieve the pressure, it builds to a point where the fuel self ignites. BOOM! You have detonation. Retard the timing to a point where peak cylinder pressure occurs just after the piston starts down the bore. You will stay out of detonation and make lots of reliable horsepower.

Compression ratio can also be a problem causing detonation. Compression ratio affects detonation, as we discussed above because it increases cylinder pressure.

Cam choice plays a role in detonation as well. The timing of closing the intake and exhaust valves control the dynamic compression ratio of the cylinder, and thus the cylinder pressure and potentially the tendency of a fuel to detonate. A cam with valve timing that fills the cylinder with more air and fuel promotes higher cylinder pressures and higher horsepower. It also increases the chances for detonation.

The temperature of your engine and its coolant can cause detonation when you get hot spots in the cylinder or combustion chamber from an inefficient or insufficient cooling system. Hot spots raise the temperature in the combustion chamber and, well you know the rest.

Detonation can also be the result of poor cylinder-to-cylinder fuel distribution. If an engine has uneven distribution of the air/fuel mixture between cylinders, the leaner cylinders are more prone to detonate. That means you need to retard the timing for the mixture of the leanest cylinder. This most often occurs on carbureted cars, but it also happens to fuel-injected cars as the injectors get clogged or just weren't built right at the factory.

If carbon builds up on the piston, valves, and combustion chamber surfaces it can cause a hot spot. Need we say more? If you really get a lot of carbon built up it can raise the compression ratio.

If you get oil in the mix, from worn or broken rings, a bad guide or ring flutter, your engine will detonate.

High air inlet temperatures can push an engine on the edge of detonation, right over the cliff. The higher the inlet air temperature, the more chance you have of detonating. Just one more reason not to put your air cleaner right by the exhaust pipes.

A pent-roof or clover shaped combustion chamber with a centrally-located spark plug and lots of quench area has the least tendency to detonate. A hemi-head/pent-roof head allows for faster combustion, allowing less time for detonation to occur ahead of the flame front.

As we have already discussed, a high octane number is an indication of a particular gasoline blend's resistance to detonation. If your engine has high compression, chances are it'll need a high octane number.

Spark plug choice is a critical factor in keeping your engine from detonating. The proper heat range and spark plug type is particularly important when using nitrous. See the sidebar in this chapter on choosing the right spark plug.

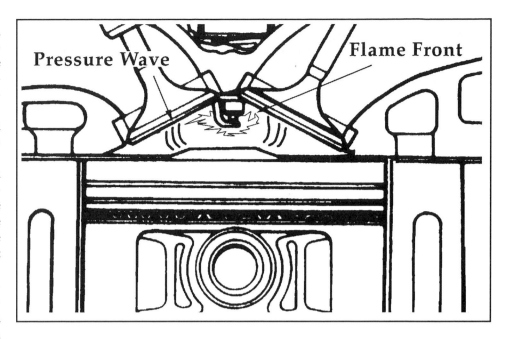

Detonation results from the generation of pressure waves in the air/fuel mix in response to the ignition of the mixture. The "knocking" or "pinging" sound of detonation comes from these pressure waves pounding against the insides of the combustion chamber and the piston top, and not from "colliding flame fronts."

The mechanism of detonation is as follows: The initial ignition of the air/fuel mixture generates a pressure wave that travels through the unburned air-fuel mix ahead of the flame front. The pressure wave hits the sides of the combustion chamber and piston tops and reflects back, just as ripples reflect off the edge of a pool. In areas where the main pressure wave and the reflected pressure waves converge constructively, the pressure is amplified, and detonation tends to occur first at these points. Areas of the combustion chamber prone to such constructive convergence are the edges of the piston crown.

Detonation occurs in these areas because the severe increase in pressure has increased the local temperature to the ignition temperature of the fuel. This ignition temperature tends to be slightly lower than that of the fuel itself because of the chemical reaction of the fuel to the rise in local heat and pressure.

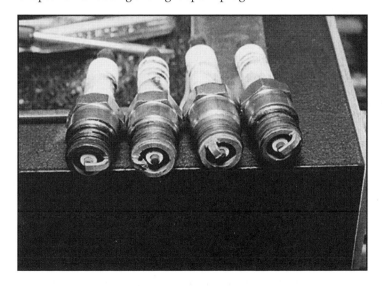

When your mixture is right, the plugs run clean and display a proper fuel ring.

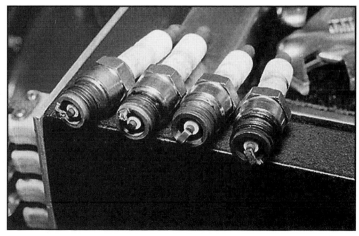

If you try to tune too lean you'll get into detonation. If you are lucky the plug's electrodes will melt, stopping the combustion process and saving your pistons and rings. These plugs have too thin an electrode for heavy doses of nitrous.

Baseline Tuning Data
for Various NOS Systems

Extra HP	Jetting N₂O/Fuel	Fuel Octane (R+M/2)	Ignition Timing	Spark Plug Heat Range
Super Powershot				
100 hp	.047/.053	92+ pump gas	Std	Std
125 hp	.055/.061	92+ pump gas w/octane booster	Std to 2° retard	Std to 1 step colder
150 hp	.073/.082	92+ pump gas w/octane booster or 100+ racing gas	2° retard	1 to 2 steps colder
175 hp	.082/.091	105 octane racing gas	4° retard	2 to 3 steps colder
Cheater System				
100 hp	.047/.053	92+ pump gas	Std	Std
125 hp	.055/.061	92+ pump gas w/octane booster	Std to 2° retard	Std to 1 step colder
150 hp	.073/.082	100+ pump gas w/octane booster or 100+ racing gas	2° retard	1 to 2 steps colder
175 hp	.082/.091	105 octane racing gas	4° retard	2 to 3 steps colder
200 hp	.093/.102	110+ octane, .74 or higher specific gravity, racing gas	6° retard	3 to 4 steps colder
250 hp	.102/.110	110+ octane, .74 or higher specific gravity racing gas	6° retard	3 to 4 steps colder
Dual Shot Cheater System, Stage 1				
100 hp	.047/.053	92+ pump gas	Std	Std
125 hp	.055/.061	92+ pump gas w/octane booster	Std to 2° retard	Std to 1 step colder
150 hp	.073/.082	92+ pump gas w/octane booster or 100+ racing gas	2° retard	1 to 2 steps colder
Dual Shot Cheater System, Stage 2				
150 hp	.063/.071	100+ pump gas w/octane booster or 100+ racing gas	2° retard	1 to 2 steps colder
180 hp	.073/.082	105 octane racing gas	4° retard	2 to 3 steps colder
210 hp	.082/.091	110+ octane, .74 or higher specific gravity racing gas	6° retard	3 to 4 steps colder
250 hp	.093/.102	110+ octane, .74 or higher specific gravity racing gas	6° retard	3 to 4 steps colder
Multiple Carburetor Cheater System				
100 hp	.033/.037	92+ pump gas	Std	Std
125 hp	.038/.043	92+ pump gas w/octane booster	Std to 2° retard	Std to 1 step colder
150 hp	.052/.059	92+ pump gas w/octane booster or 100+ racing gas	2° retard	1 to 2 steps colder
175 hp	.059/.065	105 octane racing gas	4° retard	2 to 3 steps colder
200 hp	.065/.073	110+ octane, .74 or higher specific gravity racing gas	6° retard	3 to 4 steps colder
250 hp	.073/.078	110+ octane, .74 or higher specific gravity racing gas	6° retard	3 to 4 steps colder
Big Shot System				
175 hp	.073/.082	92+ pump gas w/octane booster or 100+ racing gas	2° retard	1 to 2 steps colder
225 hp	.082/.091	92+ pump gas w/octane booster or 100+ racing gas	2° retard	1 to 2 steps colder
275 hp	.093/.102	105 octane racing gas	4° retard	2 to 3 steps colder
325 hp	.102/.110	110+ octane, .74 or higher specific gravity, racing gas	6° retard	3 to 4 steps colder
350+ hp	.120/.116	110+ octane, .74 or higher specific gravity, racing gas	8° retard	3 to 4 steps colder
2-Stage Big Shot System, Stage 1				
100 hp	.047/.053	92+ pump gas w/octane booster or 100+ racing gas	Std	1 to 2 steps colder
125 hp	.055/.061	92+ pump gas w/octane booster or 100+ racing gas	2° retard	1 to 2 steps colder
150 hp	.063/.071	100+ pump gas w/octane booster or 100+ racing gas	2° retard	1 to 2 steps colder
180 hp	.073/.082	105+ octane racing gas	4° retard	2 to 3 steps colder
210+ hp	.082/.091	110+ octane, .74 or higher specific gravity racing gas	6° retard	3 to 4 steps colder
250+ hp	.093/.102	110+ octane, .74 or higher specific gravity racing gas	6° retard	3 to 4 steps colder
2-Stage Big Shot System, Stage 2				
175 hp	.073/.082	92+ pump gas w/octane booster or 100+ racing gas	2° retard	1 to 2 steps colder
225 hp	.082/.091	92+ pump gas w/octane booster or 100+ racing gas	2° retard	1 to 2 steps colder
275 hp	.093/.102	105 octane racing gas	4° retard	2 to 3 steps colder
325 hp	.102/.110	110+ octane, .74 or higher specific gravity racing gas	6° retard	3 to 4 steps colder
350+ hp	.120/.116	110+ octane, .74 or higher specific gravity racing gas	8° retard	3 to 4 steps colder

Baseline Tuning Data
for Various NOS Systems

Extra HP	Jetting N₂O/Fuel	Fuel Octane (R+M/2)	Ignition Timing	Spark Plug Heat Range
Multiple Carburetor Big Shot System				
150 hp	.052/.058	92+ pump gas w/octane booster or 100+ racing gas	2° retard	1 to 2 steps colder
225 hp	.059/.065	92+ pump gas w/octane booster or 100+ racing gas	2° retard	1 to 2 steps colder
275 hp	.065/.073	105 octane racing gas	4° retard	2 to 3 steps colder
325 hp	.073/.078	110+ octane, .74 or higher specific gravity racing gas	6° retard	3 to 4 steps colder
350+ hp	.085/.082	110+ octane, .74 or higher specific gravity racing gas	8° retard	3 to 4 steps colder
Pro Racing Plate System, each stage				
100 hp	.047/.053	92+ pump gas	Std	Std
125 hp	.055/.061	92+ pump gas w/octane booster	Std to 2° retard	Std to 1 step colder
150 hp	.063/.071	100+ pump gas w/octane booster or 100+ racing gas	2° retard	1 to 2 steps colder
180 hp	.073/.082	105 octane racing gas	4° retard	2 to 3 steps colder
210 hp	.082/.091	110+ octane, .74 or higher specific gravity racing gas	6° retard	3 to 4 steps colder
250 hp	.093/.102	110+ octane, .74 or higher specific gravity racing gas	6° retard	3 to 4 steps colder
Multiple Carburetor Pro Racing Plate System, each stage				
Note: Special tuning combinations will be required if both stages are to be applied simultaneously.				
100 hp	.033/.037	92+ pump gas	Std	Std
125 hp	.038/.043	92+ pump gas w/octane booster	Std to 2° retard	Std to 1 step colder
150 hp	.052/.059	92+ pump gas w/octane booster or 100+ racing gas	2° retard	1 to 2 steps colder
175 hp	.059/.065	105 octane racing gas	4° retard	2 to 3 steps colder
200 hp	.065/.073	110+ octane, .74 or higher specific gravity racing gas	6° retard	3 to 4 steps colder
250 hp	.073/.078	110+ octane, .74 or higher specific gravity racing gas	6° retard	3 to 4 steps colder
Pro Fogger System				
100 hp	.018/.022	92+ pump gas	Std	Std
125 hp	.020/.024	92+ pump gas w/octane booster	Std to 2° retard	Std to 1 step colder
150 hp	.022/.026	92+ pump gas w/octane booster or 100+ racing gas	2° retard	1 to 2 steps colder
175 hp	.024/.028	105 octane racing gas	4° retard	2 to 3 steps colder
250 hp	.028/.032	110+ octane, .74 or higher specific gravity racing gas	6° retard	3 to 4 steps colder
300 hp	.032/.036	110+ octane, .74 or higher specific gravity racing gas	6° retard	3 to 4 steps colder
350 hp	.036/.040	110+ octane, .74 or higher specific gravity racing gas	6° retard	3 to 4 steps colder
400 hp	.040/.046	110+ octane, .74 or higher specific gravity racing gas	6° retard	3 to 4 steps colder
500 hp	.043/.052	110+ octane, .74 or higher specific gravity racing gas	6° retard	3 to 4 steps colder
4-cylinder Sportsman Fogger System				
50 hp	.018/.022	92+ pump gas	Std to 2° retard	Std to 1 step colder
75 hp	.022/.026	92+ pump gas w/octane booster or 100+ racing gas	2° to 4° retard	1 step colder
100 hp	.024/.028	105 octane racing gas	4° to 6° retard	1 to 2 steps colder
125 hp	.026/.030	110+ octane, .74 or higher specific gravity racing gas	4° to 8° retard	2 steps colder
150 hp	.028/.032	110+ octane, .74 or higher specific gravity racing gas	6° to 10° retard	2 to 3 steps colder
6-cylinder Sportsman Fogger System				
75 hp	.018/.022	92+ pump gas	Std to 2° retard	Std to 1 step colder
100 hp	.022/.026	92+ pump gas w/octane booster or 100+ racing gas	2° to 4° retard	1 step colder
125 hp	.024/.028	105 octane racing gas	4° to 6° retard	1 to 2 steps colder
150 hp	.026/.030	110+ octane, .74 or higher specific gravity racing gas	4° to 8° retard	2 steps colder
175 hp	-.028/.032	110+ octane, .74 or higher specific gravity racing gas	6° to 10° retard	2 to 3 steps colder
8-cylinder Sportsman Fogger System				
100 hp	.018/.022	92+ pump gas	2° retard	Std
125 hp	.020/.024	92+ pump gas w/octane booster	Std to 2° retard	Std to 1 step colder
150 hp	.022/.026	92+ pump gas w/octane booster or 100+ racing gas	2° retard	1 to 2 steps colder
175 hp	.024/.028	105 octane racing gas	4° retard	2 to 3 steps colder
250 hp	.028/.032	110+ octane, .74 or higher specific gravity racing gas	6° retard	3 to 4 steps colder
300 hp	.032/.036	110+ octane, .74 or higher specific gravity racing gas	6° retard	3 to 4 steps colder

Notes

NITROUS LEGAL RACING CLASSES RULES

The sensational growth of sport compact drag racing gives the performance enthusiast an arena to test and verify tuning and driving skills. The race track is the place to use your developing knowledge of nitrous-enhanced horsepower, not the street.

When this book was published, the two entities organizing sport compact drag racing were the National Import Racing Association (NIRA) and the Import Drag Racing Circuit (IDRC). In addition, the NHRA had just created a venue for sport compact drag racing enthusiasts.

Here is a summary of the rules governing the various nitrous-legal classes of NIRA and IDRA.

NIRA CLASSES

Power 4

Body: Full stock import or compact domestic car or truck body must be retained. Lightweight parts limited to hood and ground effects only. No cutting or drilling of body or chassis or removal of other components for purpose of lightening vehicle. Lexan or Plexiglas windows are prohibited. No tape can be used to join/cover body seams. No pre-1987 cars.

Chassis: Full stock chassis required. Roll cage or roll bars allowed only inside passenger compartment, except for trucks or as needed to be compliant with applicable safety specifications.

Wheelbase: Stock wheelbase must be retained.

Drive line: FWD, AWD, or RWD entries allowed. OEM transmission and rear end must be used. Scatter shield required if 11.99 or quicker.

Engine: Reserved for 4-cylinder entries equipped with a turbocharger, a nitrous-oxide system, or for those vehicles with superchargers and motor swaps for a total of up to two power adders. Motor-swaps plus power adders allowed. No air-cooled entries.

Exhaust: Cars MUST run mufflers for Saturday racing, otherwise, not required.

Induction: Any commercially available induction may be used, but stock configuration must be retained. Ex: Fuel-injected entries must remain fuel injected, with the same type of injection used as delivered stock.

Ignition System: Aftermarket crank triggers, two-step rev limiters, ignition amplifiers, spark computers, and dynamically adjustable or piggyback engine-management systems are allowed, but stock ECU must remain and be operational.

Nitrous: Bottles must be stamped 1800 psi minimum. Bottles must be mounted directly to the body, utilizing all mounting points on bottle points. No external heating of bottle allowed.

Interior: Front seats, door panels and door innards, dash, headliner, and carpet must remain in place. Back seat and all interior trim from driver's seat back can be removed. Windows and door switches must work as designed by manufacturer. Cars will be reinspected on the return road. Any cars found missing seats or other components shall be disqualified.

Street Equipment: DOT glass must be used. Headlights, turn signals, horn, wipers, and taillights must be retained in working stock condition. One headlight can be removed for air induction.

Tires: AWD entries must run DOT street radial tires. Cars running 11.99 or quicker must have metal valve stems. Tubes permitted. No limit on tire width at this time. Slicks ok for non-AWD entries. Absolutely no mini spare tires or non speed-rated tires may be used at any time.

Suspension: Must use one shock per wheel or retain original style suspension. Coil-overs allowed. No wheelie bars allowed.

Radiator: Electric fans allowed. Must use overflow/catch can, 1 pint minimum.

Fuel: Gasoline only. No fuel cells allowed.

Power 6

Body: Full stock import or compact domestic car or truck body must be retained. Lightweight parts limited to hood and ground effects only. No cutting or drilling of body or chassis or removal of other components for purpose of lightening vehicle. Lexan or Plexiglas windows are prohibited. No tape can be used to join/cover body seams. No pre-1987 cars.

Chassis: Full stock chassis required. Roll cage or roll bars allowed only inside passenger compartment or as needed to be compliant with applicable safety specifications, especially on cars faster than 9.99. In all cases, no car shall be allowed to cut flooring out of the vehicle. Window nets required if vehicles run quicker than 9.99 or 135 mph, as specified in NHRA Rule book.

Wheelbase: Stock wheelbase must be retained.

Drive line: FWD, AWD, or RWD entries allowed. OEM rear end must be used. After market transmissions limited to commercially-available automatics, such as Power Glides. No G-Force, Liberty, or clutchless transmissions. Scatter shield required if 11.99 or quicker. No Trans-Brakes.

Engine: Reserved for 6-cylinder entries equipped with a turbocharger, supercharger, nitrous oxide, or a combination for up to two power adders allowed.

Exhaust: Cars MUST run mufflers for Saturday racing, otherwise, not required.

Induction: Any commercially-available induction may be used, but stock configuration must be retained. Ex: Fuel-injected entries must remain fuel injected, with the same type of injection used as delivered stock.

Nitrous: Bottles must be stamped 1800 psi minimum. Bottles must be mounted directly to the body, utilizing all mounting points on bottle points. No external heating of bottle allowed.

Ignition System: Aftermarket crank triggers, two-step rev limiters, ignition amplifiers, spark computers, and dynamically adjustable and piggyback engine-management systems are allowed, but stock ECU must be retained and be operational.

Interior: Front seats, door panels and door innards, dash, headliner, and carpet must remain in place. Windows and door switches must work as designed by manufacturer. Back seat and all interior trim from driver's seat back can be removed. Cars will be reinspected on the return road. Any cars found missing seats or other components shall be disqualified.

Street Equipment: DOT-certified glass must be used. Headlights, turn signals, horn, wipers, and taillights must be retained in working stock condition. One headlight can be removed for air induction.

Tires: No limit on tire width at this time. Slicks okay. Cars running 11.99 or quicker must have metal valve stems. Tubes permitted. Absolutely no mini spare tires or non speed-rated tires may be used at any time.

Suspension: Must use one shock per wheel, or retain original style suspension. Coil-overs allowed. No wheelie bars allowed.

Radiator: No electric water pumps. Electric fans allowed. Must use overflow/catch can, 1 pint minimum.

Fuel: Gasoline only. No fuel cells.

PRO Classes

All Pro Classes run on a .400 Pro Tree.

PRO 4 Cylinder

Class designation: P/4C. Must show 9.99 license to enter this class.

All: All racers must have the sponsor decals as required by NIRA, no matter what sponsor conflicts may exist. Competitors can utilize a competing sponsor's product/logo. Pro 4 Cylinder is designed for mostly unibody FWD with up to two power adders. AWDs limited to one power adder.

Body: Full stock import or compact *FWD or unibody AWD entries only*. Domestic car or truck body style must be retained in door-slammer variety. No tape can be used to join/cover body seams. Stock general profile/shape must remain, but chop tops are allowed. Stock unibody pan must remain from front seats forward. Lightweight components limited to hood, doors, front fenders, deck lid/hatch, but one-piece front ends allowed. Headlights must remain or be painted on.

Engine: Engine must be commercially available, produced in runs of 500 or more, and 4 cylinder only. Engine must be of automotive origin. Engine must be of import origin, or be offered as OE in compact cars/trucks/SUVs as sold in North America in 2001 model year or earlier only. Engine can be equipped with a turbocharger, a nitrous-oxide system, or with a supercharger, or any combination thereof, for a total of two power adders. Displacement limited to 2.7 liters maximum. *No air-cooled or rotary entries*. Engine (block) must be of same make as vehicle competing. Hondas can use Acura motors, but must have manufacturers' identification and/or manufacturer part number. Stepped deck block configurations allowed.

Cylinder heads: No billet cylinder heads allowed. Must be commercially available, produced in runs of 500 or more. Any internal modifications allowed.

Induction: Any type of intake/fuel delivery allowed, including carbs, mechanical fuel injection, custom plenums, multiple injector entry points, etc.

Transmission: Stock or aftermarket gearboxes allowed, including sequential gearboxes.

Chassis: Full tube chassis not allowed. All Cars must retain all stock flooring from back of front seats forward. Stock flooring can be removed behind front seats, in hatch area or trunk, but sheet metal must take its place in accordance with NHRA specs. No center-drive systems. Stock engine cradle must remain. Wheelie bars allowed. Stock shock towers must remain.

Class minimum weight: 1800 lbs.. FWD cars must weigh .8 lbs per cc of displacement with driver (2 power adders). AWD entries must weigh 2400 lbs. with driver.

Wheelbase: Maximum wheelbase is 105." Wheelbase must remain within +/- 2 inches of stock.

Drive line: FWD or AWD only. Stock drive line configuration must remain. Scatter shield required if 11.99 or quicker.

Exhaust: Open headers okay, except at tracks where guidelines on decibel/noise levels exist. Cars must run mufflers for Saturday racing.

Nitrous Oxide: Bottles must be stamped 1800 psi minimum. Bottles must be mounted directly to the body, utilizing all mounting points on bottle points. No external heating of bottle allowed.

Ignition System: Aftermarket crank triggers, two-step rev limiters, ignition amplifiers, spark computers, and dynamically adjustable engine-management systems are allowed. Traction control banned.

Interior: Doors must open/close from inside and outside of vehicle. No center-drive configurations.

Street Equipment: One taillight must work. Headlights must be painted on to resemble stock or have actual units installed.

Tires: No limit on tire width at this time. Absolutely no mini spare tires or non speed-rated tires may be used at any time. Cars running 11.99 must have metal valve stems. Tubes permitted.

Suspension: Must use one shock per wheel. Coil-overs allowed. Wheelie bars allowed but wheels cannot be preloaded or touch the ground at the starting line. No cockpit adjustable, trigger-switch activated, or remote wheelie bar systems allowed. Stock shock towers must remain in front.

Radiator: Electric fans/water pumps allowed. Must use overflow/catch can, 1 pint minimum.

Fuel: Gasoline only. Must meet all requirements of Section 3.33.

Other: Scatter shields will be required on *all* FWD/AWD cars running faster than 11.99 effective January 1, 2001. See General Guidelines.

License: A valid NHRA/IHRA competition license mandatory to enter this class.

PRO FWD

Class designation: P/FWD. Must show 9.99 license to enter this class.

All: All racers must meet NIRA decal requirements. Pro FWD is designed for all-out tube chassis FWD and AWD entries.

Body: Basic stock FWD or AWD import or compact domestic car or truck body shape must be retained in door-slammer variety. No tape can be used to join/cover body seams. Stock general profile/shape must remain. Lightweight components limited to hood, doors, front fenders, deck lid/hatch, but one-piece front ends allowed. Headlights must remain or be painted-on.

Engine: Engine must be commercially available, produced in runs of 500 or more, and 4 cylinder only. Engine must be of automotive origin. Engine must be of import origin, or be offered as OE in compact cars/trucks/SUVs as sold in North America in 2001 model year or earlier only. Engine can be equipped with a turbocharger, a nitrous-oxide system, or with a supercharger, or any combination thereof, for a total of two power adders. Engines limited to 2.7 liters maximum. Engines can be equipped with a turbocharger, and/or nitrous-oxide system, superchargers, or any combination thereof for *a total of 2 power adders* maximum. *No air-cooled or rotary entries allowed.* Engine (block and head) must be of same make as vehicle competing except for certain cases (i.e. Acura engine in a Honda, Mercury engine in a Ford, etc.). Stepped deck blocks allowed.

Induction: Any type of intake/fuel delivery allowed, including carbs, mechanical fuel injection, custom plenums, multiple injector entry points, etc.

Transmission: Any commercially-available transmission allowed, including sequential gearboxes. All cars must use an appropriate scatter shield in accordance with General Guidelines, which outlines methods to construct one for FWD vehicles where no commercially-available unit exists.

Chassis: Full tube chassis allowed. NO RWD entries. Center drive systems allowed.

Class minimum weight: 1500 lbs.. FWD cars must weigh .7 lbs per cc of displacement with driver. AWD entries must weigh 2100 lbs. with driver.
Wheelbase: Maximum wheelbase is 115." Cars should be within +/- 6 inches of stock wheelbase.

Drive line: FWD or AWD only. Stock drive line configuration required (i.e.: RWD cars cannot be transformed into FWD cars). AWD may be converted to FWD. Scatter shield required if 11.99 or quicker.

Cylinder Heads: No billet cylinder heads. Must have been produced in runs of 500 or more, be commercially available. Any internal modifications allowed.

Induction: Any type of intake/fuel delivery allowed, including carbs, mechanical fuel injection, custom plenums, multiple injector entry points, etc.

Nitrous Oxide: Bottles must be stamped 1800 psi minimum. Bottles must be mounted directly to the body, utilizing all mounting points on bottle points. No external heating of bottle allowed.

Exhaust: Open headers okay, except at tracks where guidelines on decibel or noise levels exist. Cars must wear mufflers for Saturday racing.

Ignition System: Aftermarket crank triggers, two-step rev limiters, ignition amplifiers, spark computers, and dynamically adjustable engine-management systems are allowed. Traction control allowed.

Interior: Doors must open/close from inside of vehicle. Center-drive configurations allowed.

Street Equipment: Headlights must be painted on or installed as original or aftermarket units. One taillight must work.

Tires: No limit on tire width at this time. Absolutely no mini spare tires or non speed-rated tires may be used at any time. Metal valve stems mandatory. Tubes permitted.

Suspension: Coil-overs allowed. Wheelie bars allowed but wheels cannot be preloaded or touch the ground at the starting line. No cockpit adjustable, trigger-switch activated, or remote wheelie bar systems allowed. No pneumatics, hydraulics, or any other active type wheelie bar setups.

Radiator: Electric water pumps okay. Electric fans allowed. Must use overflow/catch can, 1 pint minimum.

Fuel: Gasoline, alcohol, methanol, and ethanol are permitted, provided all fire suit and other safety regulations are followed. No mixing of fuels; must match manufacturer's specifications. No hydrazine, polypropylene oxide, Nitro methane, or other fuels. If gasoline is used, it must meet all requirements of Section 3.33.

Other: See General Guidelines. Scatter shields required on all FWD cars faster than 11.99 effective Jan 1., 2001.

License: A valid NHRA/IHRA competition license mandatory to enter this class.

PRO COMP

Class designation: P/C. Must show 9.99 license to enter this class.

All: All racers must meet NIRA decal requirements. Pro Comp is designed for mostly back-halved RWD vehicles.

Body: Basic import or compact domestic car or truck body style must be retained. Vehicle must be of door-slammer variety. Stock general profile must remain but chop tops or channeling allowed. FWD: Tube chassis okay. AWD: Tube chassis okay. ALL RWD entries: Stock roof, quarter panels, doors, front fenders, rocker panels must remain. Bumpers *not* required for pre-1987 entries. Lightweight components limited to hood and bumpers; no one-piece front ends.

All: Headlights must remain or be painted on to resemble stock headlights.

Engine: Engine must be commercially available and be 4/5/6 cylinder or 2/3 rotor only. Engine must be of automotive origin. Engine must be of import origin, or be offered as OE in compact cars/trucks/SUVs as sold in North America in 2001 model year or earlier only. Engine can be equipped with a turbocharger, a nitrous-oxide system, or with a supercharger, or any combination thereof, for a total of two power adders. 6-cylinder entries limited to 3.2 liters in displacement. *No air-cooled entries allowed.* Pre-87 entries with motor swaps can only select 3TC or 2 rotor powerplants. No altered mounting points for engine or set back allowed, except as defined below. Note: An engine that came naturally aspirated standard but receives a twin-turbo upgrade AND is using nitrous is said to have three power adders, not two. (All entries limited to one engine only.)

Chassis: FWD = tube chassis. AWD = tube chassis. RWD = back-halved cars only. RWD: Stock firewall should remain. Stock floor pan should remain from firewall to behind front seats. No center-drive systems allowed. Engine should be mounted in stock location. Factory frame rails must remain intact as delivered from the factory in the engine compartment. Suspension and engine can be mounted from tubing. Engines can only be moved (forward only) to accommodate scatter shield or transmission-related safety equipment.

Weight: Cars in Pro Comp must adhere to the following weight limits:

FWD:	4 Cylinder: Must weigh 1500 lbs.
AWD:	4 Cylinder: Must weigh 1900 lbs. with or without dual power adders.
RWD:	4 Cylinder: Must weigh 1850 lbs. with or without dual power adders.
FWD:	6 Cylinder: Must weigh 1900 lbs. with single/dual power adders, 1700 lbs. without.
RWD:	6 Cylinder: Minimum weight is 2500 lbs. with up to two power adders. Add 100 lbs. for G-Force, Lenco, Liberty, or other clutchless transmissions.

RWD:
Add 100 lbs. for Methanol/Alcohol. Cars with 6 sq. ft of flooring (or more) removed add 150 lbs.
3TC/2 rotor: Minimum weight is 1900 lbs. with up to two power adders. Add 100 lbs. for G-Force, Lenco, Liberty, or other clutchless transmissions. Add 100 lbs. for Methanol/Alcohol. Cars with 6 sq. ft of flooring (or more) removed add 150 lbs.

RWD:
3 rotors: Minimum weight is 2200 lbs. with up to two power adders. Add 100 lbs. for G-Force, Lenco, Liberty, or other clutchless transmissions. Add 100 lbs. for Methanol/Alcohol. Cars with more than 6 sq. ft of flooring (or more) removed add 150 lbs.

Wheelbase: Maximum wheelbase is 115" unless OEM longer. Maximum variation left to right is 1 inch.

Drive line: FWD, AWD or RWD entries allowed. Stock drive line configuration must be retained unless vehicle is a 4 cylinder that is back halved only. No sheet metal floors beyond back halving and any tubing forward of front firewall must tie into roll cage and/or stock shock towers. A 4-cylinder entry can be converted to RWD, provided engine is of same make as vehicle being used. Aftermarket transmissions and rear ends allowed. Cars running 10.99 or quicker with independent rear suspension using dual control arm setups must use a 360-degree drive shaft safety loop at least 1 inch wide by 3/8-inch thick, regardless of the weight of the vehicle.

Cylinder Heads: Must be commercially available, produced in quantities of 500 or more, and no billet heads. Any type of internal modification allowed.

Induction: Any type of intake/fuel delivery allowed, including carbs, mechanical fuel injection, custom plenums, multiple injector entry points, etc.

Nitrous Oxide: Bottles must be stamped 1800 psi minimum. Bottles must be mounted directly to the body, utilizing all mounting points on bottle points. No external heating of bottle allowed.

Transmission: Any commercially available transmission allowed.

Exhaust: Open headers okay, except at tracks where guidelines on decibel/noise levels exist. Cars must wear mufflers for Saturday racing.

Ignition System: Aftermarket crank triggers, two-step rev limiters, ignition amplifiers, spark computers, and dynamically adjustable engine-management systems are allowed.

Interior: Only one seat required. Center drive not allowed, except in FWD entries. No other street equipment required.

Street Equipment: One taillight must work. Doors must open/close from inside and outside of vehicle.

Tires: No limit on tire width at this time. Absolutely no mini spare tires or non speed-rated tires may be used at any time.

Suspension: Coil-overs allowed. Wheelie bars allowed on all cars but wheels cannot touch the ground at the starting line. Four link suspensions allowed.

Radiator: Electric water pumps okay. Electric fans allowed. Must use overflow/catch can, 1 pint minimum.

Fuel: Gasoline, alcohol, methanol, and ethanol permitted, provided all fire suit and other related safety regulations are followed. No hydrazine, propylene oxide, Nitro methane, or other fuels. If gasoline is used, it must meet all requirements of Section 3.33.

License: A valid NHRA/IHRA competition license mandatory to enter this class.

PRO Import

Class designation: P/I (9.99 and quicker only). Must show 9.99 license to enter this class.

All: All racers must meet NIRA decal requirements. All cars must meet 9.99 NHRA standards, including licenses, to be allowed on the track. Pro Import is for all-out tube framed entries. Weight restrictions depend on the powerplant.

Body: Import or compact import or domestic car or truck body style must be used. Altered wheelbase allowed. Cars should loosely resemble stock vehicles. Vehicle must be of door-slammer variety, no rails or dragster-type vehicles. Call NIRA for specific information. Body must be 1990 or newer. PRIOR to beginning construction of your project, see General Technical Guidelines. (*Examples of bodies NOT allowed: Mustang, Camaro, Intrepid family, Taurus family, Grand National, Regal family, Lumina family, Monte Carlo family, Aurora family, Catera, Corvette, Lincoln, Intrigue, Grand Prix, etc., Grand Am. Acceptable platforms include Ford Focus, Dodge Neon, Mercury Cougar, Ford Contour, Chevy Cavalier, Pontiac Sunfire, and other similar cars.*)

Engine: 4 cylinder entries: Engine must be commercially available. Engine must be of automotive origin. Engine must have come from a vehicle in the 2001 model year or earlier. Multiple power adders allowed with no weight penalty. No Fontana-style blocks. No aftermarket billet blocks. Unlimited power adders. 6 cylinder entries: Engine must be commercially available. Engine must be of automotive origin. Engine must be of import origin or be of OHC design. Engine must have come OEM from a compact car/truck or SUV (as defined by JD Power) in the 2001 model year or earlier. Engine can be equipped with a turbocharger, a nitrous-oxide system, or with a supercharger or any combination thereof, for a total of two power adders. Entries limited to 3.8 liters in displacement maximum. No billet engine blocks. See General Technical Guidelines. Dual power adders allowed with no weight penalty. All entries limited to one engine only. 8 cylinder entries: Not allowed. 2 rotor entries: Allowed in any configuration. 3 rotor entries: Allowed with weight penalty. 4 rotor entries: Not allowed.

Chassis: Reserved for full-tube chassis vehicles, or for vehicles that do not meet minimum requirements for Pro Comp. Minimum weights are as follows: (NIRA reserves the right at any point in the season to add weight in order to provide greater parity among cars in this class.)

Weight: Cars in Pro Import must adhere to the following weight limits:

FWD: 4 cylinder: Must weigh at least 1450 lbs. with unlimited power adders.

FWD: 6 cylinder: Must weigh at least 1600 lbs. with up to two power adders. Air-Cooled 4 cylinder: Must weigh at least 1500 lbs. with or without power adders.

RWD: 2 rotor: Must weigh at least 1800 lbs. with unlimited power adders.

RWD: 3 rotor: Must weigh at least 2200 lbs. with up to two power adders.

RWD: 4 cylinder: Must weigh at least 1700 lbs. with unlimited power adders.

RWD: 6 cylinder: Must weigh at least 2300 lbs. with up to two power adders.

Wheelbase: Altered wheelbase permitted but car must resemble stock vehicle. Maximum wheelbase is 122" inches.

Drive line: Stock drive train configuration NOT required. Any aftermarket transmission and rear end allowed. Cars running 10.99 or quicker with independent rear suspension using dual-control arm setups must use a 360-degree drive shaft safety loop at least 1 inch wide by 3/8-inch thick, regardless of the weight of the vehicle.

Cylinder heads: Any commercially-available cylinder head may be used. Billet heads allowed, so long as they are commercially available.

Induction: Any type of intake/fuel delivery allowed, including carbs, mechanical fuel injection, custom plenums, multiple injector entry points, etc.

Nitrous Oxide: Bottles must be stamped 1800 psi minimum. Bottles must be mounted directly to the body, utilizing all mounting points on bottle points. No external heating of bottle allowed.

Transmission: Any commercially-available transmission allowed.

Exhaust: Open headers okay, except at tracks where guidelines on decibel/noise level exist. Cars must wear mufflers for Saturday racing.

Ignition System: Aftermarket crank triggers, two-step rev limiters, ignition amplifiers, spark computers, and dynamically adjustable engine-management systems are allowed. Telemetry allowed. Data logging allowed. Any other electronics, air shifters, etc. allowed.

Interior: Can be full race. Doors must open/close from inside and outside of vehicle.

Street Equipment: None required.

Tires: No limit on tire width at this time. Absolutely no mini spare tires or non speed-rated tires may be used at any time.

Suspension: Full race suspension allowed. Wheelie bars allowed but wheels cannot touch the ground at the starting line.

Radiator: Electric water pumps okay. Electric fans allowed. Must use overflow/catch can, 1 pint minimum.

Fuel: No limit on fuel type other than NHRA guidelines. Gasoline and alcohol and other alternative fuels allowed. Equipment requirements per NHRA guidelines MUST be met in order to run alternative fuels. No Nitro methane. This includes driver apparel, fire suppression systems, firewall requirements, etc.

License: A valid NHRA/IHRA competition license mandatory to enter this class. License commensurate with car's ET required. EX: Cars running 7.50 or quicker must have a higher level of license.

IDRC Classes

Toyo Tire Street Class

The IDRC Street Class pioneered by *Sport Compact Car* magazine requires all cars run on performance radials, through the mufflers, and carry current registrations. This IDRC class gives the local "Kings of the Street" a chance to become national heroes.

All vehicles in this class maintain the factory chassis construction. To date, no one has broken the 9-second barrier in competition. Competitive cars currently run in the 10s and 11s at sea-level tracks. The race is on to see if and when it will be possible for a Street Class car to dip into the 9s.

For fair and entertaining competition, the Street class (along with all IDRC heads-up classes) runs a .400 Pro Tree along with a Sportsman-type ladder during the elimination rounds. All events are run in single-elimination fashion. Red lights result in automatic disqualification, as does crossing the centerline.

Fields will be made up of the 8 or 16 quickest competitors from the qualifying rounds. No make-up runs will be permitted for racers who miss their qualifying round. If a qualifier elects not to compete or is unable to make the last call to the staging lanes, the next available alternate will be selected until a full field of 8 or 16 is present.

All Quick class vehicles must pass the safety tech inspection issued by the track. Most tracks follow NHRA or IHRA safety regulations. The safety inspection is separate from the IDRC class qualification inspection that will precede or follow the tech inspection. Vehicles will only be eligible after passing safety inspection and being classified as eligible Quick class vehicles.

It is the driver's responsibility to make sure the vehicle meets weight requirements. Vehicles will be weighed after each qualifying and elimination round. Vehicles not making minimum weight will be disqualified during elimination rounds or will have their run made void during qualifying. All vehicles must reach scales under their own power. No support vehicle may assist before the scales.

Eligibility: All vehicles must pay racer entry fee. The racer on the tech card for the vehicle must also be the driver. Additional drivers will pay full race entry fee and must notify officials that there will be two drivers. The driver who qualifies a vehicle must also be the driver in elimination rounds.

Registration: All Street class cars must be currently registered.

Engine : Only one internal-combustion gasoline engine permitted in vehicle. Engine manufacturer must match vehicle chassis manufacturer. Brother company substitutions are allowed, such as Lexus/Toyota, Nissan/Infiniti, Honda/Acura. Domestic manufactured vehicles (Ford, GM, Chrysler) are limited to four-cylinder engines. Engine must be located and configured in OEM location. Setting engine forward or back is allowable when and only when modified engine mounts attach to factory mounts on the frame or cross member. Changing engine from transverse configuration to conventional is not allowed. Engine

type (number of cylinders) and the number of power adders will establish minimum weight breaks along with drive configuration (FWD, RWD, AWD).

Power Adders: Engines may be equipped with up to two power adders. Power adders include nitrous-oxide-injection systems, turbocharger systems, and supercharger systems. Redundant power adders such as twin-turbochargers or multi-stage, nitrous-oxide systems count as a single-power adder. Thus, a twin-turbo engine using a three-stage nitrous system would still count as only two power adders.

Intercoolers, cool cans for fuel systems, and compressed-nitrogen gas systems used to cool the intercooler are not counted as power adders. Any compressed gas used on the vehicle is subject to inspection. If found to be an oxide (like nitrous oxide), it will be counted as a power adder.

Exhaust: All Street class vehicles must run at least one muffler with an exhaust system that exits behind the rear wheels.

Fuel: All vehicles must run on gasoline. Pump and racing gasoline are acceptable. Gasoline may not have Nitro methane, propylene oxide, or Nitro propane added. All fuels are subject to testing by IDRC officials.

Transmissions — FWD: Any transmission allowed. Clutchless, pro-shifted, and sequential transmissions subject to 150-pound weight penalty.

Transmissions — RWD/AWD: Standard transmissions must retain H-pattern. Standard transmissions must also allow downshifting (example: a G-Force transmission would not be legal for this class). Air shifters are also illegal. No aftermarket sequential transmissions will be allowed. Clutchless and pro-shifted standard transmissions are not legal. Non-OEM transmission replacements are subject to a 100-pound weight penalty. Examples would include a Chevy Power glide in a Toyota Supra.

Chassis, All Basic: All Street class vehicles must be an import chassis with functional doors, barring the following exceptions. Exceptions will be made for domestic-labeled, joint-manufactured vehicles that have a USA-available, import counterpart. Examples include but are not limited to: Chrysler Conquest, Dodge Colt, Dodge Stealth, Eagle Talon, Ford Probe, Mercury Capri XR2, and Plymouth Laser. Additionally, any front-wheel-drive, four-cylinder-powered vehicle from any manufacturer (including Domestics — Chevy, Chrysler, Ford) is legal for competition.

All Street class vehicles must retain factory chassis. Vehicles original built with a front-wheel-drive configuration must maintain front-wheel-drive configuration. No rear-wheel-drive conversions are permitted. Chop tops are permitted.

Glass: All Street class vehicles must maintain the factory glass in all locations.

Suspension & Chassis — FWD:

Front: Wheel tubs are not permitted. Upper mounting point for strut assemblies must be in factory location. Further, the entire reinforced portion of the shock tower member must be retained. This would include the entire portion that is welded to the unibody frame. Top of strut assembly must mount to top of strut/shock tower, as did the factory unit. Adjustable caster/camber pillow ball mounts are acceptable. Lower control arms may be strengthened and altered providing that factory mounting at frame is not changed in location. Lower mounting point for strut may be modified for improved caster or camber. Strut tower braces, lower tie bars, sway bars, and limit straps are permitted.

Rear: The entire frame structure must remain in rear. Factory independent rear suspensions must maintain independent configuration. Upper mounting point for strut assemblies must be in factory location. Further, the entire reinforced portion of the shock tower member must be retained. This would include the entire portion that is welded to the unibody frame. Top of strut assembly must mount to top of strut/shock tower, as did the factory unit. Adjustable caster/camber pillow ball mounts are acceptable. Lower control arms may be strengthened and altered. Lower factory mounting at frame may be changed. Lower mounting point for strut may be modified for improved caster or camber. Strut tower braces, lower tie bars, sway bars, and limit straps are permitted.

Suspension & Chassis — RWD/AWD

Front: Upper mounting point for strut assemblies must be in factory location. Further, the entire reinforced portion of the shock tower member must be retained. This would include the entire portion that is welded to the unibody frame. Top of strut assembly must mount to top of strut/shock tower as did the factory unit. Adjustable caster/camber pillow ball mounts are acceptable. Lower control arms may be strengthened and altered providing that factory mounting at frame is not changed in location. Lower mounting point for strut may be modified for improved caster or camber. Strut tower braces, lower tie bars, and limit straps are permitted.

Rear: Retention of the OEM rear end is encouraged. If rear end from a different manufacturer is used, a weight penalty of 100 pounds will be assessed to minimum weight requirements. Back-half conversions and tube-chassis configurations are not permitted. Wheel tubs are also not permitted. For vehicles weighing over 2000 pounds that

are factory equipped with an Independent Rear Suspension (IRS) and running quicker than 10.99, solid-axle rear conversions are permitted as long as the factory wheel wells (both inner and outer) are not modified in any way. Strut tower braces, lower tie bars, sway bars, and limit straps are permitted. Rear suspension must maintain a minimum of 1 inch of travel. All rear suspensions must use at least one hydraulic shock per wheel. Wheelie bars must be detachable.

Tires: All Street class vehicles must use D.O.T. radial tires. Tires must measure less than 10.5 inches in tread width, not in section width. Maximum tire height is 28 inches. No slicks allowed.

Wheelie Bars: No wheelie bars are allowed.

Minimum Weight Requirements (Driver and Car):

	4cyl/2r	5cyl	6cyl/3r	8cyl/4r
Cylinders/Rotors				
FWD (0 power adders)	1700	1800	1900	2200
FWD (Nitrous Only)	1800	1900	2000	2300
FWD (1 power adder)	1900	2000	2100	2400
FWD (2 power adders)	2100	2200	2300	2600
RWD (0 power adders)	2100	2250	2400	2800
RWD (Nitrous Only)	2300	2450	2600	2900
RWD (1 power adder)	2400	2550	2700	3000
RWD (2 power adders)	2600	2750	2900	3200
AWD (0 power adders)	2100	2250	2400	2800
AWD (Nitrous Only)	2300	2450	2600	2900
AWD (1 power adder)	2400	2550	2700	3000
AWD (2 power adders)	2600	2750	2900	3200

Weight Penalties:
Non-OEM rear end +100 pounds
Aftermarket Transmission +100 pounds
FWD Sequential Transmission +150 pounds

Nitto Tire Turbo Magazine Quick Class

The original "heads-up" import drag racing class continues to be the sport's most popular. Pioneered by *Turbo* magazine, this class has evolved to present leading-edge technologies while

still maintaining its original purpose — to showcase the performance available from today's production compacts. All vehicles in this class maintain the factory chassis construction. The highly developed Quick class rules allow many different makes and models to be competitive in the same class. This allows for manufacturer rivalries, as well as the constant front-wheel-drive versus rear-wheel-drive showdowns. Competitive cars currently run in the 9s or 10s at sea-level tracks. The race is on to see if and when it will be possible for a Quick class car to dip into the 8s.

For fair and entertaining competition, the Quick class (along with all IDRC heads-up classes) runs a .400 Pro Tree along with a Sportsman-type ladder during the elimination rounds. All events are run in single-elimination fashion. Red lights result in automatic disqualification, as does crossing the centerline.

Fields will be made up of the 8 or 16 quickest competitors from the qualifying rounds. No make-up runs will be permitted for racers who miss their qualifying round. If a qualifier elects not to compete or is unable to make the last call to the staging lanes, the next available alternate will be selected until a full field of 8 or 16 is present.

Eligibility: All vehicles must pay racer entry fee. The racer on the tech card for the vehicle must also be the driver. Additional drivers will pay full race entry fee and must notify officials that there will be two drivers. The driver who qualifies a vehicle must also be the driver in elimination rounds.

All Quick class vehicles must pass the safety tech inspection issued by the track. Most tracks follow NHRA or IHRA safety regulations. The safety inspection is separate from the IDRC class qualification inspection that will precede or follow the tech inspection. Vehicles will only be eligible after passing safety inspection and being classified as eligible Quick class vehicles.

It is the driver's responsibility to make sure the vehicle meets weight requirements. Vehicles will be weighed after each qualifying and elimination round. Vehicles not making minimum weight will be disqualified during elimination rounds or will have their run made void during qualifying. All vehicles must reach scales under their own power. No support vehicle may assist before the scales.

Engine: Only one internal-combustion gasoline engine permitted in vehicle. Engine manufacturer must match vehicle chassis manufacturer. Brother company substitutions are allowed, such as Honda/Acura, Lexus/Toyota, or Nissan/Infiniti. Domestic manufactured vehicles (Ford, GM, Chrysler) are limited to four-cylinder engines. Engine must be located and configured in OEM location. Setting engine forward or back is allowable when and only when modified engine mounts attach to factory mounts on the frame or cross member. Changing engine from transverse configuration to conventional is not allowed. Engine type (number of cylinders) and the number of power adders will establish minimum weight breaks along with drive configuration (FWD, RWD, AWD).

Power Adders: Engines may be equipped with up to two power adders. Power adders include nitrous-oxide-injection systems, turbocharger systems, and supercharger systems. Redundant power adders such as twin-turbochargers or multi-stage, nitrous-oxide systems count as a single power adder. Thus, a twin-turbo engine using a three-stage nitrous system would still count as only two power adders.

Intercoolers, cool cans for fuel systems, and compressed-nitrogen gas systems used to cool the intercooler are not counted as power adders. Any compressed gas used on the vehicle is subject to inspection. If found to be an oxide (like nitrous oxide), it will be counted as a power adder.

Fuel: All vehicles must run on gasoline. Pump and racing gasoline are acceptable. Gasoline may not have Nitro methane, propylene oxide, or Nitro propane added. All fuels are subject to testing by IDRC officials.

Transmissions — FWD: Any transmission allowed. Clutchless, pro-shifted, and sequential transmissions subject to 150-pound weight penalty.

Transmissions — RWD/AWD: Standard transmissions must retain H-pattern. Standard transmissions must also allow downshifting (example: a G-Force transmission would not be legal for this class). Air shifters are also illegal. No aftermarket sequential transmissions will be allowed. Clutchless and pro-shifted standard transmissions are not legal. Non-OEM transmission replacements are subject to a 100-pound weight penalty. Examples would include a Chevy Power glide in a Toyota Supra.

Chassis — All Basic: All Quick class vehicles must be an import chassis with functional doors, barring the following exceptions. Exceptions will be made for domestic-labeled, joint-manufactured vehicles that have a USA-available, import counterpart. Examples include but are not limited to: Chrysler Conquest, Dodge Colt, Dodge Stealth, Eagle Talon, Ford Probe, Mercury Capri XR2, and Plymouth Laser. Additionally, any front-wheel-drive, four-cylinder-powered vehicle from any manufacturer (including Domestics — Chevy, Chrysler, Ford) is legal for competition.

All Quick class vehicles must retain factory chassis. Vehicles originally built with a front-wheel-drive configuration must maintain front-wheel-drive configuration. No rear-wheel-drive conversions are permitted. Chop tops are permitted.

Suspension & Chassis — FWD:
Front: Wheel tubs are not permitted. Upper mounting point for strut assemblies must be in factory location. Further, the entire reinforced portion of the shock tower member must be retained. This would include the entire portion that is welded to the unibody frame. Top of strut assembly must mount to top of strut/shock tower, as did the factory unit. Adjustable caster/camber pillow ball mounts are acceptable. Lower control arms may be strengthened and altered providing that factory mounting at frame is not changed in location. Lower mounting point for strut may be modified for improved caster or camber. Strut tower braces, lower tie bars, sway bars, and limit straps are permitted.

Rear: The entire frame structure must remain in rear. Factory independent rear suspensions must maintain independent configuration. Upper mounting point for strut assemblies must be in factory location. Further, the entire reinforced portion of the shock tower member must be retained. This would include the entire portion that is welded to the unibody frame. Top of strut assembly must mount to top of strut/shock tower, as did the factory unit. Adjustable caster/camber pillow ball mounts are acceptable. Lower control arms may be strengthened and altered. Lower factory mounting at frame may be changed. Lower mounting point for strut may be modified for improved caster or camber. Strut tower braces, lower tie bars, sway bars, and limit straps are permitted.

Suspension & Chassis — RWD/AWD:
Front: Upper mounting point for strut assemblies must be in factory location. Further, the entire reinforced portion of the shock tower member must be retained. This would include the entire portion that is welded to the unibody frame. Top of strut assembly must mount to top of strut/shock tower as did the factory unit. Adjustable caster/camber pillow ball mounts are acceptable. Lower control arms may be strengthened and altered providing that factory mounting at frame is not changed in location. Lower mounting point for strut may be modified for improved caster or camber. Strut tower braces, lower tie bars, sway bars, and limit straps are permitted.

Rear: Retention of the OEM rear end is encouraged. If rear end from a different manufacturer is used, a weight penalty of 100 pounds will be assessed to minimum weight requirements. Back-half conversions and tube chassis configurations are not permitted. Wheel tubs are also not permitted. For vehicles weighing over 2000 pounds that are factory equipped with an Independent Rear Suspension (IRS) and running quicker than 10.99, solid-axle rear conversions are permitted as long as the factory wheel wells (both inner and outer) are not modified in any way. Strut tower braces, lower tie bars, sway bars, and limit straps are permitted. Rear suspension must maintain a minimum of 1

inch of travel. All rear suspensions must use at least one hydraulic shock per wheel. Wheelie bars must be detachable.

Tires: All Quick class vehicles may use racing slicks or D.O.T. tires, provided specified tread width is no more than 10.5 inches on slicks. D.O.T. tires must measure less than 10.5 inches in tread width, not in section width. Maximum tire height is 28 inches.

Wheelie Bars: No wheelie bars may be preloaded. The IDRC recommends a minimum 1/2-inch clearance when measured on a flat plane. Wheels are subject to inspection by starting line officials following the burnout. All wheels must be able to spin freely when checked. No mechanisms of any type may be employed to alter the height, clearance, or geometry of the wheelie bar during the run. All wheelie bars must be detachable.

Minimum Weight Requirements (Driver and Car)

	Cylinders/Rotors		
4cyl/2r	5cyl	6cyl/3r	8cyl/4r
FWD (0 power adders)			
1700	1800	1900	2200
FWD (Nitrous Only)			
1800	1900	2000	2300
FWD (1 power adder)			
1900	2000	2100	2400
FWD (2 power adders)			
2100	2200	2300	2600
RWD (0 power adders)			
2100	2250	2400	2800
RWD (Nitrous Only)			
2300	2450	2600	2900
RWD (1 power adder)			
2400	2550	2700	3000
RWD (2 power adders)			
2600	2750	2900	3200
AWD (0 power adders)			
2100	2250	2400	2800
AWD (Nitrous Only)			
2300	2450	2600	2900
AWD (1 power adder)			
2400	2550	2700	3000
AWD (2 power adders)			
2600	2750	2900	3200

Weight Penalties
Non-OEM rear end +100 pounds
Aftermarket Transmission +100 pounds
FWD Sequential Transmission +150 pounds

A'PEXi Outlaw Class

As many Quick class racers have wanted to go beyond what the Quick class rules allow, the Outlaw class was developed to support these racers. Today, this class is arguably the most popular with the crowds as it has produced some of the biggest names in import drag racing, such as Saruwatari, Papadakis, Buschur, and Paisley. Today, the Outlaw class features some great rivalries between the full-tube frame, front-wheel-drive vehicles and the back-halved, rear-wheel drives. The current class record stands at 8.13 and most competitors run deep into the 8s. The race is on to see if and when it will be possible for a Outlaw Class car to dip into the 7s.

For fair and entertaining competition, the Outlaw class (along with all IDRC heads-up classes) runs a .400 Pro Tree along with a Sportsman-type ladder during the elimination rounds. All events are run in single-elimination fashion. Red lights result in automatic disqualification as does crossing the centerline.

Fields will be made up of the 8 quickest competitors from the qualifying rounds. No make-up runs will be permitted for racers who miss their qualifying round. If a qualifier elects not to compete or is unable to make the last call to the staging lanes, the next available alternate will be selected until a full field of 8 is present.

Eligibility: All vehicles must pay racer entry fee. The racer on the tech card for the vehicle must also be the driver. Additional drivers will pay full race entry fee and must notify officials that there will be two drivers. The driver who qualifies a vehicle must also be the driver in elimination rounds.

All Outlaw class vehicles must pass the safety tech inspection issued by the track. Most tracks follow NHRA or IHRA safety regulations. The safety inspection is separate from the IDRC class qualification inspection that will precede or follow the tech inspection. Vehicles will only be eligible after passing safety inspection and being classified as eligible Outlaw class vehicles.

It is the driver's responsibility to make sure the vehicle meets weight requirements. Vehicles will be weighed after each qualifying and elimination round. Vehicles not making minimum weight will be disqualified during elimination rounds or will have their run made void during qualifying. All vehicles must reach scales under their own power. No support vehicle may assist before the scales.

Engine: Only one internal-combustion gasoline engine permitted in vehicle. Domestic manufactured vehicles (Ford, GM, Chrysler) are limited to four-cylinder engines. Changing engine from transverse configuration to conventional is allowed. Front-wheel-drive to rear-wheel-drive conversions are permitted. Engine type (number of cylinders) and the number of power adders will establish minimum weight breaks along with drive configuration (FWD, RWD, AWD).

Power Adders: Engines may be equipped with up to two power adders. Power adders include nitrous-oxide-injection systems, turbocharger systems, and supercharger systems. Redundant power adders such as twin-turbochargers or multi-stage, nitrous-oxide systems count as a single power adder. Thus, a twin-turbo engine using a three-stage nitrous system would still count as only two power adders.

Intercoolers, cool cans for fuel systems, and compressed-nitrogen gas systems used to cool the intercooler are not counted as power adders. Any compressed gas used on the vehicle is subject to inspection. If found to be an oxide (i.e. nitrous oxide), it will be counted as a power adder.

Fuel: All vehicles must run on gasoline or alcohol. Pump and racing gasoline are acceptable. Gasoline may not have Nitro methane, propylene oxide, or Nitro propane added. All fuels are subject to testing by IDRC officials.

Transmissions — FWD: Any transmission allowed.

Transmissions — RWD/AWD: Any transmission allowed.

Chassis — All Basic: All Outlaw class vehicles must be an import chassis with functional doors, barring the following exceptions. Exceptions will be made for domestic-labeled, joint-manufactured vehicles that have a USA-available, import counterpart. Examples include but are not limited to: Chrysler Conquest, Dodge Colt, Dodge Stealth, Eagle Talon, Ford Probe, Mercury Capri XR2, and Plymouth Laser. Additionally, any front-wheel-drive, four-cylinder-powered vehicle from any manufacturer (including Domestics — Chevy, Chrysler, Ford) is legal for competition. Chop tops are permitted.

Chassis — FWD: Full-tube-frame vehicles are permitted. Any chassis modifications allowed as long as car remains front wheel drive.

Chassis — RWD/AWD: No full-tube-frame, rear-wheel-drive or all-wheel-drive vehicles are permitted. Vehicles may have a tube or boxed-style back-half conversion. Front of vehicle may use aftermarket struts. Factory firewall, A-pillars, and rocker panels must be maintained.

Tires: Unlimited.

Wheelie Bars: No wheelie bars may be preloaded. The IDRC recommends a minimum 1/2-inch clearance when measured on a flat plane. Wheels are subject to inspection by starting line officials following the burnout. All wheels must be able to spin freely when checked. No mechanisms of any type may be employed to alter the height, clearance, or geometry of the wheelie bar during the run. All wheelie bars must be detachable.

Minimum Weight Requirements (Driver and Car)

	Cylinders/Rotors		
4cyl/2r	5cyl	6cyl/3r	8cyl/4r
FWD (0 power adders)			
1400	1550	1700	2000
FWD (Nitrous Only)			
1500	1650	1800	2100
FWD (1 power adder)			
1600	1750	1900	2200
FWD (2 power adders)			
1700	1850	2000	2300
RWD (0 power adders)			
1700	1850	2000	2400
RWD (Nitrous Only)			
1900	2050	2200	2600
RWD (1 power adder)			
2000	2150	2300	2700
RWD (2 power adders)			
2200	2350	2500	2900
AWD (0 power adders)			
1700	1850	2000	2400
AWD (Nitrous Only)			
1900	2050	2200	2600
AWD (1 power adder)			
2000	2150	2300	2700
AWD (2 power adders)			
2200	2350	2500	2900

JE Pistons Pro Class

This class is currently open to all Pro Import door slammers running 9.49 or quicker. All cars must be full-tube-frame design. There are no restrictions on fuel or number of power adders. Engines must be from an import manufacturer; 4-cylinder domestic engines are allowed. As this class grows, additional regulations will be instituted to assure proper growth and fair competition.

NITROUS SOURCE GUIDE

A.1 TURBO Industry Inc.
Turbo Cars, Parts, & Accessories
2621 Pico Boulevard, Unit G
Santa Monica, California 90405
Ph: 310-827-4800
Fax: 310-828-2070
Toll Free: 800-535-8872
email: a1turbo@hotmail.com

Accel
Mr. Gasket Co.,
10601 Memphis Avenue , #12
Cleveland, OH 44144

Advanced Clutch Technology
P.O. Box 93425
Palmdale, CA. 93590-3425
Ph: 661-947-7791
Fax: 661-947-5998
sales@advancedclutch.com

Advanced Engine Management
2205 126th Street, Unit A
Hawthorne, CA 90250
Ph: 310-484-2322
Fax: 310-484-0152

Aeroquip Industrial Group
Performance Products Division
P.O. Box 700
Maumee, OH 43537-0700
Ph: 419-891-5100
Fax: 419-891-5159
www.aeroquip.com

Apex Integration Inc.
17091 Daimler Street
Irvine, CA 92614
Ph: 949-224-1680
Fax: 949-224-1681
www.apexi.usa.com

Applied Technologies & Research, Inc.
17040 S. Highway 11
Fair Play, SC 29643
Ph: 864-972-3800

AEROCHARGER Turbo Systems
Division of Aerodyne Corporation
8 Apollo Drive
Batavia, NY 14020
Ph: 716-345-0055
Fax: 716-344-5623
www.aerocharger.com

ARP Automotive Racing Products.
531 Spectrum Circle
Oxnard, CA 93030
Ph: 805-278-7223
www.arp.bolts.com

ATK Engines
3210 S Croddy Way
Santa Ana, CA 92704
email: sales@atkengines.com
email: custserv@atkengines.com

Borla
5901 Edison Dr.
Oxnard, CA 93033
Ph: 877-Go-Borla
www.borla.com

Bosal USA, Inc.,
14 Troy Hills Road,
Whippany, NJ 07981
Ph: 800. –631-7271
Fax: 973-428-8856
www.bosalusa.com

Blitz Performance Products
4879 E. La Palma Avenue Suite 206
Anahiem, CA 92807
Ph: 714-777-9766
Fax: 714-777-9763

B&M Racing and Performance Products
9142 Independence Avenue
Chatsworth, CA 91311
Ph: 818-882-6422
Fax: 818-882-6694

Baer Racing
3108 W. Thomas Road
Suite 1201Q
Phoenix, AZ 85017
Ph: 602-233-1411
Fax: 602-352-8445
email: brakes@baer.com
www.baeracing.com

Brakeman
2455 Blanchard Road
Camarillo, CA 92012
Ph: 805 491-2185
email: brakeman@hotmail.com

BREMBO North America
1585 Sunflower Avenue,
Costa Mesa, CA 92626
Ph: 714-641-0104
Fax: 714-641-5827

Buschur Racing
24 W. Main Street
Wakeman, OH 44889
Ph: 440-839-1900
Fax: 440-839-5088

Carrera Shocks
5412 New Peachtree Road
Atlanta, GA 30341
Tech Support: 770-451-8811
Orders only, 24-hr recorder: 800-RACE-4-IT
Fax: 770-451-8086

Clutch Masters High Performance Center
1330 Glassell, Unit N
Orange, CA 92867
Ph: 714-288-8811
Fax: 714-288-9093

East Coast
217.85 98th Avenue
Queens Village
New York NY 11428
Ph: 718-217-0139
Fax: 718-217-0894

Comptech USA
4717 Golden Foothill Parkway
El Dorado Hills, CA 95762
Ph: 916-939-9118
Fax: 916-939-9196

Cone Engineering
10883 Portal Drive,
Los Alamitos, CA 90720
Ph: 714-828-8728
Fax: 714-828-6942

Crane Cams, Inc.
530 Fentress Blvd.
Daytona Beach, FL 32114
Ph: 904-252-1151
Tech Support: 904-258-6174
Fax: 904-258-6167

CROWER CAMS & EQUIPMENT CO., Inc.
3333 Main Street
Chula Vista, CA 91911-5899
Ph: 619-422-1191
Fax: 619-422-9067

Cunningham Rods
550 W. 172nd Street
Gardena, CA 90248
Ph: 310-538-0605
Fax: 310-538-0695
email: staff@cunninghamrods.com

DC Sports
286 Winfield Circle
Corona, CA 91720
Ph: 909-734-2030
Fax: 909-734-2792

Dinan
150 South Whisman
Mountain View, CA 94041
Ph: 650-962-9401
www.dinanbmw.com

Drag Performance Products
Ph: 323-721-9689

Dunrite Converters
4509 Shirley Avenue, Unit B
El Monte, CA 91731
Ph: 626-442-1404

EFI Systems, Inc.
3790 Highway 92, Suite 210
Acworth, GA 30102
Ph: 770-529-3202
Fax: 770-529-3203

Electromotive, Inc.
9131 Centreville Road ,
Manassas, Virginia 20110
Ph: 703-331-0100
Fax: 703-331-0161

Elf Race Fuel
Competition Fuels Inc.
304 Gasoline Alley, Suite D
Indianapolis, IN 46222
Toll Free: 800-ELF-FUEL

Earl's
189 West Victoria Street
Long Beach, CA 90805
Ph: 310-609-1602

Product Sales / Support
Evans Cooling Systems
P.O. Box 434
Parkerford, PA 19457-0434
Tech Support: 610-323-3114
Toll Free: 888-990-2665
Ph: 610-970-0286
email: ecs@evanscooling.com

Evans Engineering Center
253 Route 41 North
Sharon, CT 06069
Fax: 860-364-0888
email: webmaster@evanscooling.com

EXTRUDEHONE corporation
1 Industry Boulevard
P.O. Box 1000,
Irwin, PA 15642
Ph: 724-863-5900
Fax: 724-863-8759
Toll Free: 800-367-1109
email: exhone@extrudehone.com

Flex.a.lite
P.O. Box 580
Milton, WA 98354
Ph: 253-922-2700
Fax: 253-922-0226
Toll Free: 800-851-1510

F&L Co., Inc.
1537 E. Del Amo Boulevard
Carson, CA 90746
Ph: 310-603-2200
Fax: 310-603-2257

Fidanza Flywheels
4285 Main Street
Perry, Ohio 44081
Ph: 440-259-5656
Fax: 440-259-5588

Flowtech division of Holley
AIRMASSExtreme Exhaust Systems
2605 West First Street
Tempe, AZ 85281
Ph: 480-966-1511
Fax: 480-966-1197
email: info@airmassexhauStreetcom

Fuel Safe Systems
C/O Aircraft Rubber Manufacturing, Inc.
63257 Nels Anderson Road
Bend, OR 97701
Ph: 541-388-0203
Fax: 541-388-0307
www.fuelsafe.com

G.Force Engineering
2311 West 205th Street, Suite 102
Torrance, CA 90501
Ph: 323-585-2852
Fax: 323-587-0119
Toll Free: 800-262-6267

Goodridge USA Inc.
20309 Gramercy Pl.
Torrance, CA 90501
Toll Free: 800-662-2466
Fax: 310-618-0909
www.goodridge.uk.com

Greddy Performance Products
9 Vanderbilt
Irvine, CA 92718
Ph: 949-588-8300
Fax: 949-588-6318
www.GReddy.com

Gude Performance
28780 Vacation Drive
Canyon Lake, CA 92587
Ph: 909-244-3533
sales@gude.com

HAHN RaceCraft
1981 D Weisbrook Drive
Oswego, IL 60543
Ph: 630-801-1417
Fax: 253-830-7558
email: sales@turbosystem.com

HASport Performance/Honda Auto Salvage
4039 E Winslow
Phoenix, AZ 85040
Ph: 602-470-0065 (HASport Performance)
Ph: 602-470-0789 (Honda Auto Salvage)

HKS USA Inc.
2801 East 208th Avenue
Carson, CA 90810-1102

Holley Tech Service,
P.O. Box 10360,
Bowling Green, KY 42102-7360.
Ph: 270-781-9741.
email: help@support.holley.com.
www.holley.com

Hypertech, Inc.
3215 Appling Road
Bartlett, TN 38133
Ph: 901-382-8888
email: techsupport@hypertech.inc.com.
email: sales@hypertech.inc.com

HPC West
Corporate Headquarters.
550 W. 3615 S.
Salt Lake City, UT 84115
Ph: 801-262-6807
Fax: 801-262-6307

HPC Central
400 N. Glade Avenue
Oklahoma City, OK 73127
Ph: 405-789-2888
Fax: 405-789-2885

HPC Southwest
6313 W. Commonwealth Place
Chandler, AZ 85226
Ph: 480-753-1320
Fax: 480-753-1329

HPC Queensland
Lot 45 Strathwyn
Brendale 4500, Queensland
Australia
Ph: 61-7-3881-0885
Fax: 61-7-3881-0887

HPC Victoria
6 Watson Road Industrial Park
Leongatha, 3953 Victoria
Australia
Ph: 61-0-3566-24719
Fax: 61-0-3566-24719

HPC New Zealand
Unit O
62 Mahia Road
Manurewa
New Zealand
Ph: 64-9-267-1007
Fax: 64-9-266-3388

Hose Techniques (US)
1603 Border Avenue,
Torrance, CA 90501
Toll Free: 888-999-2817
Order Line: 310-320-2660
Tech Line: 310-328-2800
Fax: 310-533-7077
email: hosetech@pacbell.net

HoseTechniques (Japan)
HPS HoseTechniques Japan
39.9 Izumi, 1 Chome
Suginami.ku
Tokyo, Japan 168-0062
Ph: 03-3322-8888
Fax: 03-3324-7566

Iceman Cool Air Intakes
Knight Engineering
45322 North Trevor Avenue
Lancaster, Ca 93534
Ph: 661-940-1215
Fax: 661-940-1217

Ingalls Engineering Co.
34 Boston Court
Longmont, CO 80501
Ph: 303-651-1297
Fax: 303-651-1298
Toll Free: 800-641-9795

JE Pistons
15312 Connector Lane
Huntington Beach, CA. 92649
Ph: 714-898-9763
Fax: 714-893-8297

JG Engine Dynamics
431 S. Raymond Avenue
Alhambra, CA 91803
Ph: 626-281-5326

Jackson Racing
7281 Westminster Avenue
Westminster, CA 92683
Ph: 714-891-1113
Fax: 714-895-6873

Jackson Racing Superchargers
440 Rutherford Street
Goleta, CA 93117
Ph: 888-888-4079
Fax: 805-692-2523

Honda /Acura Service & Installations
7281 Westminster Avenue
Westminster, CA 92683
Ph: 714-891-1113
Fax: 714-895-6873

Jacobs Electronics
500 North Baird Street
Midland, Texas 79701
Ph: 800-627-8800
Toll Free: 800-825-3345

Johnny Mac Motor Sports Inc.
4220 E. River Road
Dayton, OH 45439.1459
Ph: 937-298-2856
Fax: 937-298-2876

JET.HOT
Corporate Headquarters
55 East Front Street
Bridgeport, PA 19405
Toll Free: 800-432-3379
Ph: 610-277-5646

JET.HOT (South)
5602 Orchard Road
Pascagoula, MS 39581

JET.HOT (West)
1840 West Drake Drive
Tempe, AZ 85283

JET Performance Products
17491 Apex Circle
Huntington Beach, CA 92647
Ph: 714-848-5515
Fax: 714-847-6290
email: Sales@JetChip.com

K&N Engineering Inc.
561 Iowa Avenue
P.O. Box 1329
Riverside, CA 92502-1329
Ph: 800-858-3333
Fax: 909-684-9060
www.knfilters.com

Kaaz Limited Slip Differentials
935.A Sunset Drive
Costa Mesa, California 92627
Ph: 949-631-0990,
Fax: 949-631-0909
email: newportcars@kaazusa.com
www.kaazusa.com

Kirk Racing Products
1433 Montgomery Highway
Birmingham, AL 35216
Ph: 205-823-6025
Fax: 205-823-6550
email: info@kirkracing.com

Knight Engineering
45322 North Trevor Avenue
Lancaster, CA 93534
Ph: 661-940-1215
Fax: 661-940-1217

LC ENGINEERING, Inc.
1880.B Commander Drive
Lake Havasu City, AZ 86403
Ph: 520-505-2501
Fax: 520-505-2503
email: dave@lcengineering.com

Lightspeed Racing
6644 San Fernando Road
Glendale CA 91201
Ph: 800-624-7223
Fax: 818-956-5160
email: Info@LightspeedRacing.com

Magnecor
2550 Oakley Park Road, Suite 200
Walled Lake, MI 48390
Ph: 248-669-6688
Fax: 248-669-2994
www.magnecor.com

Majestic TurboChargers, Inc.
Waco, Texas
Toll Free: 800-231-5566

Mackin Industries
Importer of Tanabe components
9921 Jordan Circle
Santa Fe Springs, CA 90670
Ph: 562-946-6820
Fax: 562-944-7719

Malvern Racing
271 Malvern Farm Dr.
Charlottesville, VA 22903
Ph: 804-971-9668
Fax: 804-971-5652

Mugen Co. Ltd.
2.15.11 Hizaori.cho, Asaka.shi
Saitama 351-8586, Japan
Ph: 0-48-462-3111
Fax: 0-48-462-3100
www.mugen.honda.co.jp

Mugen North American distributor:
King Motorsports Unlimited
105 E. Main Street
Sullivan, WI 53178
Ph: 414-593-2800
Fax: 414-593-2627

MazdaTrix
2730 Gundry Avenue
Signal Hill, CA 90806
Ph: 562-426-7960
Service, Parts: 562-426-4460
Fax: 562-426-9646

Moroso
80 Carter Drive
P.O. Box 1470
Guilford CT 06437-0570
Ph: 203-453-6571
Tech Line: 203-458-0542

Marren Motor Sports, Inc.
49 Burtville Avenue, Unit 3A
Derby, CT 06418
Ph: 203-732-4565

Neuspeed/Neumann Distributing
3300 Corte Malpaso
Camarillo, CA 93012
Ph: 805-388-8111
Fax: 805-388-0030

Nitrous Express
4623 Lake Park Drive
Wichita Falls, TX 76302
Ph: 888-463-2781
Fax: 940-767-7697

Nitrous Works
1450 McDonald Road
Dahlonega, GA 30533
Ph: 706-864-8544
Fax: 706-864-2206

NOS
2970 Airway Avenue
Costa Mesa, CA 92626
Ph: 714-545-0580
Fax: 714-545-8319
Tech Line 714-546-0592
email: nosinc@earthlink.net

Optima Batteries Inc.
17500 East 22nd Avenue
Aurora, Colorado 80011
Ph: 303-340-7440
Fax: 303-340-7474
Toll Free: 888-867-8462

Pacesetter Performance Products
2841 W. Clarendon Avenue
Phoenix, AZ 85017
Ph: 602-266-1964
Fax: 602-650-1136
Toll Free: 800-472-7337
email: tech@pacesetterexhauStreetcom

Paxton Automotive Corp.
1250 Calle Suerte
Camarillo, CA 93012
Ph: 805-987-8660
www.paxtonautomotive.com

Place Racing
1611A San Bernardino Road
Covina, CA 91722
Ph: 626-966-4888
Fax: 626-967-4846
www.placeracing.com

Perma.Cool
671 East Edna Place
Covina, CA 91723
Ph: 626-967-2777

Performance Research
1539 Dolgner Place
Port of Sanford, FL 32771
Ph: 407-321-6036
Fax: 904-672-0114
email: prinet@perfresearch.com

R.T. Quaife Engineering Ltd.
Vestry Road
Otford, Sevenoaks, Kent
TN14 5EL England
Ph: +44-0-1732741144
Fax: +44-0-1732741555
email: info@quaife.co.uk

Ryane Motorsports
3185 East Main Street
Ashland, OR 97520
Ph: 541-482-4822
Fax: 541-482-4834

Racing Sports Akimoto
18239 S. Figuroa Street
Gardena, CA 90248
Ph: 310-532-4588
Fax: 310-532-4588
email: Info@avanche.com

Redline Weber
6300 Gateway Drive
Cypress CA 90630
Ph: 800-733-2277
Fax: 714-995-5899
email: redline@redlineweber.com

RSR
4789 Wesely Street
Anahiem, CA 92807
Ph: 714-779-8677
www.racingbeat.com

The Racer's Group
29181 Arnold Dr.
Sonoma, CA95476
Ph: 707-935-3999
Fax: 707-935-5889

Random Technologies
1313 Temple Johnson Road
Loganville, GA 30052
Ph: 707-978-0264

RC Engineering
1728 Border Avenue
Torrance, CA. 90501
Ph; 310-320-2277
Fax: 310-782-1346
email: rc@rceng.com

Red Line Synthetic Oil Corporation
6100 Egret Court
Benicia, California 94510
Ph: 707-745-6100
Fax: 707-745-3214
Toll Free: 800-624-7958
email: redline@redlineoil.com

Rev Hard Mfg.
7407 1/2 Fulton Avenue
N.Hollywood, CA 91606
Ph: 818-764-4312
Fax: 818-764-6519

Rod Millen Motosports
17471 Apex Circle
Huntington Beach, CA 92647
Ph: 714-847-2158
Fax: 714-848-6821

Royal Purple
3648 FM 1960 West, Suite 110
Houston, TX 77068
Ph: 281-880-7788
Fax: 281-880-7584
www.synerlec.com

Split Second
2824 S. Willis Street
Santa Ana, CA 92705
Ph: 949-863-1359
FAX: 949-863-1363
email: splits@pacbell.net

Stage 8 Fasteners
15 Chestnut Avenue
San Rafael, CA 94901
Ph: 415-485-5340
Fax: 415-485-0552
Toll Free: 800-843-7836
email: stage8@well.com

Stillen
3176 Airway
Costa Mesa, CA 92626
Ph: 714-755-6688 x257
Fax: 714-540-1826
email: info@stillen.com

STR Performance Products
2355 Foothill Blvd. Suite 501
LaVerne, CA 91750
Ph: 909-394-4719
Fax: 909-394-2339

Superchips Inc.
134 Baywood Avenue
Longwood, FL 32750
Ph: 407-260-0838
Fax: 407-260-9106
email sales dept
email tech dept

Thermal R&D Mufflers
7624 Winnetka Avenue
Canoga Park, CA 91306
Ph: 818-998-4865
Fax: 818-998-3161

Thermotec
P.O. Box 96
Greenwich, OH 44837
Ph: 419-962-4556
Toll Free: 800-274-8437

TWM Induction
325D Rutherford Street
Goleta, CA 93117
Ph: 805-967-9478
Fax: 805-683-6640
email: twmindsb@aol.com
www.tmwinductions.com

Toyota Racing Development
1382 Valencia Avenue
Tustin, CA 92780
Ph: 714-918-7526
Fax: 714-259-1140
www.trdusa.com

TESLA Electronics
1728 Wellesley Avenue
West Los Angeles, CA 90025, U.S.A.
Toll Free: 877-887-2681
Fax: 301-665-1831
email: info@turboxs.com
www.gtechpro.com

Turbonetics Inc.
5400 Atlantis Court
Moorepark, CA 93021
Ph: 805-529-8995
Fax: 805-529-9499
www.turbonetics.com

Turbo Clutch
RPS Performance Products
9820 Owensmouth Avenue, Suite # 14
Chatsworth, CA 91311
Ph: 818-993-9174
Fax: 818–993-9177

TurboXS
623 Dual Highway PMB 120
Lagerstown, MD 2174
email: sales@turboxs.com
email: tech@turboxs.com

Tri-Flo Performance Exhaust
by B&B Fabrication
23045 N 15th Avenue
Phoenix, AZ 85027
Toll Free: 888-228-7435
email: info@bbtriflo.com

Unorthodox Racing, Inc.
45 D Nancy Street
West Babylon, NY 11704
Ph: 631-253-4909
Fax: 631-253-4907
email: info@unorthodoxracing.com

VENOM™
8625 Central Avenue
Stanton, CA 90680
Ph: 714-828-1406
Fax: 714-828-0964
Toll Free: 800-959-2865

VP Racing Fuels, Inc.
16 Brookhill Drive
P.O. Box 9999
Newark, DE 19714
Ph: 302-368-1500
Fax: 302-368-1869

Wiseco Piston, Inc.
7201 Industrial Park Boulevard
Mentor, OH 44060-5396
Fax: 800-321-3703

Jim Wolf Technology
212 Millar Avenue
El Cajon, Ca. 92020
Ph: 619-442-0680
Fax: 619-579-8160
email: websales@jimwolftechnology.com

X.TEC
Ph: 519-659-3853
Toll Free: 800-961-XTEC

XRP
5630 Imperial Highway
South Gate CA, 90280
Ph: 562-861-4765

ZEX Innovation
3406 Democrat Road
Memphis, TN 38118
Toll Free: 888-817-1008
email: zex@compcams.com

Zen Motorsports
4025 Spencer Street, Suite 304
Torrance, CA 90503
Ph: 310-542-3821
email: info@zen.motorsports.com